Wisdom G.I.F.T.S.

Finding and Embracing The Legacy In Our Lessons

PRESENTED BY

KIM COLES

HC
Haute Coles Publishing

Haute Coles Publishing
Woodland Hills, California

Published by
Haute Coles Publishing
6303 Owensmouth Ave., Suite 1048
Woodland Hills, Ca 91367
www.HauteColes.com

Wisdom G.I.F.T.S.
Finding and Embracing The Legacy In Our Lessons
ISBN 979-8-9853729-0-8

www.wisdomgiftsbook.com

Dedication

To anyone who has ever felt silenced.
The world needs your voice and your wisdom.

Forward

As a young girl, I was such a big fan of outings to visit family. Whether it was a car trip to Hackensack or Plainfield, New Jersey, to see my dad's relatives for Thanksgiving, or a plane ride to Raleigh, North Carolina, to see my mother's side of the family for reunions, I *always* enjoyed myself.

In particular, I loved listening to the more senior members of the family. Well, I suppose *everyone* is your senior when you are a pre-teen! I had funny and fabulous aunties, loud and crazy uncles, and a few queenly grand aunties, too! They all had wonderful rich stories and memories to share. I enjoyed hearing them multiple times over the years as I listened intently for new details that may not have been revealed in the last 20 or 30 times they had told them. I asked a lot of questions. I still do. Either I'm super curious, just plain nosey, or perhaps I'm listening for the nuances. You know, the beautiful bits and pieces of the fabric of life that make us, well… US.

I think that those times spent enraptured with those treasured elders made me respectful of aging. I saw them and their lives as delicious, full of lessons learned, challenges overcome, and wisdom gained. I wanted to be wise and full of glorious insight. I wanted to be able to have a keen understanding of how things were supposed to be or could have been, and I wanted cautionary tales to tell. I knew then that I wanted to be able to tell lots of stories and make others feel the way that I felt back then. They made me feel that anything was possible and that I was unstoppable.

Their stories were about having fun, taking youthful risks, having strong faith, and "overcoming" to become resilient.

I had an 80-year-old great aunt who took up belly dancing when she was 75, so she could keep up with her 65-year-old boyfriend. Yaaaasss, Aunt O'Celia! My mother's eldest sister, Inez, told stories about sneaking out to go to dances and not making it home in time for curfew, only to get caught sneaking in a back window… more than once.

My mother, Bernice, had a story about a brutally cold winter when money was scarce, and they had run out of coal to heat the house. There was no money to purchase more coal. The family would have to sleep fully clothed with piled-on extra blankets, and everyone had bad colds. Each day, my mother, the youngest, would crawl under the house to see if she could scrape up a few handfuls of leftover coal. Miraculously, she would discover just enough to keep the family warm that night. And the next, and the next. The miracle continued until there was enough money to buy more coal.

My dad, Cliff, shared his painful lessons about racism as a young Marine. He was sent to the segregated training facility called Montford Point, where the conditions were less than ideal, and he was treated very unfairly. As a kid growing up in racially-diverse Brooklyn, NY, he could not understand why all races could not serve in the military together. President Obama honored the group of courageous Black men who integrated the Marines during 1942-1949 with The Montford Point Marines Bronze Medal, which is a duplicate of the Congressional Gold Medal. He proudly displayed that medal until his passing.

From these stories and more, I soaked up the wisdom of staying in a space of playful joy, when to follow (or not follow) the rules, how to have unshakeable faith, and how to persevere.

I came to understand that life was meant for living out fully and allowing your experiences to fill you up and build you up and for you to find and share meaning.

I think of wisdom as something that you get to add to a beautifully-decorated, sturdy ornate trunk that you get to take with you on the journey of life. In this trunk are all the things you know, all the stuff you've experienced, and your good judgment that can be used to make good decisions ... mainly because you have made some bad decisions, also!

Do you know what else goes into the trunk? Compassion and self-knowledge, insights, and plain old common sense.

Now, it is said that wisdom comes with age, but who wants to wait that long? In my deep respect for wisdom, I'm grateful to have come to understand that one does not have to be an elder to be wise. I believe that wisdom can come at any age and any stage. Young people have experiences and lessons learned, and incredible insights that I also enjoy listening to and tapping into. In fact, I think that younger generations appreciate it when older folks are willing to listen and learn from them, as well.

I'd like to share a few things from my trunk:

Examine your past for mistakes. Your mistakes have a lot to teach you. In fact, I have taken the perspective that my "mistakes" have been some of my best lessons.

Perspective is everything! Be open to new ideas and viewpoints. As Wayne Dyer said, "If you change the way you look at things, the things you look at change."

Examine and celebrate your past for success. What did you do right? Can you do that again? Looking at past victories builds wisdom and confidence, too.

Be patient when trying to understand others. We are on different paths, and compassion will open you up to learn from another's journey.

Ask questions when you don't understand something. I remember thinking that I would look "cool" if I acted like I knew everything already. I soon discovered that I was limiting myself. Asking questions opens our world to more.

Seek wise mentors, role models, and/or coaches. Learn from those who have already walked the path that you want to walk. You are not supposed to do this thing called life all alone.

Wisdom is yours to share. Your stories and experiences matter and can open up so much for others. Everything that has happened TO you has happened FOR you. Share what you know; it is part of your legacy!

This is really the reason for this book; I wanted these wonderful authors to share what they have learned and experienced in life.

I hope that you will be inspired and empowered to see yourself within their stories. Each of them is strong, capable, smart, faith-filled, and, yes, full of wisdom… **Just like you!**

Look for all of the wisdom in *your* journey and *your* stories, and when you are through reading this book, I have a special treat for you!

On page 377 you will get access to my free course, "What's Your Story?" It will help unlock some powerful and meaningful stories from *your* life. My wish is that you are ready and willing to share the GIFTS of your wisdom with the world.

Share your takeaways with me @kimcoles on Instagram and LinkedIn or @realkimcoles on Facebook.

Woo woo woo,
Kim Coles

Kim Coles

Visionary Author

Brooklyn native, Kim Coles, is an Actress, Comedienne, Host, Author, and Motivational Speaker who starred as sweet but naive "Synclaire James" on the iconic comedy series, "Living Single." The groundbreaking show aired for five seasons on FOX, and Coles received an NAACP Image Award for "Outstanding Lead Actress in a Comedy Series." Coles' TV credits include "Frasier," "MadTV," "In Living Color," "A Black Lady Sketch Show," "Home Economics," and "The Soul Man," as well as hosting appearances on "Pay It Off,",

"In The Loop With iVillage," and "The View." Coles' two critically-acclaimed one-woman shows, "Homework" and "Oh! But Wait, There's More," sold-out theaters from coast to coast and showcased Coles' skilled storytelling to inspire, empower, challenge, support, and motivate audiences. Growing demand for her gifts encouraged Coles to design and build popular community-based personal development coaching programs. She loves helping her clients to Radiate and Captivate by telling their authentic stories. With gratitude, appreciation, and a "Woo Woo Woo," Coles embraces her Surreal Life living in Los Angeles.

To connect with Kim, go to kimcoles.com

What Happens To A Dream Deferred? *

By Judge Leonia Lloyd

It was 2013 and I had just boarded a plane that was leaving Detroit, Michigan, to take me to a place that I had dreamed about. It wasn't a tropical island or a country in Europe, which are wonderful places to visit. It was a place that I had never in my wildest dreams counted on seeing while living on this earth. It was the birthplace of my mother, Rock Hill, South Carolina, which is 25 miles south of Charlotte, North Carolina. The Rock Hill population in 1920 was 8,800. My mother was born a few years later in 1922. The population of Rock Hill in 2021 had skyrocketed to 76,818.

Rock Hill was always in my thoughts as a place to one day visit, because I had visited Memphis, Tennessee, the birthplace of my father, who showed us his Memphis history, but I hadn't seen my mother's birthplace. My twin sister, Leona, and I, often pleaded with our mother to go with us to Rock Hill and show us her hometown, but the answer was always "NO." Wild horses couldn't have dragged my mother to Rock Hill. She loved showing us her mother's funeral photo album and explaining to us, for the 100th time, who was in the pictures and their fascinating life stories. She explained, as she looked at the pictures of her mother in the casket, that the pain was too unbearable for her to return. Trying to explain her reasoning resulted in her crying like a baby.

At that point we knew we had pushed too hard, so we stopped questioning her about the possibility of all of us taking a trip together to Rock Hill. We needed to give her some space and possibly revisit the topic another time. So, we passed the Kleenex tissue box back and forth between the three of us and quickly changed the topic so my mother's smile would return once more, as she continued the stories about her family.

Our mother described her mother, Fannie S. Chisolm, who was born in 1886, as a strong woman that was way ahead of her time.

Fannie and her husband, Anderson Chisolm, simultaneously owned two houses, located across the street from each other. They also owned a gas station with a convenience store that was located next door to one of their houses in Rock Hill. This area of the city stood out from the more rural areas close by because they were blessed with having modern day amenities, like running water and automobiles. My grandmother, who was fortunate enough to have an automobile, allowed my mother, who was only 12, to drive the car on dirt roads to run errands for her. This area was populated predominantly by African Americans.

Even as a business entrepreneur, my grandmother still found time to raise her eleven children. My grandmother was a strong believer in education, so seven of her children graduated from college. My mother, Mattie, was one of the four exceptions. She graduated from a hospital- based diploma program and successfully passed the Florida RN State Board Examination and obtained her license as a registered nurse. Two of her brothers received the required training and became licensed funeral directors, who owned and operated their funeral homes where each resided. One was located in Massachusetts and the other in South Carolina. Her remaining brother became an ordained Minister in Rock Hill.

Our mother emphasized that her mother's true inner beauty was the way she improved life for others, which was heightened when the Great Depression came in 1929-1939 and affected nearly every country in the world with unemployment, poverty, banking panics and homelessness. Fannie led by example and taught her children the true meaning of helping others. In her store, her children watched her give away food, clothing and other items that people so desperately needed to survive.

It came as no surprise to me that all her children entered professions that were dedicated to serving the public, i.e., a nurse, minister, teachers and funeral directors. Public service was in their DNA.

However, one of her sons, William Mason Chisolm, born in 1905, stood out as an extraordinarily generous human being.

An article in The News & Reporter, written by Makeda Baker, beautifully described the many facets of my Uncle William:

...one of South Carolina's unsung heroes who was born in 1905 in Rock Hill into a large family. William Mason Chisolm was by no means an ordinary man... During a time of enforced segregation, disenfranchisement, and racial restrictions, William Chisolm refused to allow the separate and unequal societal mandates to dictate or define his life, purpose or responsibilities. He was a graduate of Drake University in Des Moines, Iowa, in the 1920's, when very few people of color were afforded any type of a college education. He traveled internationally, including studying at Spain's University of Madrid and at Heidelberg in Germany. Besides being a singer and pianist, he reportedly spoke seven languages. Aligning himself with Northern philanthropists, he used this social relationship to help provide for and improve the lives of those in need in Rock Hill and surrounding communities. These provisions included monies to help finance neighborhood centers and clothing for those in need...He established sewing, cooking, and piano classes... During the 1930's he began, in Rock Hill, what was called The Durkee Institute, a formalized training program likened to Tuskegee Institute, according to a 1938 Evening Herald article. Culinary and professional housekeeping skills were taught here... For those living in rural areas of town, Mr. Chisolm, in ensuring access to city water, paid for water lines to run from the city to those in the country. He designed numerous buildings that were built along Saluda Street in the area of Heckle Boulevard, including his home which for years stood as a directional landmark for the community. One of the greatest acts of benevolence bestowed upon the community by Mr. Chisolm was the purchasing of a bus for the express purpose of getting rural students to the few segregated schools in the area. Not only did he use personal funds to buy the bus, but used those same funds to pay the driver. Though he left no children, Mr. Chisolm left a legacy that has long been remembered and not forgotten.

My uncle, though never married during his 57 years, accomplished far more than the average man. Even though the Klan burned down many of the structures he built, including the schools for Black children, it would not stop him from helping his community. His commitment to the community was incomprehensible and his level of achievement had lasting effects on the lives that he helped and were felt for generations to come. The blueprint of Fannie's generosity was deeply embedded in William and his siblings.

Nevertheless, the Klan did not care for Fannie's or William's acts of kindness to their community. It was not unusual to see the Klan coming into their town, burning crosses on the front lawns.

However, one night when the Klan stormed into their town, they had targeted the Chisolm family. My grandmother immediately ordered my mother, who was 8 years old, and her little sister, my Aunt Net, who was 3, to hide under the bed so no one could find them.

My mother, very protective of her younger sister, followed her orders as she hid and covered her baby sister. I can only imagine the fear in my mother's little heart, while hiding and silently listening to the crackle of the flickering flames from the cross burning in her front yard. Simultaneously, the Klan targeted my grandmother's other home across the street and set it on fire. As that home went up in blazing flames, the family had to have heard the creaking and groaning of timbers and the contracting of the frame that once supported the structure of the house, glass popping and shattering. People were screaming and running, while clouds of smoke billowed through the neighborhood. Fortunately, at this time only three of the eleven children were still living in the family house because the older children had left to marry, attend college or to establish a foundation for their lives.

When the Klan left, the house, without the convenience store or gas station, was reduced to smoky ruins. Everything in that house was destroyed. But thank God, there was no loss of life for the Chisolm family.

You would think with a loss like that, my grandmother, out of fear, would have withdrawn, but instead she was more determined to help families who were impoverished and had absolutely nothing.

My mother's sweet memories of her mother were a timeless treasure and would never fade, but the memories of pain she and her family endured was the reason she would never return.

My mother died in 1998 at the age of 76. My twin sister, Judge Leona L. Lloyd, died unexpectedly in 2001 from arteriosclerosis at the age of 51, so the possibility of us going to Rock Hill as a team died with her. The idea of going to Rock Hill by myself, without personally knowing any of my remaining relatives, would have amounted to a hopeless fishing expedition in search of information and possibly ending in rejection. Twelve years after my sister's death, unbeknownst to me, fate had determined my future trip to Rock Hill. As fate would have it, my trip to Rock Hill would come to life in 2013. It all started when my unknown cousin, Pamela (Pam) Chisolm, sent a letter introducing herself to me and stated she was a detective for the Washington D.C. police department.

She further explained how we were related and that we were second cousins. Very intrigued by her letter, I called her, and we talked for over an hour. However, the big surprise came at the end of our conversation when she told me about the upcoming family reunion. Even though she acknowledged it was short notice, she still wanted to send me the reunion information. She said, "I hope you can come; I would love to meet you."

She sent a chart of the family tree, a picture of my grandmother's burial site and a picture of our great grandmother. Hoping for an affirmative response, she sent information about the upcoming Chisolm family reunion. Even though it was three months away, I immediately called her and said enthusiastically, "I am coming, I wouldn't miss this for the world." This would be a great chance for me to connect with my unknown relatives in Rock Hill. I immediately booked my flight and made room reservations in the same hotel as Pam.

Travel day had finally arrived. I was about to catch my flight to Rock Hill. Thanks to my unknown cousin Pam, the trip of my dreams was happening. To say I was excited would be an understatement. Rock Hill did not offer commercial passenger airline service, so Pam met me at the Charlotte airport. I was anxious to meet my cousin, Pam.

Later that evening Pam introduced me to my other unknown cousin, Allen. Pam and Allen were also cousins and had known each for quite a while. They teamed up as my informal tour guides and showed me the best Rock Hill had to offer, as well as, places that were connected to my family history. I saw the extensive parcels of land that were once owned by the Chisolm's and were now repurposed as large residential communities. Pam, also the family historian, said that at one time the Chisolm family owned about 50% of Rock Hill. I was both speechless and proud.

I was astonished when Pam showed me the street sign named "Chisolm" and then she took my picture standing next to it. Touring Rock Hill, I got a chance to see the growth and progress of Rock Hill since the time my mother lived there as a child.

In the afternoon, we proceeded to the family reunion picnic where I met a lot of relatives. I was introduced as "William Chisolm's niece" because everyone seemed to know my Uncle William. Being from Motown, I joined the dozens of cousins on the dance floor that had formed hustle dance lines. Pam was taking pictures of me dancing and spinning around. Between the jumping music and the mouth-watering food, everyone was having a ball!

Later that evening was the big family reunion dinner, during which 500 elegantly dressed family members got together to celebrate the solidarity of the Chisolm family and its cohesiveness. This was the most important family get-together meal of the year. Filled with excitement, I looked across the ballroom that was filled with family and love. The master of ceremonies had me stand as he introduced me as Judge Leonia Lloyd, from Detroit, and the niece of my uncles, A.D. and William Chisolm. Judging from their applause, I felt very warmly received. After the dinner, I proudly took pictures with several groups of second and third cousins, who questioned me about my role as a judge. The young ones were giddy and beaming with pride as they posed for pictures with me, capturing a special moment in time.

I got a chance to meet and talk to relatives who knew my Uncle William and they gleefully shared with me firsthand knowledge of his kindness and generosity to his community. When the reunion dinner ended, I returned to my hotel room. I laid across my bed and reflected on my unbelievable fun-filled weekend that was packed with the amazing history lessons of the Chisolm family tree. My eyes filled with water as I thought about my mother and Leona and desperately wished they were there.

This was my final night in Rock Hill and my trip was coming to an end the next day, but I had one more place to visit and that was my grandmother's burial site. It was crucial that I see her statue that her son, Napoleon, the funeral director, had erected. Sadly, my mother had never seen the statue, but this was my chance to see it for her.

However, that night was one big nightmare. I tossed and turned as I dreamed about the burning cross on the front yard of my grandmother's house, as well as her other house, torched by the Klan. I dreamed I was there with my mother under the bed when she was a little girl and I was trying to protect her and her baby sister.

Finally, morning arrived, and I awoke from this horrible nightmare with an urgency to go see my grandmother, the woman who left a 'legacy of the gift of giving' to her children and grandchildren.

When my cousins arrived to pick me up, I was packed and ready, but I immediately asked them to take me to Grandmother's burial site at the cemetery and Allen responded, "no problem, I know where it is located."

When we arrived at the cemetery and started walking towards the site, my cousin, Allen said, "there is a statue of an angel marking her gravesite." I said, "No, it is supposed to be a statue of my grandmother!" As I approached the statue, I excitedly said, "it is my grandmother, look at her hair, her rimless glasses, her smile and her little hoop earrings." She looks exactly like her portrait that my mother displayed in our house for years. She was beautifully draped in a flowing gown with her hands clasped together in prayer, so, I can see why Allen thought she was an angel. Like Allen, I, too, thought she was an angel, because of all her good deeds for others. Gazing at my grandmother's face, I was mesmerized and hauntingly drawn to it. As I came closer, I began to slowly touch her face. I stared at it for the longest time in a trance and then, like a bolt of lightning hitting me, I then realized why I was staring at her. The face on the statue bore an unbelievable likeness to me and my twin sister, Leona. The resemblance left me breathless.

Looking further, I saw two tablets, one on each side of her statue with inscriptions on it that shared the most descriptive values she possessed:

Tablet 1: A pioneer devoted to building character, educationally, morally, and religiously. Seeking her own in other's good.

Tablet 2: A civic leader devoted to improving and uplifting the lives of others.

To preserve this wonderful memory, I took several pictures standing next to the statue of my grandmother. I talked to her as if I had known her for years. I told her that Leona and I followed in her footsteps by selecting professions that serve mankind and help transform lives, i.e., teachers, lawyers, and judges. I continued to tell her that as a Drug Court and Veterans' Treatment Court Judge, I dispensed justice in a unique way that would help and uplift and restore lives that had been destroyed by drugs and/or alcohol.

Looking at her with admiration and much thought, I smiled and said to her: "The fire started by the Klan was meant to destroy your life's work, but instead it made you stronger and like a phoenix you rose from the ashes."

As I left the grounds of the cemetery, with every step I took, I felt at peace because the spirits of my mother and my sister surrounded me like a warm blanket.

I have traveled all over the world but this was a trip of a lifetime that connected me historically to my past. I was fortunate to have finally met my amazing grandmother, Fannie Chisolm, and as her proud descendant, I will continue to help mankind in a way that would make my ancestors proud.

***My dream, even though deferred, was definitely not a dream denied!**

The G.I.F.T.S. of Wisdom I Learned

TRIUMPH

When I returned home, I felt my trip was triumphant because, by learning about the achievements of my family, I now understood how my family, many years ago, had instilled in my DNA, the greatest gift to give the world, which was to be of service to it.

*Hughes, Langston, Dream Deferred (Harlem) 101 Great American Poems

https://www.onlinechester.com/content/salute-mre-william-m-chisolm, "A Salute to Mr. William M. Chisolm" by Makeda Baker, March 4, 2014, updated March 5th)

* * *

Judge Leonia J. Lloyd

Leonia found the meaning to her life by helping others when she became a teacher, lawyer, judge, motivational speaker. She did this while holding on to her core values of respect, humanity and justice in the face of racism and sexism. She earned her Bachelor of Science Degree and a Juris Doctorate at Wayne State University. Determined to help the disenfranchised, as well as unknown musical artists, Leonia, and her twin sister, Leona, set up their own law firm. They acquired and negotiated multimillion dollar recording contracts that resulted in their artists earning gold and platinum records.

Elevating the lives of those who appeared before her was her goal as a Drug Treatment Court Judge. She helped implement the second Veterans Treatment Court in Michigan. Serving on the board of the Michigan Southeastern Veterans Stand Down, she brought the court to Homeless Veterans so they could be free to live powerful lives.

Assisting law students that needed financial aid, she endowed the *Wayne State University Twins for Justice Scholarship fund.*

Judge Lloyd authored a memoir, "Your Honor, Your Honor," that garnered several literary awards in the United States, England and Canada.

Visit her at www.judgeleonia.com, LinkedIn at Judge Leonia Lloyd and her YouTube channel - Judge Leonia Lloyd

Intentionally Reinvented

By Ernetta Caldwell

Traveling through this journey called life, I experienced many ups and downs and felt like I was on a never-ending merry-go-round.

There were times I felt like things were spinning out of control, then other times they could be calm and smooth along the road.

I've experienced many childhood traumas - foster care, teen pregnancy and would later experience going through the devastation of a divorce.

At that point, I really lost myself, and felt remorse. I blamed myself and felt like I was at fault for the many life experiences and unmet expectations that broke my heart.

Many days the pain was so real, the clouds were so gray. I had to dig deep within, surrender to God and really learn how to pray.

God gave me the wisdom to know that he would fight my every battle. He taught me how to stand strong and forgive those that have done me wrong.

Giving thanks at all times and showing gratitude became my living song. I had to learn how to love myself and know my worth, because of all that I have gone through I could have been riding in a hearse.

I really knew that things could have been worse but I pulled from the strength deep within and was willing to win. My faith, courage and wisdom wouldn't let me down.

I held my head high and no longer walked with a frown.

There was one key factor that helped me to remain optimistic through the many challenges that I faced. God gave me wisdom, peace and his healing grace.

He showed me that he was intentional for me to experience the things that I went through. For many days I questioned him "Lord, Why me, what is it that you have for me to do?"

What I've learned is there is nothing wasted with God. The good, the bad and the ugly, he will use it all to mold you into the person that he wants you to become.

I now walk in my purpose to share my story with others with the gift of intention. Not to mention, I used to be afraid to share my truths.

I really didn't think that they would impact anyone and there was no use. I would rather hide the physical, mental, sexual and emotional abuse.

I didn't want anyone to judge me by sharing my story and using my voice.

Rivers of tears would start to fall from my eyes. I knew there were so many others hurting and feeling pain, and hiding in disguise.

This quote spoke to my heart. "One day, you will tell your story of how you overcame what you went through, and it will be someone else's survival guide." (Author Unknown). I knew I had to reach back and not hide my story, because, through it all, God gets the glory.

I will share with you the steps I had to take to get through and overcome many of life's adversities. These things I couldn't have learned through any major universities.

They came from my own personal experiences, heartaches and pain.
One thing remains is that God's word has never changed.
Take my life lessons and hold them close to your heart and know that God has always held you close right from the start. He will not let you go and will lead your paths. Just trust Him each and every day and I pray for His blessing over you in every way.

Be intentional with your prayer life.

> "Therefore I tell you, whatever you ask for in prayer, believe that you have received it, and it will be yours." Mark 11: 24 (NIV).

From when I was a little girl, I knew that there was power in prayer. Witnessing my mother on her knees praying and calling on Jesus always sparked my attention. She set the intention for me to know that prayer helps you get through the tough times that you may face in life.

Let me take you back to when I was in third grade. There was a high bar above the doorway in the girls' bathroom. Many of the girls would swing on the bar when we knew the teacher wasn't watching us. I remember climbing up on the bar and I started swinging. A classmate took both of my legs and gave me a push so I would swing higher. The next thing I knew, I hit the hard cement bathroom floor and realized I had broken my left arm when I wasn't able to push up on it. I looked at my deformed arm and screamed **JESUS** at the top of my lungs. The whole school heard me from one end to the other. This would be the start of my own personal prayer life that was taught by my mother to simply call on the name of Jesus in the time of need.

There is no wrong or right way to pray. It's all about having a conversation with God. God knows your heart so prayer is a way for us to language what is on our heart as an affirmative request or declaration.

Being intentional with your prayer life is a commitment and requires that you honor your word to God and yourself. Here is how you create a prayer life: set up a time and place that you can meet with Him daily. I like to call it "A Mandatory Meeting With Myself and God." This is where you do not let anyone or anything get in the way of your meeting with God on a daily basis. The keyword is **mandatory.** I came up with this because I noticed that my day would be off balance and would not go as smoothly without meeting with God daily. The space could be in a closet, at a kitchen table or a special area in your home. During this meeting you want to pour out your heart to God, sharing your hurts, pains, brokenness, desires, dreams and goals. In His presence is where you will gain clarity and direction for your life. Have a journal and pen handy so you can take notes and write down your request to God, as well as the answers you will receive back from him. If you skip a day, don't be hard on yourself, just pick up your meetings where you left off.

Be intentional with your faith.

> "Now faith is the substance of things hoped for, the evidence of things not seen." Hebrews 11: 1 (KJV).

It is so easy to lose faith and hope in the time of life's hardships. There are many things that will come unexpectedly and knock you off your feet. The key is to stand back up, keep the faith and know that God is fighting your every battle.

Becoming a teenage mother at the age of fifteen, there were many people that doubted that I would be able to graduate from high school and live a successful life. I started to believe what I was hearing and felt as though my life was over. The turning point was every day when I looked into my little boy's brown eyes, I knew that I had to work harder and persevere toward my goals. I broke past my limiting beliefs, walked by faith and knew that I could do anything that I put my mind to.

Keeping the faith helped me to trust in God and have a positive mindset. Believing in myself helped me to succeed to great levels in my life. Over the many years, I learned to utilize faith-building strategies, such as, reading my Bible, doing prayer/meditation, saying affirmations, and renewing my mind daily. Having faith helped me to break past many barriers that could have kept me immobilized in fear and never reaching my full potential.

Be intentional in forgiving.

> "For if you forgive other people when they sin against you, your heavenly father will also forgive you." Matthew 6:14.

There are times that people will hurt us and our reaction is to want to hurt them back. We've all heard the saying "Hurt people, hurt people," but I am a true believer that "healed people, heal people." The number one key I have found is that you have to first extend forgiveness to yourself and then forgive others. Remember, forgiveness is not for the other person's benefit, it is really for you, in that it allows you to move forward in your life. Forgiveness is a freedom that will remove you from being in bondage to bitter pain.

Being violated, betrayed and going through a divorce really challenged me to dig deep within my heart to find forgiveness. Releasing forgiveness helped me to not carry the weight of the pain that I was feeling deep down in my soul. One way to forgive is to write a letter to the person that has hurt you or go to God in prayer and ask how to release and forgive yourself and that person.

Be intentional with your thinking.

> "For as he thinketh in his heart, so is he." Proverbs 23:7

If you are constantly thinking negative thoughts, you will manifest a negative life. As a little girl, I dreamed of being an actor. Acting was a gateway from the traumatic childhood that I had experienced. I would use my imagination, by acting, to remove myself from painful situations. Changing my thoughts helped me to stay optimistic and my life turned out better than I could ever have expected. In fact, today I am an actress and have been a part of productions such as "Black Kids White Mama," "A House Full of Secrets" and have been on tour with the 2017 gospel image award-winning stage play "Bad Manners At The Dinner Table." Being intentional with my thoughts made this dream come true. It is so important to keep your thoughts on God and His unchanging word.

Changing your thinking could start with you saying positive affirmations daily, meditating on scriptures that speak to your heart, and being around other positive people that see the best in you.

Be intentional in loving yourself.

> "I will praise thee; for I am fearfully and wonderfully made; Marvelous are thy works; and that my soul knoweth right well." Psalm 139:14

Showing love to God and others is so important, but you can't forget to show love to yourself. It is so easy to find yourself nurturing, caring and giving to others, that you tend to forget about you. You can find yourself feeling empty and depleted because you have poured into others but never poured back into yourself.

If you are anything like me, it is hard to say no to others' needs and wants. I had to learn quickly, after experiencing burnouts and overwhelm, to take my power back, put me first and love me. You have to show yourself grace and embrace who you are. When God created you, He had a plan and purpose for your life. Why is this so important to know? It is very important because YOU are important and when you love yourself you will show up in this world as the best version of YOU!

Ways to show yourself love are by starting from the inside out – eating a well-balanced diet, getting enough rest, saying "**NO**" and spending time alone, with just yourself.

Be intentional about loving.

> "Let love and faithfulness never leave you; bind them around your neck, write them on the tablet of your heart. Then you will win favor and a good name in the sight of God and man." Proverbs 3:3-4.

You may be asking yourself, "how could I love someone when they are not loving me back?"; or you may say, "I have given my heart to someone time and time again, only to end up hurt." I have been there as well. Even though I experienced going through the devastation of a divorce, I was willing to take the risk to love again.

I am now remarried to the love of my life, also known as my "Mr. Right." It was about me being intentional with loving God, myself, and others and love came and found me. I started a workshop called "Dating God Until Mr. Right Comes." The intent was to teach single women to manifest the love that they want to attract. The Bible tells us to never let love and faithfulness leave us. Even when you feel like someone doesn't deserve your love, love them anyway. Love always wins in the end.

Be intentional about not living in your past.

> "Brethren, I count not myself to have apprehended: but this one thing I do, forgetting those things which are behind, and reaching forth unto those things which are before." Philippians 3: 13

It is so easy to get caught up in the things that we have gone through in our past. We could find ourselves being stuck and find it hard to move forward. Going through my divorce, I lost all hope and didn't see life after the loss of my marriage. I started digging deeper into my past to the trauma I had experienced as a little girl and blamed myself for the unforeseen things that were happening to me. Doing that made me question my future and life's purpose.

One day, my little girl encouraged me to create a vision board and, because of her faith and me creating a vision board, my life changed dramatically. Who would have known cutting out pictures and pasting them on a board would change the whole direction of my life. It helped me to not only hope for a better future but to also believe that better days were ahead of me if I only believed and stopped living in my past.

Through this experience and my little girl's faith, I am the creator of the "Prayer Vision Box." It's about focusing on your future by creating your prayer vision board and getting clear where you want to go in your future. It's all about your prayers manifesting into tangible realities. Frame your future by going after your prayers, dreams and goals by taking faith-filled action steps to move you forward from your past. I am passionate about leading women through workshops to let go of their past and look ahead to their bright futures. My motto is "Pray it, Believe it, See it." It's time to release your past, refocus and reframe your future.

God allowed me to go through many different experiences because He knew that I would turn around to help someone else. God has intentionally reinvented me to be the woman that I am today. I would not be who I am if I had not gone through the various adversities that I have faced. God is very intentional and has the master plan for our lives. When you go through different storms in your life, just trust and believe that God will use it for your good. The key is to keep moving forward and have faith that things will get better. The very thing that you want to fight against is the very thing that God will use to elevate you to your purpose. My hope is that you would learn from the wisdom and guidance that God has given me. Please know that the road wasn't easy but it was worth it. My pain pushed me into my purpose and now I am unstoppable. I now use the gift of my voice to encourage, inspire and lead women to a life of freedom and transformation. It all starts with surrendering to God and allowing His will to control your life. Release control and take the faith-filled action steps to move you closer to your dreams and the fulfillment of your life's purpose. My heart's desire is to see you win and become the best version of YOU.

A Prayer for You:

> Dear Lord Jesus,
>
> I ask that every reader who would read this chapter would gain new wisdom and insight. Help them to be intentional with knowing that anything that they face throughout their lives, they can get through as long as they have you. Lord, I ask for healing and restoration. I ask for guidance and direction. I ask that forgiveness will come easy and self-love will be a must. Lord, whatever they will face in this season, allow them to do so with strength and the knowledge that you cover them with your grace. Pain is uncomfortable and sometimes can make us question our existence, but Lord we know that you said in Jeremiah

29:11 "For I know the plans I have for you," declares the Lord, "plans to prosper you and not to harm you, plans to give you hope and a future." So God, give them hope and a future to lead them to their expected end with perseverance and endurance to win this race called life. Help them come out better, not bitter and have a renewed heart. Give them unspeakable joy, peace, love and prosperity. Allow their latter years to be greater than their former years. Lord, when their mind reverts back to their past, help them to quickly renew their minds and look forward to their futures. I ask all these things in Jesus' name. -Amen

Be Blessed and know that I am praying for your success
—Ernetta Caldwell

I leave you with the words of
my phenomenal Coach, Kim Coles.

"Everything that happened **to** you, happened **for** you."

* * *

Ernetta Caldwell

Ernetta Caldwell is an actress, bestselling author, inspirational speaker, entrepreneur, and registered nurse, who currently works as a school nurse in South Carolina, serving children within her community. She spoke at the "Power Up Summit" with Kim Coles, Lisa Nichols, Forbes Riley and Chrisette Michele.

Her book, "A Journey To A Healed Heart: Healing Through A Painful Divorce," is about overcoming dark places to find your destiny. She is the CEO/Founder of Beauty for Ashes, LLC, where she inspires women to reinvent themselves to be all that God created them to be by transforming their mind, body, and spirit to be in alignment with God's purpose for their lives.

She is a transformation coach, empowering women to take faith-filled action steps to live out their dreams and walk in their purpose. She is the creator of the "Prayer Vision Box," which is all about being intentional with prayer and creating a vision plan for your life and your future. "Pray it, Believe it, See it."

She is passionate about her goal to help others in need and complete her God-given assignments while on earth.

To learn more, follow on all social media platforms @ErnettaCaldwell - stay connected at www.ErnettaCaldwell.com.

Unleash The Power Of Your Authentic Self

By Vanessa Perry

"The very best that you can do for the whole world is to make the best of yourself"
—Wallace Wattles

The first time that I read this quote, it immediately enlarged my perspective of myself. I had never imagined me impacting and adding value to the whole world. I could see myself making a difference in my local community, but the whole world? Huh, and it is so.

I was born, took my first breath in the North, in Chicago. From my first clear memories of human interaction, around the age of three, I quickly understood that I was in a hostile environment. My natural gifts of discernment and observation were dominant, I am a seer. I was born into a large female-dominant family. There were generations of abuse, neglect, bitterness, and pain. Emotional intelligence within the family was almost non-existent. The purity of my authentic self had been gagged, buried and left for dead. My father would visit as often as he could. He returned to Chicago on leave from the US Army when I was about ten years old. He and my mother remarried, and we were off to be stationed and live in Hanau, West Germany, for five years. The relocation was what my soul needed. I truly felt like the world had opened and said 'welcome home.' All was made new, the air even felt cleaner in Germany. Experiencing the diversity of people, culture, and language was the pivot that I never knew that I needed. Living in Germany was a magnificent life-changing experience. While I was busy soaring on eagle wings in Germany, learning to speak German, thriving at a German-American middle school, playing sports, I was not paying attention to the deterioration of my new and improved family. Peace, love, and happiness were no longer residing in our home. My eagle's wings had been clipped and I was labeled as "my father's daughter." I had no idea who else my mother wanted me to be, but I was marked for the rest of my life. And, once again, my authentic self, the me I was destined to be began to slip away. I didn't know it then, but I began to slip back into the girl that I was in Chicago. Somehow, she crossed the Atlantic Ocean and found me in Germany. This time I didn't have a fight in me. I allowed my adaptive self to stay, and I made peace with the pain.

"Your task is not to find yourself, but to seek and find all of the barriers within that you have built against your authentic self"
–Vanessa Perry

Fast forward, being my fathers daughter, I too joined the US Army. I served three years with one combat deployment. After an honorable discharge I returned to Virginia as a new woman. The military introduced me to the leader and the humanitarian in me. I got my eagle wings back. Although all my adaptive layers were not singed off by the flames of trial and transformation, I could still connect emotionally to the authentic me I was destined to be.

After receiving an honorable discharge from the military, arriving in Virginia, I was wide open for the possibilities concerning my career. I was ecstatic about building and creating my life and my community. Although the military planted the seed of leadership and had begun to nurture that seed, I found myself without mentorship and accountability. I had tasted the fruit of growth and setting my intentions, but I still was not clear on what mountain I wanted to conquer. I was not clear on what career path that I wanted to take. Back then Administrative Temp Agencies were booming. I signed up at five different agencies within a 60-mile radius. I struck gold, I was in my sweet spot, I thrived! I would get hired and walk in the door as a receptionist or administrative assistant and within a very short period of time the company would buy out my Temp contract and hire me as Executive Assistant, Program Manager or some other lofty position. I remember this one time when I was hired as a receptionist for a snooty Jewish attorney. As I sat back in the large butter-soft leather chair while he was listing the perks of his offer to me as Executive Assistant, I could hear my inner voice asking, "gosh, who am I? What am I capable of? What is it that other people see in me?" It asked these questions because at the time, I didn't have ambition, I didn't have goals. I just showed up. Whatever I put my hands on prospered. It was all so easy for me. The inner me was stuck in survival mode. All I wanted was to pay the bills, have a safe clean place to live and food on the table. I was repeating the cycle of surviving. I survived Chicago, I survived Germany, I survived one combat deployment in the military. I was an overcoming survivor. The problem with that is that you live a life of avoidance. Avoiding, leaving and escaping unpleasant situations, people and places.

My journey of finding myself began in Richmond, Virginia. I was the Owners' Agent and Property Manager of an 11-million-dollar, 156 unit apartment complex. The two managing owners would stop by once every two weeks to go over the books. The three of us sat in my office, as usual, chatting it up. Owner number 1 was extremely happy, almost giddy. Owner number 2 says, "we just left the accountant's office. When we hired you, the property was valued at $11.1 million, now, less than three years later, it's worth $14.2 million. Who are you working with? Do you have a team that we don't know about?" It felt like time had stopped and the earth stood still as the three of us sat there staring at each other. His voice started to sound like the teacher on Charlie Brown, "womp, womp…womp, womp, womp." When I snapped out of wherever I was in my head, I heard him explain, "…of course it's great that the value increased, we're just wondering how are you doing it?" As I answered his question, I felt like I was talking to myself as opposed to talking to him. "I love what I do, I'm passionate about it. It's work but the ideas and creativity flow and I execute. That's all! I have fun and enjoy what I do." Now I understood that he was inquiring about the marketing, upgrades and the leasing strategies but I was speaking to the spirit and the mindset that I was in as I executed all that went into increasing the value of the property.

After giving me my bonus check, the owners left. From that day forward I looked at myself with a renewed sense of being. In less than three years I had increased someone else's vision by $3.1 million. I did not have a vision outside of working in someone else's vision. I was satisfied going all in, over and beyond, for another person's vision. My barrier was being satisfied with being average. I was a beast at executing and overcoming another person's vision and desires. At that point, I had never been told that I could be great, a successful business owner or a co-creator of my own life.

For the next seven years I was distracted with finding myself, discovering who Vanessa was. Most of the time when we set out to find ourselves, it's an external journey. In the military, if a person was lost there was a team put together to find that person. It was called a search and rescue mission. The challenge with being on a search and rescue mission to find yourself is that you tend to find other people's ideas and opinions of you. Also, you run the risk of having a knee-jerk reaction to what is working for others, like their career choice, the 5,000 square foot house they bought, or their fancy sports car. We all have two identities. The first is the higher self. This is the authentic self, spirit, soul, true self, or inner self. The second is the lower self. This is the external self or physical self. It includes everything else, including your body, personality, words, and behavior. The goal should not be to *find* yourself; the goal should be to *release* your authentic self. To release your authentic self requires a shedding of the barriers of ignorance, disappointment, pain, shame and unforgiveness for yourself and others. These negative experiences have planted seeds of limitation and distortion within your subconscious mind and fortified you against your authentic self. This beautiful journey of releasing your authentic self, thankfully, takes time. And over time the *releasing* becomes an *unleashing.* This unleashing becomes an intentional, powerful flow of your higher authentic self. It does not happen all at once. Think of the life of the Caterpillar and the Butterfly. When the Caterpillar is born, it is born with everything it needs on a cellular level, to become a butterfly or a moth. The Caterpillar is released into the chrysalis stage and over time is unleashed back into the world as a beautiful butterfly or moth. The difference between a butterfly and a moth is that one lives by daylight, and the other lives by moonlight. However, both are unleashed back into the world to experience the remainder of their life from a higher perspective as their higher authentic self. What limiting beliefs do you have? What are your internal barriers?

When you are authentic, you wear integrity as a crown. The choices that you make align with your values, so you seldom have to second-guess yourself. Who you are, what you do, and what you believe in - all of these perfectly align. Authenticity is living your life according to your own needs and values rather than those that family, friends and society expect from you. Living authentically offers several benefits, including respect, your true purpose, and happiness and well-being.

Being your authentic self can feel risky or scary at times. We are surrounded, day in and day out, by the filtered and the edited, the glamourous and the exciting. As we take in more and more of what other people are doing, we get lost in a world of comparison. This leads to tough questions: When is my time going to come? Why doesn't my life look like that? What's wrong with me? And just like that, these thoughts and feelings seep deep into our subconscious, planting seeds of feelings of inadequacy. So how do we take off the mask we've been wearing and start to live a life of authenticity?

To succeed in being authentic, you first must know who your true self actually is. And this requires mindfulness, self-awareness and self-acceptance. Here are some tips to help you express your authentic self:

1. **Observe yourself objectively**. Be the fly on the wall and observe yourself. Watch yourself as you live in the present moment, observing how your adaptive self reacts under pressure, how it responds to challenges, and what it believes. Take time and practice noticing which of these responses feel authentic and which ones feel inauthentic. Which responses are adaptive versus authentic? Now you can begin to notice the falseness and begin to see the hope of truth.

2. **Examine family belief systems.** Think back to episodes in your childhood that led you to stop believing and being your authentic self and instead caused you to adopt some other way of existing and coping. When we examine where our behaviors come from we can learn a lot about our authentic selves.
3. **Identify your actions versus beliefs.** If you catch yourself using banter and being cynical, ask yourself whether you really believe the words that you speak. Are you just saying these things because someone else taught you to? Remember, the adaptive self just wants to fit in. So it can often act in ways that are inconsistent with our authentic selves. There is power in noticing the discrepancies between our beliefs and our actions.
4. **Explore your values.** What do you live for? Explore your values and figure out some ways to start living them.
5. **Love yourself and have compassion and empathy for others.** It takes self-love for our authentic selves to emerge. Love is just a breath away. To increase your love, simply set aside some time to take numerous deep breaths each day. Slowly take a deep breath in and when you are feeling fully relaxed and receptive, call love to yourself from your environment. With each breath imagine your breath is infused with loving energy. Draw love into your lungs and disperse it throughout your body, sending

it directly to your authentic self. As you sit quietly with your eyes closed and relaxed, as other people come to mind you can send them loving thoughts. I call this love breaths.

6. **Develop yourself in authentic ways.** As you pursue your goals, pause and ask yourself if you are pursuing the right goal, in the right way, for yourself? If not, you will likely find yourself months or years in the future having a hard time enjoying the process or the outcome.
7. **Learn to listen to your inner guidance or intuition.** People call their inner guidance many things; the spirit, the soul, God, higher self and so forth. The key to discovering your authentic self is following this inner guidance. You were born with this inner guidance, so try to keep an open mind and ear for the guidance that you hold within you.
8. **Find your life purpose.** Authenticity and purpose are closely linked. So open yourself up to living authentically and your purpose is likely to become more clear.

Acting in ways that show your true self and how you feel is the beginning of being authentic.

Authenticity is your gift to the world, your gift to yourself. We aren't fighting over the dull light of acceptance and competition. Instead, we step into the eternal illumination of our life's purpose and legacy.

"Be authentically you. The world doesn't revolve around you, but it depends on you. Be consistent. Be your best self. Show up every day like the sunrise, wearing your finest garment, and be ready to shine brightly in every life and every circumstance that you touch."
—L. Obeng

✡ ✡ ✡

Vanessa Perry

Vanessa Perry is a passionate leader and professionally certified Transformational Life Coach, Consultant and Trainer, committed to empowering people and transforming lives. Perry serves her community as a Nurse-Whole Health Coach for the Federal Government, and is a US Army Combat Veteran.

Perry's journey to becoming a Coach began in 2010. She is a Certified Coach, Speaker, and Trainer with Maxwell Maximized Leadership. She is also a Facilitator of The Global Youth Initiative, a Maximized Leadership Program that equips, empowers, and inspires youth to have a positive self-image, to respect themselves and others, to be a positive influence and to fail forward toward success.

Vanessa Perry is also known for designing and facilitating mindset-shifting conversations that make a practical difference in people's lives, developing teams and training leaders to effectively deliver their ideas. Her coaching session will equip you with the power and authority to step into your authentic self.

* * *

The Day When Life Had Other Plans

By Adonia Dickson

"Sometimes it's the journey that teaches you a lot about your destination."
—Drake

It was a typical warm summer day in June. Nothing extraordinary was going on. I don't recall having plans to do anything exciting. I don't remember precisely when the thought came, but when it did, my heart dropped into my stomach. It was a feeling like no other. It was the day that everything changed. I felt lightheaded and queasy. It felt like I was on a rollercoaster, being jerked and twisted up and down and all around. That heart-drop feeling quickly became a suddenly brutal reminder that my period was late!

I tried hard to remember the last time "Flow" had visited me. My thoughts took me into a tailspin. The first day of my cycle, which sometimes turned into two days, was pure HELL. Hell might be a slight exaggeration, but I don't think it was too far off. How could I forget something like that?

The severity and intensity of the cramps would literally knock me off my feet. The only degree of comfort I could find was to lie down and curl up in an effort to escape the pain. I never really enjoyed the taste of warm milk, but for some reason it would lull me to sleep and relieve the cramps. I usually only suffered for one day, but even one day was too long.

I was close to two weeks late. I thought, could it be possible that I am…? Instantly, my heart was racing, head was pounding, breathing was heavy, I was in full blown panic mode. I caught myself repeating, I cannot be pregnant! Not me! I was one of the "good girls." One, who would be called "a goodie two shoes." I was the person who mean girls falsely accused of being "stuck up." If they got to know me, they would not think I was stuck up at all. The same girls accused me of thinking I was cute and thinking I was better than everyone else. That was the anthem some of the bullies would sing. Little did they know how low my self-esteem was. And referring to myself as "cute" was nowhere in my vocabulary.

"The experience" that resulted in my period being late, was my first time. It was very awkward, and my boyfriend and I didn't know what we were doing. And besides, we "kinda" really didn't do that much, so we thought. Nothing happens the first time, right? Come on; it was my first weird, clumsy, embarrassing encounter that was quickly interrupted by the return of my mother and brother from the store.

Our saving grace was my brother, who came into the house first. He must have known something was going on. His loud voice gave us a vocal warning that he and mom were home, giving us just enough time to get ourselves together. Thank goodness we hadn't fully disrobed. I believe my brother was trying to protect me. He didn't want me to get in trouble. Years later, we laughed about it. I don't know how or what he knew, but my brother told us that he knew "something" was going on.

My mind was playing ping pong as I contemplated the possibility of my missed period turning into an unplanned pregnancy. Pregnant at sixteen? This can't be! And right at the time, I was moving into my Senior Year in High School. But the pregnancy test had other plans in mind. It definitively confirmed that I had a tiny human being, currently the size of a seed, growing inside of me.

Congratulations, I just became a statistic. I was a pregnant teenager. And to make things worse, this naïve, ugly, self-conscious girl would now have the responsibility to raise, support, protect, love, and teach this innocent child about this sometimes-cruel world that she, too, was still trying to figure out. What on earth was I going to do?

While in the depth of my deepest fear, being young and inexperienced, I knew that there were at least two choices I could make. One is to keep this little person growing inside me or terminate that kernel of life and return to being a naïve sixteen-year-old trying to navigate this gigantic world; a teenager who had just ended her junior year in high school, a teenager who should be looking forward to her senior year and all the excitement, fun, and celebration that comes with such a milestone. My story tells you what I chose.

I was not equipped to raise a child. Terminating the pregnancy crossed my mind and I thought about it repeatedly, but I convinced myself that this was an option I should not explore.

Making a decision quickly became a priority, but I was not ready to choose. I had not told a soul, not even my boyfriend/"baby daddy." Deep down, did I think this nightmare would magically go away? No! I knew something had to be done, but didn't know what.

I remember when mom came and picked me up from my boyfriend's house. Our ride home started quietly, but seconds later, mom flat-out asked me if I was pregnant. I was stunned, embarrassed, and ashamed; I knew I had let mom and myself down. Fear paralyzed me. How did mom know? I suppose the empty pregnancy test box I threw in the garbage was a sure giveaway! Now my shameful secret was out. Quietly, with tears streaming down my face, I confirmed that I was, in fact, "with child." Mom teared up and started to cry, too.

The rainbow inside this dark cloud was my mother's calm response and support. She never yelled or raised her voice. In her composed, but firm voice, she asked, "What are we going to do about this?" I cried more, with such sorrow for the disappointing circumstances. It took me several minutes to compose myself. As if finding out I was pregnant wasn't enough, I had to tell mom that terminating the pregnancy may no longer be an option because I was too afraid to say something sooner. And that keeping the baby was likely my only option due to how far along I thought I was. There were more tears, silence, and hugs.

Mom and I talked through the options, knowing that our attention may be best served to figure out how we would prepare to welcome a new baby into our lives. Mom scheduled a doctor's appointment for me to get an official pregnancy diagnosis, leading to confirmation and the date when this little human being was expected to arrive.

September enters, and my Senior Year of high school begins. By then, I was a little over three months pregnant, and I still wasn't showing a baby bump and, indeed, wasn't ready for what came next. Little did I know that girls who got pregnant in high school were sent to an "alternative school." This school was full of "bad kids," the troublemakers who cut school, got into fights, and who were the bullies who caused all kinds of problems. The remainder of the students were pregnant girls, who were also bullies and problem students. I wasn't a problem student.

Graduating from high school is a rite of passage. It's an important celebrated event in a teenager's life that opens doors, leading to the introduction of the responsibilities and opportunities of adulthood. I was determined not to let my circumstance prevent me from the graduation experience. Graduation was mine to have, and it would be an affair I would get to enjoy! I was so hell-bent on taking my walk across that graduation stage, no barricade or obstruction could have stopped me!

I was NOT going to that alternative school. I was not that kid! I had nothing in common with them; well, except that I was a pregnant teen. Unquestionably, I refused to go! I was not a troublemaker. I didn't get into fights, cut school, nor did I cause trouble for anyone. Heck, I was quiet, shy, had a handful of friends, and minded my business, and I actually liked school.

Fortunately, considering my record, and partially because there was a new program on campus called, A School Within a School, I was allowed to stay. I was grateful that concessions were granted, but I felt isolated because I wasn't in the classes I expected to have with friends. My class schedule was adjusted, but my subjects remained primarily the same.

I had hoped to go to college, but it didn't appear to be an option with a baby on the way. What had I done? I wondered what the baby and my life would look like? Would my friends still be my friends? Fear and doubt consumed me. I was scared, very, very scared.

The days passed by at a rapid pace. My routine began feeling a little more normal, if that's possible. Days turned into weeks, weeks into months, and before I knew it, I was facing about six weeks or so until the baby's arrival. According to the doctor, there was no reason to be worried, the baby was healthy. I had only gained about 15 pounds. I wondered, should I be concerned?

The baby was growing and developing as expected. It's a girl, and she was due April 1st, April Fool's Day, of all days, and two months before Senior Graduation. I struggled to keep up with my schoolwork. Carrying this baby made me tired. Nonetheless, I would graduate if it was the last thing I would do!

My due date was a little less than two weeks away. It was a Saturday afternoon, the third week in March. I was hanging out at my boyfriend's family's house. He and his brother were outside playing basketball. Shortly after that, he and I bounced the ball around, and I took a few shots. After my stomach was accidentally confused with the basketball several times, I quit playing.

My boyfriend's father was cooking us dinner. We watched movies that evening, and I fell asleep on the sofa. His stepmother made up the extra bed for me, and I spent the night. I slept okay, but around 5:00 am, I woke up feeling pressure around my belly. It wasn't painful, but it was slightly annoying.

Everyone started to awaken and were getting excited, betting I was in labor and trying to guess when the baby was coming, but I wasn't convinced. The annoyance became more frequent, but it still wasn't painful. I felt no pain and, remember, the baby wasn't due until April Fool's Day.

Around 9:00 am, the pressure intensified, still no pain, but increased discomfort remained. Nevertheless, my boyfriend's stepmother suggested it would be a good idea to go to the hospital to get checked out. I thought everyone was making too big of a deal about the situation but ultimately agreed to go while I thought, could this be it?

On our way to the hospital, I called my mother, who lived about 15 minutes away. It was then that I started to feel nervous and scared. The hospital was only a few miles away. When we arrived, I was swiftly taken into a room, given a gown, temperature checked, and examined.

The nurse shouted out I was six centimeters dilated and that the baby was on her way. What happened to April 1st? One hour and thirty minutes later, a 6lb, 6oz baby girl blessed us with her presence.

The baby came so quickly that when my mom arrived, it was just in time to see me rolling down the hallway back to my room. There was excitement and fear dancing through me. I am a mom now. What did I know about taking care of a baby? I did want to be a good mother.

Two days later, I was released from the hospital with the baby in tow. Both families were excited, while I was filled with anxiety. Mom quickly got down to business and said that first thing next week, she would take me to the Welfare Department to apply for AFDC (Aid for Families with Dependent Children). Shame, undeniably, does not sufficiently describe what I felt. I had never imagined that I would be on the other side of the window asking for help. It's hard to describe the devastation and humiliation that washed over me.

Society condemns people who receive public assistance. They think they're lazy and don't want to work. For many, that is not their truth and is the reason why I didn't want to ask for help. I was embarrassed and had become a person who needed help. I believed I wasn't society's stereotype, but I needed help, like it or not. My now seventeen-year-old self, along with my already low self-esteem, took a deeper nosedive, if that's even possible. Never in a million years did I think I would need welfare and food stamps. Again, I became another statistic!

We all need help from time to time. My circumstances weren't any different. The first time I used food stamps, it felt like a living nightmare, one I couldn't escape. It felt like eyes were glaring at me and burning into my heart. Those eyes, undoubtedly, were judging and stereotyping me. That was the day I resolved to get off welfare in one year. I didn't know how, but damn it, I would do it.

No matter what it took, I was going to persevere. I had no idea how, but my principles were much greater than the humiliation that I was unwilling to accept.

One year later, I got a job and, according to the county, made enough money that I was no longer eligible for public assistance. I never felt prouder to receive my notice of ineligibility. My pride was short-lived after realizing that there still wasn't enough money at the end of the month. However, both families and friends helped me in several ways. As the African Proverb says, "it takes a village to raise a child." I was blessed to be surrounded by a wonderful village!

You might be wondering where the baby's daddy was? He joined the Army. Initially, I was angry and hurt that he left me alone to raise our daughter. I felt abandoned, but I now believe taking him away from the evil streets saved his life. Months later, we got married. We tried, but we struggled. Two kids raising a baby wasn't the ideal situation.

It took multiple break-ups for us to realize our marriage wasn't going to work, not from the lack of trying. We were two young, naïve kids, who didn't know who we were, while forced to act like grownups, trying to figure out this thing called life. We were different in many ways and weren't aligned.

There was a beautiful Cinderella-like ending to our love story. We remain good friends and respect one another. From time to time, we still have our intense disagreements, and they magnify our differences and support our decision that it was more favorable to remain friends and supportive co-parents.

I am grateful that I was surrounded and loved by family, friends, and genuinely good people who helped raise my daughter and me. Perhaps some might say I was one of the lucky ones.

What I know for sure is that we can change the direction of our life by a simple choice. One of my favorite quotes comes from Zig Ziglar.

"The three C's of life: Choice, Chance, Change. You must make a choice, to take a chance, or life will never change."
—Zig Ziglar

Some of my greatest life lessons came from this unplanned experience of becoming a teenage mom. Most importantly, it is proof that it unequivocally does take a village to raise a child. Whether linked by blood or otherwise, family and friends were everything for us.

Enduring tough, challenging times, and being faced with many moments where I wanted to give up, including contemplating taking my life, I am now graced with the privilege to leave you with a powerful lesson that took me years to learn.

My G.I.F.T.S. of WISDOM

Our current condition does not dictate our next minute, hour, day, night, week, month, or year. If I were to say nothing else, I really want you to get this. You can make a choice in an instant that can CHANGE, or perhaps, SAVE your life! No matter how bad, there is always hope and possibility. You have choices! What will you choose?

From the depth of my soul, I know that one choice can change your life. As long as there is still breath in your body, you can decide to make a choice and take the actions necessary to change your life! Good or bad, it starts with ONE choice.

One of the things I learned that made a difference for me, was to write a love letter to myself. I had to forgive myself and love myself first! Writing a love letter to yourself might be one of the single most important steps you take toward self-love. Include in your letter what you like about yourself. Identify some of your successes and the things you do and have done well!

Stop and celebrate yourself for those things. Give yourself a great big hug! If you draw a blank, ask friends, family, peers, co-workers, etc., to tell you what they like about you. You owe it to yourself to wrap yourself in self-love first. You deserve it! **SELF-LOVE** is a choice! Do not wait. Do it now!

No matter your age, whether you are 16, 17, 20, 30, 40, 50, or beyond, know that your fabulous life is right before your eyes, so CHOOSE! Irrespective of what happened in the past, how you started does not have to be how you finish. Your fabulous life is waiting on you.

"Life is a matter of choices, and every choice you make, makes you."
—John C. Maxwell

* * *

Adonia Dickson

Adonia Dickson is a human resource influencer who assists aspiring and emerging leaders. She earned a Bachelor's degree in Business Management from the University of Phoenix and has 16 years of Human Resource experience.

Adonia is a bestselling author of *"What I Wish I Knew At 5 Years Old: 10 Lessons to Get You Unstuck and Create Your Best Life."*

Her services include coaching and personal development. Redesigning and becoming friends with your negative self-talk is an area of focus in every product she creates. Her core values are planting seeds of hope and being a person who cares about people.

Adonia life's purpose is to help develop individuals and leaders into exceptional people and positively impact, inspire, and help improve the lives of everyone whose path she crosses. You can visit her online at https://awe-inspiringleadership.com/

Miracles In Action

By Angela Alexander

**"There's a time to weep, And a time to laugh;
A time to mourn, And a time to dance."**
~ Ecclesiastes 3:4

I turned the television on, the five o'clock morning news had just started. Suddenly that drum roll sound that indicated breaking news caught our attention. The screen turned solid blue, with bold red letters that read, "Special Report." Our eyes fixed on the television. We heard the announcer state: "African-American woman found deceased early this morning in her Lakewood apartment."

My body turned cold as ice. I felt my blood drain from the top of my head to the sole of my soul. The newscaster purposely didn't say a name, but with every fiber of my body, I knew he was talking about my best friend, my sister, Alice.

Two weeks prior, our brother David was released from jail and needed a place to stay. Alice opened her home to him. Their agreement was that he would stay during the week. On the weekend when she had her children he would stay at a local shelter. That plan worked for a couple of weeks until David no longer saw the need to leave. He had been diagnosed with schizophrenia and bipolar disorder from the age of twelve. The problem was that he was released from jail without his medication. He started hearing voices and began to self-medicate with drugs and alcohol. Because I decided not to read the report, all I know is that she came home from work to discuss his going to the shelter, and she didn't make it out alive.

My world was DEVASTATED! I Was Emotionally SHATTERED! I had nightmares of my sister and I fighting our brother together. I woke up nightly in cold sweats. I didn't want anything to do with David. I couldn't even muster up enough energy to hate him. My heart literally ached! Every ounce of energy was required to grieve for my sister. At the time, a freight train could have hit me, and the pain wouldn't have compared to what I was going through. I couldn't even say the words "Alice is dead" out loud.

Still, her memorial service had to be planned. I decided that I did not want to wake up one day and regret that I had not participated. There were no second chances, or choices for me. Alice and I had been partners my entire life, and now that her earthly journey was completed, I would do for my sister what I knew she would have done for me. My family agreed that her memorial service would not be a funeral but rather a celebration of her life.

David loved our sister. When he found out what he had done he was extremely remorseful, and had to be put on suicide watch.

The following year my brother's trial began. Some family members were summoned to testify for the defense, others for the prosecution. We didn't allow this to divide us; the situation was already tough enough. None of us mumbled one negative word toward my mother for standing up for her son.

I was subpoenaed for the prosecution regarding a phone conversation I had with David the evening of Alice's death. Because I was called as a witness, I was not allowed to hear anyone else's testimony. During the two-week trial, I spent day after day secluded. The lawyers prepared me to take the stand, but as it turned out, my testimony wasn't needed. I was grateful! It was still too painful to discuss Alice's death, let alone be aggressively questioned. I was allowed to hear the closing arguments, which was more than enough for me.

David was sentenced to life in prison. We received Alice's purse that was held in evidence. Behind several layers in her wallet I found a letter she had addressed to God. From the content, I could tell it was written about a week before she passed.

> "Dear God,
>
> Hello it's me, Alice. I need you, and I can't handle my affairs without you."

After reading the first sentence, all of the grief I had carried over the past year lifted instantly. This was a conversation between God and Alice. This letter wasn't about me, her children or, for that matter, our brother

David. She was going through a whole lot here, and the next week she was home in heaven. I continue to miss my sister beyond words, but because of her letter, I was no longer angry.

David wrote to our family asking for forgiveness. I forgave and loved my brother. I had to separate the man from his behavior. He would have never hurt Alice if he was in his right mind.

Early on, you couldn't even say David's name in my father's presence. It took years for him to visit David in prison. During the first visit, my father didn't even look at him, and no words were exchanged. But his presence spoke volumes. Over the years, my family forgave David at different stages. Now we laugh, talk, send emails and photos. We knew this is how Alice would have wanted it.

I was a reservist in the Air Force. On April 1, 2000, four years after my sister had passed, I was in Japan on military duty. I was working with a group of people. Our Lieutenant approached and said, "Sergeant Alexander, I need to speak with you." I was thinking, is this an April Fool's Joke? We entered an office where I was introduced to a priest, who nervously held paperwork from the Red Cross. The priest told me that my husband and four children had been in a car accident. From the looks on their faces I knew this was no April Fool's Joke.

The priest told me my family was driving down the highway. A car cut them off. Our truck hit the center divider. Upon impact, everyone was knocked unconscious. Our truck rolled backwards, fell 25 feet below, and landed upside down on top of two parked vehicles with people inside. Our truck fell on their engines and not their roofs. The people in the parked vehicles were extremely shaken up. Praise God they were alright!

The police, ambulance, and the fire-fighters with their jaws-of-life, came to the site. My daughter Angela, who was eleven, was in and out of consciousness.

"Where's your mother?" a police officer asked.

"My mother's in Japan," Angela responded in a daze.

The police officer just thought she had hit her head way too hard and was delirious. He retrieved our address from my husband's driver's license, and came to our home. Praise God I wasn't there. If so, I would have run somewhere and not have heard God's voice. In Japan, I had no choice but to be still and know that God is still God.

The priest said,

"Your husband, Surie, is okay, but he's in the hospital. Your daughter, Angela, she's okay, but she's in the hospital. Your daughter, Angelina, she's okay, but she's in the hospital. But your two eight-year-old sons, Murice and Roger, didn't make it."

I felt as if time just stopped, and no one was in the room, but God and me.

I recalled a prayer my children said before going to bed.

"Now I lay me down to sleep. I pray the Lord my soul to keep. If I should die before I wake, I pray the Lord my soul to take."

I don't know, maybe because I wanted to hear from my sons so badly, I felt in my heart as if I heard them say, "No, Mommy, that priest is wrong! We prayed to the

Lord our soul to take! We did make it! We're here with J-e-s-u-s!" God was sending me so much love, and so much peace that there was no room for pain. The people in the room were watching and waiting for my world to turn upside down. Instead, they witnessed my world still in alignment with the One we call our Heavenly Father.

About an hour into that flight home, I remembered a letter Murice wrote about a month before. Murice was in the third grade. He had a math test at school, finished early, and received his 'A'. While he was waiting for his classmates to finish, he wrote a letter to Surie and me.

He ran in the house from school and shouted, "Mommy, Mommy, Daddy, I wrote you a letter! I wrote you a letter!"

The three of us sat at the foot of my bed as I read his letter aloud.

"Is he talking about us?" my husband and I asked. His letter was so special, all he did was edify his parents. Murice not only expressed that he loved us, he explained why he loved us. It was a precious moment that we'll always cherish.

"Murice, thank you so much for sharing your feelings, we love you too. I'll treasure your letter forever. I'm also going to buy two frames and frame your letter." I said as we held hands.

"Mommy, buy three frames, because I'm going to write you another letter!"

The Holy Spirit must have told him I was going to need some more help. Murice ran to his room and wrote another letter addressed to, "Dear Mom." At the end of all three pages, he wrote the words, "by-by."

As soon as I arrived home from Japan, I went directly to my dresser, retrieved Murice's letter, and read it for everyone who came to share their condolences.

Years prior, my husband had suffered a severe brain aneurysm. During this time he was still in the hospital. When our truck crashed, Surie hit his head. All the progress he had made from therapy over the years was immediately gone. Again, he couldn't read, write, didn't remember the alphabet, and his speech was slurred. All of this was in addition to grieving our sons.

Angela needed ten staples in her left knee, and Angelina wore a shoulder brace for about two hours. Their pain was more emotional than physical.

The Thursday before my sons' double memorial service, I stood in my kitchen and cried, and prayed.

"Dear God,

Thank You so much for Murice's incredible goodbye letters. It's truly the reason I can stand here right now. I need to know that Roger was also visited by the Holy Spirit. God, I need to know that You are in control."

I felt one word in my spirit, and that word was "search."

Family and friends came from all over for their service. They saw me searching. The problem was I didn't know what I was looking for. I searched my home for over three hours, and didn't find anything that I had prayed for, trusted, and believed I would find.

However, as only God can create it, as only God can orchestrate it, that evening was an open-house at my children's elementary school. We went to all four of their classes. Their classmates wrote heartfelt, tear-stained, condolence letters and cards to our family. Murice's class was extremely emotional. Then we went to Roger's second grade class. Mrs. Blassey shared her sincere sympathy.

"What did Roger do for the open-house?" I asked. Her students' projects were displayed on the wall.

Little did I know God had designed this opportunity for Roger to write his good-bye letter. I saw Roger's project, and immediately knew it was what I had searched for! Roger had cut out the shape of a house. Inside he described heaven, and told me that dead men joy, and dead men jam. Wow, I almost fell to my knees! I knew my sons were joyfully jamming with Jesus!

Roger's letter was the answer to my prayers that I had just prayed for hours earlier that day. Murice didn't know about Roger's letters, and Roger didn't know about Murice's letter. They individually listened to the Holy Spirit and obeyed.

While I was writing my children's memorial program, God revealed that Alice, Murice, and Roger's letters* were written to soothe my soul, but more importantly to share.

(The full letters are displayed in my autobiography titled, Miracles in Action; children's book, Never Too Young, and documentary film, MiraclesInAction.com.)

Immediately, I heard that inner voice, "You're not a writer, or a public speaker."

And that's when the arguments began!

I gave God a laundry list why I couldn't, shouldn't and wouldn't. For months I rehearsed, nursed, and owned all those negative thoughts, because I couldn't even say Murice's and Roger's names without a lump in my throat. For over six months, I was in agony as I walked in disobedience. It wasn't God who I doubted, but myself. Finally I woke up and said, "I surrender all. God use me as You choose to." Then God told me how to share my testimony through His eyes.

The lessons I learned from my sister's passing helped prepare me for my sons' passing.

At the time, I had fifteen years in the Air Force. I asked God to give me the strength to stay in the military five more years so I could retire. God granted me that strength, and gradually transitioned me from military to ministry.

Now I'm an Author, Inspirational Speaker, Grief Coach, and Executive Producer of my documentary film titled, *Miracles in Action ~ Turning Pain into Power and Grief into Peace.* My grief coaching program is A 90-Day Transformation From Grief To Peace.

7 Steps from Grief to Peace

1. **Seek God First.**

   The first time I felt my heart was when it broke into a million little pieces. That was the day my sister passed. Ask God to heal your broken heart, and worship Him during your healing process.

   Scripture: But seek ye first the kingdom of God, and his righteousness; and all these things shall be added unto you. ~ Matthew 6:33

2. **Speak life over yourself and your situation.**
   Be in agreement with God's words and your own words. The enemy needs your collaboration to cancel your dreams. Don't allow your own words to be used as ammunition against yourself.

   After my husband Surie suffered a brain aneurysm, the doctor told me on Dec. 3rd that I would probably be a widow by Christmas. I immediately denounced that and spoke life over him that he would live and not die.

   Scripture: For I know the plans I have for you, declares the Lord, plans to prosper you and not to harm you, plans to give you hope and a future. ~ Jeremiah 29:11

3. **Search for your miracles, and praise God in the midst of your storm.**
   You can search for your miracles or your misery; the choice is yours, but whatever you want, wants you. Know that whenever and wherever there's a crisis, Christ is!

   Alice's, Murice's, and Roger's letters gave me that peace that I had been searching for. Receiving and finding all three of their letters meant more to me than any amount of money they could have willed. Why? Because peace is priceless.

   After finding out my sons had passed, I thanked God in the midst of my storm that my whole family hadn't passed away. Be grateful for everything. God has a supernatural way of multiplying and magnifying even your small prayers into huge testimonies.

Death is inevitable, but misery - that's optional. "God is good all the time, and all the time God is good."

That's not just a saying. I truly believe that statement, even on my darkest day.

4. **Give and/or receive forgiveness.**
   Forgiveness is simply mandatory for your sanity. It will set you free. Forgiveness doesn't mean the person was right, or you have to spend time with them. It's perfectly fine, and in some cases necessary, to forgive from a distance.

   Hating my brother didn't make him feel any worse than he already did. Unforgiveness and hatred is heavy. Holding on to both would really just have blocked my blessings.

   "Forgiveness is like releasing someone from prison, then finding out you were the prisoner."

5. **Listen to inspirational, and/or praise and worship music.**
   The ministry of music is therapeutic, helpful, and healing. Write the lyrics down, meditate and reflect on the message.

   After my sister passed I didn't want to talk to anyone, and I didn't want anyone talking to me. However, the ministry of music soothed my soul. I listened to a song by Patti LaBelle called, Love Never Dies. I played that song over and over again until it penetrated my soul. Four years later, when my sons passed, I knew in my core that the love I have for Murice and Roger would never die. The lyrics helped me to realize that your spirit just transforms from form to formless.

Scripture: Hear, O kings! Listen, O rulers! I will sing to the Lord; I will sing praise to the Lord God of Israel. ~ Judges 5:3

6. **Take a daily walk, or exercise.**
   Getting out of the house will help you from becoming isolated, withdrawn, depressed, lonely, or homebound. When you exercise, your body releases chemicals called endorphins that make you feel better.

   After my sons passed, my husband and I made a point to walk on a treadmill or outside in the sunshine, even as tears fell.

7. **Attend grief coaching - individual or group sessions.**
   Fellowshipping with others who are grieving could be extremely beneficial, especially if they are further along in their grieving process. Some may even be living the peace you deserve and desire.

Scripture: There's a time to weep, And a time to laugh; A time to mourn, And a time to dance . ~ Ecclesiastes 3:4

Scripture: Jesus said, "I am the resurrection and the life. He who believes in Me, though he may die, he shall live. And whoever lives and believes in Me shall never die. Do you believe this?" ~ John 10:27 and 28

✡ ✡ ✡

Angela Alexander

Angela Alexander is an Inspirational Speaker, Author of three books, a Grief Coach, and Co-Producer of her documentary film, *Miracles in Action*. While Angela was in Japan on military duty, her family at home was in a horrific car crash. Sadly, her two eight-year-old sons passed away instantly at the scene. Although her sons had passed away instantly, God allowed both to have written and left behind incredible good-bye letters. God revealed that their letters were written to soothe her soul, but more importantly to share and help others who are grieving.

She offers *A 90-Day Transformation From Grief To Peace* program. Angela has retired from the Air Force. She loves warm weather, hikes, and ocean-view vacations. She's been endorsed by Les Brown, Lisa Nichols, Pastor John Gray, Marilyn McCoo, Billy Davis, Jr., and more. Receive your free gift, and contact Angela for speaking engagements and grief coaching at MiraclesInAction.com.

Wisdom and Gratitude

By Cleopatra A. White, CPA, MBA

The gratitude that I feel and have felt over my lifetime makes me who I am today. My wisdom gift is GRATITUDE. Here I give you a few of my challenges and how I handled them. Ultimately, I am grateful for these experiences because they have made me stronger, bolder, and more compassionate.

When did you last do something you thought you would never do in a million years? Well, I was faced with such a dilemma. Although a little apprehensive at first, I brought my mom to my home when she could no longer live by herself. Then, I thought it would be like back in the day, the good old days, when we would shop on Canal Street, or make some of my favorite Caribbean dishes, or just reminisce.

It turned out to be anything but that.

As her short-term memory faded, she could only recall her younger days. I would find out from her through the only memory she had left, her long-term memory, things I had never known, that as a young woman, my mom had won awards in culinary school. She was also quite the accomplished seamstress. She even designed and sewed her beautiful wedding gown when she and my father got married. But she had her struggles, too. Shortly after suffering through the pain of my baby sister's crib death, when I was just a toddler, she divorced my father and immigrated to the United States from Guyana. She settled in Brooklyn, New York, where she worked several jobs before finding her love of nursing and married my step-dad. Tragedy struck again, when her oldest sister, Olive, in London, was murdered, and then within a few months she found out my step-dad's aunt had been murdered in their home in Brooklyn. And if that wasn't enough, just a few years later, while pregnant with twins, a boy and a girl, and I being a teenager, she and my step-dad separated.

Not only did mom now find herself a single parent with three children to support, she also had her mother, who had recently moved to the United States. But mom came to America for a better life and that's what she would have.

Growing up, I admired her tenacity and was inspired by her sheer will. I would learn from her as she bought her first home, put two children through college, and kept food on the table and a roof over our heads. We celebrated the holidays with the most delicious meals and the nicest Christmas presents. My sister and I enjoyed music and dance classes, and we even traveled back to Guyana several times. My brother proved to be a handful, but mom tried to be both mom and dad since my step-dad was not in the picture. She did her best and got him through high school. Mom and I bonded on our love of shopping, which are some of my favorite memories of spending time with her. She knew all of the bargain shopping areas in New York City. Then, coupled with her wonderful sense of style and an eye for color, she would pick out the most adorable outfits. Long after I left home, she would find and send me the most fashionable pieces that my coworkers would compliment me on.

Of course, she and I had our battles, like most mothers and daughters. We were more alike than I cared to admit. We both thought we were right, resulting in some of our more colorful disagreements. We argued about what I wore, decisions I made, or places I wanted to go. It wasn't until I left for college, got married, and started a family of my own, that I understood the magnitude of what she had been through and what she had on her plate. It all caused her to be fearful of everything, made it hard for her to let her guard down, and prevented her from having close relationships, including with me. When my brother confided in me that he had attempted suicide several times, I also realized the depth of trauma and mental challenges that had occurred in mom's life was passed down from generation to generation and left scars on all of us. I recalled my grandmother threatening to kill herself on a number of occasions, so much so, it became a way of how she coped with stress. She herself had raised six children as a single parent when her husband left to be with another woman. She suffered the brutal murder of one child, and within a few months, the death of her younger sister. I vowed to break the cycle of mental anxiety. A healthy relationship cannot be based on fear and fear of being hurt emotionally.

Several years after my grandmother died and the twins moved out, I started to notice that things weren't quite right with mom. Since I lived about 200 miles away and didn't see her that often, it was easy for her to explain inconsistencies. When I would press her on why she couldn't remember my phone number, she would say she couldn't find her address book. Or when I returned her calls, she couldn't remember why she called me. But it soon became evident that something was terribly wrong when she couldn't remember to refill her medication. The first opportunity I got to get away from work, I went to see her. I was shocked and dismayed when I saw that she had lost over 50 pounds, looked weak, confused, and disheveled. I barely recognized her. My mom's memory had deteriorated so badly that she barely knew me. This vibrant, capable, and talented woman I once knew growing up, was now almost totally dependent.

It was clear that she needed around-the-clock care. I was afraid to ask but my husband spoke up and said she was coming to live with us. His family had been grateful to be able to care for their elderly at home and he was not in favor of putting my mom in a nursing home. Mom was now living with me. My life was hectic enough with a senior management position at work, managing rental properties, teaching, taking care of my family, and now, a caregiver. I had no idea what I was getting myself into. Mom's situation was much worse than I thought. I discovered she was in the late stages of Alzheimer's disease. Until then, I knew very little about the disease, only what I had heard in the news, i.e., seniors not able to find their way home. I did not know the nuances of simple things that can appear like everyday occurrences, such as misplacing keys, forgetting names, or skipping meals, except they get worse. This diagnosis meant a series of doctors' and specialists' appointments, hospital visits, medication changes, and nursing staff arrangements. My mornings included getting her up, washed and dressed, then making sure she took her medication. This meant repeatedly telling her that she hadn't taken it, until she finally took it. She would then eat breakfast and settle down to watch television.

Late afternoon and bedtime, however, were unpredictable and manic. Mom would get ready for bed, then, almost immediately, she would start packing to "go home." This would turn into a desperate need to get out of the house, followed by turning all the lights on and stripping the sheets off the bed. Some afternoons I dreaded coming home, fearing how bad the situation would be. Increasingly, she stayed up all night. She banged on the walls or paced the floors incessantly. Her condition made her totally disoriented about where she was, the time of day, and even the year. With very little short-term memory left, she lived mostly in the past. On any given day she thought she was still living in Guyana, her mother was alive, or she was at work. She often asked me if she and I were working on the third floor of the nursing home that day, or if we had a ride home. Mostly she thought I was her oldest sister and referred to my husband as Olive's husband.

Outings were hit or miss. Then mostly misses. Her doctor's office recommended home visits after she verbally attacked another patient who reminded her of my brother. I told myself that I was still holding it down, but it wasn't until mom went missing that I reexamined how I was managing my life and decided things had to change.

When the security guard brought mom to our door at seven o'clock one morning, we had no idea she had left the house. She had been gone for about an hour. She must have gotten up, but when she didn't see us, she became disoriented, walked out the front door, became even more confused, and kept walking. In addition to getting help to have more eyes on mom, our home security would eventually consist of deadbolt locks, window blocks, and wireless cameras.

While she lived with me, although she wouldn't know it, mom and I had the relationship I had hoped for, for a brief time. She went out to dinners with my family and me, greeted and interacted with guests in my home, and bonded with her grandchildren. She would offer to make those delicious Caribbean dishes. I would tell her how delightful it would be, but she forgot almost as soon as she mentioned it. Through her living in the past, I would come to know her oldest sister, whom I had never met. Much of her memories were about them as kids and young adults. Happily, she would recall a party they attended, or the school event they went to.

I journaled to cope with the uncertainty of each day, which was the way I had previously dealt with difficult periods in my life. I wrote about how mom's doctors' visits went, the really bad days, and the times of despair. I also wrote about the joyful times, like our Mother's Day brunches, church on Easter Sunday, and holiday meals. She loved the outfits, along with the matching purses I bought her for these occasions.

I discovered that one in five Americans are providing adult care and experiencing increased health issues as a result. I realized that the rest of our family either didn't understand my mom's condition or chose to be in denial. When I had no one to turn to, I found comfort in support groups. These are people experiencing or have experienced the same. They provided caring, advice, or just a friendly ear. There was also a slew of information related to caregivers. They emphasized I was not alone, the importance of caring for myself in order to be able to care for loved ones, and getting respite breaks.

In the three years mom was with me, I started to take regular vacations to all-inclusive resorts in the Dominican Republic and Mexico and cruises to the Caribbean. I'm so glad that I was able to get agencies like the Visiting Angels to come in to help with mom because these opportunities to get away worked wonders for my mental health, rejuvenated me, and made me ready to be a better caregiver for mom and still be present for my family. I felt more relaxed and less anxious as the days went by as I began to immerse myself into regular exercise, lowering my blood sugar level, reflecting on being grateful for the life I was given, the people in my life, and the opportunity to help others. This was a great boost to my mental health and outlook on life.

Mother Teresa said, "I know God won't give me anything I can't handle..." I firmly believe this because, as my plate was full and running over, my step-dad's health deteriorated and I became his long-distance caregiver.

Interestingly, although we were estranged and had not seen each other in over 30 years, we cherished our time when we reconnected. It brought closure to both of us, and for that I will be forever grateful. My mom would eventually have very little memory of him, if any.

My trials and tribulations didn't end there. While I was getting a hold of the reins on my personal life, my work life started to unravel. Shortly after just starting a new job, I had three departments added to my workload, none of which I knew anything about. Imagine being tossed into the deep end of the pool, but didn't know how to swim. The new staff did everything they could to make my life miserable. Again, I managed as best as I could.

But it wasn't until one of the new staff I supervised, a female Asian employee, filed a discrimination grievance against me, that my universe altered. I was not expecting this. I was crushed. My first thought was to curse her out. Who would blame me? Or, they could stereotype me as the angry Black woman. I blinked back tears as I read the charge. *Don't let them see you cry.* It didn't matter how hard I worked. It came down to, I am now being questioned about my actions, like a criminal. They recommended I enroll in sensitivity classes before the hearings started. How am I going to deal with this, then go home to whatever's waiting for me there? I drafted letters and emails to express how I felt. Not only don't I discriminate, but I had never had any type of grievance filed against me. AND, it wasn't true. So we went through hearing after hearing from the informal department resolution, and on to the State. I thought all the hard work I had put in to get to this position was gone. I decided I wasn't going to let this break me. All that I had within me… praying, meditating, and journaling, I used to keep my sanity, my cool, and my job.

Co-workers and friends rallied around me. Of course, I continued to write in my journal. I thought this could be in my memoirs one day. To relieve the stress of the situation, I started to use daily positive affirmations. I had read somewhere that positive affirmations help you persevere and keep faith in yourself through a difficult time. One of my favorites is "I am strong enough to handle what's happening to me right now," or "This situation is difficult, but I have the skills and abilities to deal with it." I came to realize my super powers to combat challenges were already within me. Just like a superhero springing into action, these extraordinary/ordinary tools paid off. Zap with a personal affirmation when the Human Resources officer scheduled the grievance meeting, zing with gratitude when my boss reassured me that she supported me, or zoom with self-care in the form of meditation after being overwhelmed in a hearing that lasted three hours. Since I still had a job to do and was still supervising this employee, hitting the gym after work for a Zumba class did wonders. It relieved me of all that pent up frustration of the long drawn out grievance process. I'm not sure why, but I knew I had to keep going. My husband and I would meet friends for dinner after work on Fridays and I would fill them in on the latest episode. Although we laughed about things, like the time the employee's husband wanted to testify instead of her, or when she amended her grievance to include that I no longer came by her office to chit chat with her, I was dying inside. Eventually, the charges were so ridiculous that the committee had no other choice but to rule in my favor. The case ended. Later that year I was promoted with a $20,000 salary increase. Although my mom's condition continued to deteriorate, I had the resources in place to cope.

Mom passed peacefully in her sleep at home one late October afternoon, just shy of her 80th birthday. As I stood in the cemetery at her graveside that rainy day, reflecting on the past three years, I thought that my mom had lived an amazing life.

I am involved in many activities and have more life challenges than ever before. I am so grateful to be able to use my experience to create a space to help others who may feel they have nowhere to turn. You are never alone. I am, and continue to be, inspired by the women who endured in spite of the hands they were dealt; the mothers, daughters, pioneers. Know that, inside of you, you have what it takes to be the best and to live in your purpose. Managing your emotions, being self-aware, and building bonds are important ingredients in dealing with your personal and professional lives. Believe in yourself!

I have humbly tapped into my life's journey, spirituality, and the wisdom of a Black woman. I reflect on tensely navigating the corporate world and the life of organizing and finding balance, grounding, center and the impact on my years, months, and days. I found this so profound and enlightening that I now teach this system to others.

In my gratitude, I've created ways that I can help my fellow sisters who have busy lives like mine, are dutifully raising a family, and/or have been introduced to the "sandwich" generation, to manage and exceed beyond their dreams. One of these ways is in the form of a course to "reclaim your time" by identifying time steals, chunking tasks into small manageable portions, and making self-care a priority. Remember, you are beautiful and appreciated. I wish you all the best.

* * *

Cleopatra A. White, CPA, MBA

Cleopatra is the author and creator of *The Black Planner*. It is a guide in the form of a day planner to simplify priority planning and strategic goal setting. Cleopatra is a certified public accountant in the State of Maryland and holds a Master's of Business Administration degree. She is a University Administrator and Adjunct Associate Professor in Accounting, where she not only teaches accounting but also mentors her students in the skills of time management.

Cleopatra was the caregiver for her ailing mom where she developed the resources that would later become *The Black Planner.* She had to find a way to cope with her busy, complicated, and unmanageable schedule. Fortunately, many have found this resource to be extremely helpful.

Whether she is teaching, taking care of her family, or making scrumptious dishes from her Caribbean roots, she can be found working on her plans and goals to keep her demanding life well organized. She is a passionate advocate, sponsor, and supporter for women's and children's issues, which she finds very rewarding.

You can visit her online at https://www.facebook.com/LifestylesinBlack

The Arranged Marriage

By Dr. Peggie Etheredge Johnson

"All that happened to you, happened for you!"
~Kim Coles

These words captured my attention and caused a commotion within my heart. The road of escaping pain is far greater than evaluating the purpose. Tucking it all away and praying for it to remain hidden there forever had become commonplace. But this quote challenged me to answer the question by facing my reality. *Suppose everything that happened to you REALLY happened for you?* Thinking about the question caused the floodgates of tears and emotions to return so quickly that I almost screamed. We were triumphant!

I was mentally returning to my past and the circumstances that caused God to arrange a marriage—after a whirlwind period of dating, divorced from the love for details, replaced with love for God and blind trust, two of the most unlikely people would be married. This marriage would take us to unimaginable places.

I instantly jolted back to the time God aligned the heavens to create the arrangement of my unusual marriage.

The process of sifting through the details of discovery began immediately. I understood the force behind the question and quote. Was it worth digging for more information to discover the "how" and "why?" Well, I did not need to look far or long. Like an old dusty treasure chest waiting to be dusted off to reveal its beauty, the information I needed was waiting to be removed. The veil that hid these treasures was developed intentionally to contain and conceal the secrets and sources of my journey.

Discovery!

I pursued freedom. After high school, I moved from my hometown to attend college and encountered a considerable distraction. Within two months, I had fallen in love with this distraction dressed in a suit! Did I say, "whirlwind?" How did this happen? Simply, God! God knew who I was, the love and healing I desperately needed, the path I was to take, and whom I was to take it with. Dating and marriage were not even on my radar, yet it happened!

God had other plans for both of us, and when our paths crossed, I did not recognize him. He met none of the qualifications on my list. He was not riding a physical white horse, and there was no shining armor, my fairytale wishes. My eyes betrayed me because they were veiled.

The Veil

I came on the scene, occupied with nurturing invisible wounds from a recent breakup, family wounds, grief from the death of my savior sister, and discontentment over leaving my two-year-old nephew behind. Not only were these wounds open, but they were also oozing. I was doing my best to protect each from additional injury, fearful of exposing secret wounds. So, I hung the veil of protection with great care; the lesions were physically invisible, after all.

The physical veil is visible and represents material worn to protect and conceal. Its physical covering surrounds, shrouds, and hides secrets. Although veils are much like masks, they are different in suppressing so much more. In contrast, the spiritual veil is invisible and intended to cover, conceal, disguise, or protect what is invisible to the physical eye but known in the spiritual dimension.

While hiding behind the spiritual veil, I was separated from every wound's truth, source, extent, and depth. The veil shielded me from further disclosure and damage. The veil also covered the period of spiritual warfare that engulfed my life from birth. I refused to acknowledge these things, but I also convinced myself that they did not matter. Therefore, denying myself the opportunity to heal and experience forgiveness. God was setting me up for healing, trusting, and loving again. His take-over of my journey was not hostile but designed to reveal that all that had happened to me was actually happening for me.

The Journey

Arriving in the city took all the courage and strength I had left. I was broken and needed mending, unaware of the fragile condition of living in city life. I did not know the ropes and constantly depended on my younger nephew to help me navigate the city.

I had my share of wisdom. I knew God, how to pray, and make my own decisions, or so I thought! God has a way of allowing us to believe we are all of that until He removes the cover. He has a Kingdom Agenda that is in stark contrast to our earthly goals. I was about to rediscover who I was.

Wisdom is the quality of experience, knowledge, and sound judgment coupled with an understanding of how to apply each to life, consisting of various systems and degrees. One can have spiritual wisdom and lack street wisdom or organizational wisdom and lack intellectual wisdom. Wisdom is to be sought after, desired, and learned through the fear of God and by simply asking Him. His answer may arrive in the form of an individual.

Leaving home was my relentless dream, my escape from far too many things to mention. Fortunately, I was not without family and friends in this new environment. So, I accepted the invitation of a friend to attend her family church and considered this an opportunity to run into the arms of God for relief.

The Encounter

As I walked up the steps, the fear and excitement of the unknown caught up with me. If I could turn around and walk away at that moment, I would have. The reality of that thought quickly took flight because I had no idea where I was, how I would leave, or where I would go.

I was the guest, my friend the host. I entered this church and realized this had been my beloved sister's place of worship before her transition. I anticipated experiencing what she and my brother loved about this place. I longed to meet people who knew and loved her during her illness. I was finally here! Reaching the top step, we entered the open door. A male usher greeted us as we found seats near the back. Settling down, I felt eyes looking at me from several directions. I was able to calm myself to listen and observe. Suddenly, I noticed a note passed to my friend, who chuckled after reading it. Glancing in her direction, I wondered if I should inquire. No need, she looked at me and smiled, then whispered her cousin wanted to know, "who is the girl with you?" I smiled upon discovering the usher was her cousin, and he was interested in my identity. I wondered why, but did not entertain the thought at the moment.

After dismissal, he made his way to us and others who introduced themselves. He was my future husband, but I did not recognize him. There were no fireworks, no light from heaven announcing he was 'the one.' There was absolutely no indication of who he was and would become. Without our permission, God began to expose His arrangement that night. Phone numbers were exchanged, although I had no intention of calling him. He began phoning, and soon he was picking me up for service, a friendly gesture, I thought. Soon, we talked regularly and spent a great deal of time together at church functions.

God's Plans

For I know the thoughts that I think toward you, says the Lord, thoughts of peace and not of evil, to give you a future and a hope. Then you will call upon Me and go and pray to Me, and I will listen to you. And you will seek Me and find Me when you search for Me with all your heart. (Jeremiah 29:11-13, NKJV)

God's plans are not always visible or known to us. He works behind the scenes in hidden places, such as the heart, to fulfill His desires in our lives. I did not immediately recognize that God turned my future husband's eyes and compassion toward me. After one month of talking, he boldly informed me that the Lord told him I would be his wife. His words did not move or disturb me because my relationship with God had developed early, it was still intact, and I knew His voice! I politely looked him in his eyes and said, "Well, He did not tell me that." It fell on deaf ears as he suggested we fast and pray to see what God says. I readily agreed. He was speaking my language now! I was positive that I already knew the answer, and this young man would soon learn that he was not about to mislead me into something as unreasonable as marriage to him, a stranger! I tried to convince myself that God had not spoken to him, which would be an easy win! Later, I learned that he had consulted God and the wisdom of his grandmother and a Church Mother. Both of them affirmed that I was to be his wife.

Can you imagine how dumbfounded I was when the answer I received was "YES?" God precisely informed him. The fact that he was willing to carry out God's orders in such a short period without knowing me was impressive. Now, I am wondering, what was the Lord doing? What is He up to? Why and how can this be God's plan for me? I just got here! We are both in college! According to the world's standards, we had nothing! Absolutely nothing except the clothes on our backs. Even though I thought we had nothing, we had more than most, we had one another, and we had God! I contended with the Lord and myself until I was worn out, then I surrendered. Yes, LORD! He won me over! I fell in love with this handsome, loving, and caring gentleman. He was talkative, inquisitive, and had a great mind!

God's Stress-Free Finance-Free Marriage!

God was orchestrating and arranging my marriage to save my life, again!

He purchased the ring, and wedding plans began. Everything was happening so fast. We planned a long engagement, but God decided it would be short. I now know that a long commitment would have been the death of our relationship due to increasing opposition. Then our wedding plans were interrupted due to organizational restrictions. Although tiring and offensive, we withstood the hurdles. God had an escape plan, so we eloped and informed everyone about it six months later. Our greatest challenge, the accusation that we were pregnant, was the only acceptable reason for eloping. However, time would prove what we could not verbalize. We were not sexually intimate before marriage, and the first child would arrive three years later.

Every trial, opposition, and accusation had spiritual implications, but they only increased our faith and prayer life. The obstacle pushed us closer together as God openly defended us against every allegation as we labored to become one.

The answer to the surge of questions regarding time, housing, transportation, and finances was merely a prayer away. We had to learn that our help for survival was God's responsibility, and often He did not allow support to come from other sources. Why? My perspective: He knew the secret conversations that declared our decision to marry was foolish and would not survive. He was not allowing anyone to take His credit. So, step by step, He revealed His plan and the big picture for us, year by year and day by day. We were not always privileged to know in advance. He miraculously provided all that we needed and more.

Before Our Physical and Spiritual Eyes

As His map unfolded before our very eyes, we were the recipients of God's plan! We were young, and we faithfully stood against an invisible army that accused us of being unwise. We contemplated; when is it unreasonable to follow God? We were in love, and we were on a journey with no answers, only questions. We learned valuable lessons: 1) trust and obey, 2) our understanding is futile, 3) praying together in the Spirit moves mountains, and 4) God answers every question and wins every battle.

Our journey began with blind faith and trust in God. The enemy marked us for failure, but God never fails! His plan, purpose, and position are perfect, even when they seem imperfectly impossible! He provided, protected, and perfected His will in us before everyone's eyes.

We remained two limited people willing to submit our lives to God. We followed Him and disregarded what others were thinking, saying, and doing. We had two vital advantages: 1) we knew things others did not know, 2) we saw things others did not see in the physical and spiritual dimensions. God prepared us to experience the unthinkable and fulfill the impossible as the unexpected manifested in our sight.

We were destined and chosen to see and meet, heal from our brokenness together, and go wherever He sent us! God arranged our marriage, and our worldwide adventures are priceless!

Life, Love, Legacy

> *"All good men and women must take responsibility to create legacies that will take the next generation to a level we could only imagine."* ~Jim Rohn

Often, we look at one another and ask, what happened? How did we get here so quickly? We are still together, not because of anything we did, but because of what God did. Influential people predicted our failure, and we would have failed grandiosely if left to our wisdom. However, God did not listen to them, and neither did we. Eventually, they understood that God had arranged our marriage!

God delivered us from everything that came against us. He sent mature, wisdom-filled, loving, and understanding spiritual fathers and mothers. They nurtured us in every stage and phase. He sent strangers to mentor, inspire, and support us through some of our darkest days and empowered us with knowledge and the gift of discernment as we built our lives, love, and legacy.

The road less traveled was easily chosen without much hesitation. It enabled us to become church planters, global travelers and learners, speakers, counselors, mentors, coaches, comforters, ministry leaders, a social worker, a college professor, entrepreneurs, teachers of teachers, spiritual immune system strategists, founders of a global non-profit, The Lea Project, and so much more in ministry, the marketplace, and missions.

Regardless of our accomplishments, our most outstanding achievement is the gift of our three sons, three daughters-in-love, five grandchildren, five grand-dogs, Goddaughters, and spiritual children. We pray they go further and experience more tremendous success than we ever dreamed of or imagined!

Life, Love, Legacy Extended

The marriage God arranged was not easy. We experienced many things through ministry to and with others: grief, loss, storms, life, sorrow, and false accusations, all tied up in spiritual warfare. We experienced joy, laughter, praise, and worship while living through great miracles, signs, and wonders with our Warring Angels! We prayed, loved, and nurtured the spiritually wounded. We wept with those who wept and grieved with those in sorrow. We wiped tears, fed the homeless, and visited the prisons. We witnessed wombs opened, babies born while counseling loved ones and strangers. Our spiritual gifts ministered to others through prophecy, healing, wisdom, love, support, serving, mercy, and forgiving with no apologies. We donated our resources of time, treasures, and talents, expecting nothing in return. And most notably, we led many to Salvation in Christ.

We were discouraged and encouraged, but we kept the faith. We kept moving! We were homeless with two children and one on the way, experienced vehicle repossession. We kept the faith. There were even times when we did not like one another, but love prevailed! Through the good, bad, ugly, and beautiful, God was right there, guiding, providing, healing, and restoring! We believed! We received!

The Secret Sauce

You may wonder, what was the secret sauce? How did you do that? There is no secret sauce! The secret that is not a secret is God with us and in us! He reveals Himself to all who seek Him and obey His directions. God is always available! He used many things and people to contribute to our triumphant success!

Our Wisdom Pearls

1. God First, Family Second
2. We are not one another's God
3. We are in covenant agreement with God
4. We compete to serve and respect one another
5. We seek Godly counsel when needed
6. We trust and forgive one another
7. We embrace God-Detours (divine changes to plans)
8. We prayed!!!

Eventually, God answered my 'Why' question through this quote; *"all that happened to me happened for me!"* Amazing!!! Without my permission, God planned my entire life. The family wounds developed my relationship with God. My sister's death refocused my eyes on God as Savior. The high school breakup ensured the move. The church invitation arranged my encounter with destiny.

One Final Thing

Mistakes are lessons learned! We made our share. One thing I would do differently is to seek professional counseling to deal with family wounds and cultural differences. Otherwise, relics remain to infect the marriage and other relationships. Yes, God is a counselor and healer. Sometimes physical counseling is as necessary as spiritual counseling.

The years passed quickly, and it seemed like yesterday when I walked down the steps of a closed-door relationship and up the steps to an open-door relationship that became the revolving doors of our lives. One door was closed, but another door opened!

Today, we do not look back and wonder how we made it more than fifty years. Instead, we look forward and know it was God's Grace, and *all that happened to us, happened for us!* We defied the odds and triumphantly stood together, only because God made provisions for *the marriage He arranged!*

Of the many WISDOM G.I.F.T.S.
I am most GRATEFUL for TRIUMPH
through God's grace.

✡ ✡ ✡

Dr. Peggie Etheredge Johnson

Dr. Peggie is a serial entrepreneur and owner of Kingdom Of Pearls. She is a writing and life coach and has successfully assisted several clients to publish books. She is a transformational speaker, educator, spiritual immune system strategist, teacher of teachers, beauty consultant, author of *Kingdom Of Pearls: Recovering the Wounded Heart,* and co-author of eight best-selling anthologies, and creator of the course, The Spiritual Immune System Under Attack.

She studied at Bonner College, Columbia International University, and Capella University. She is the recipient of the iChange Nations' highest award in Global Leadership and is a global traveler of more than 20 countries. She enjoys reading, writing, teaching, blogging, researching, and spending time with her fabulous grandchildren.

She is a faculty instructor who is passionate about children and families in poverty. She answers the call to serve them locally and globally in the area of education through her non-profit, The Lea Project.

Dr. Peggie is the wife of a pastor, and they reside in Columbia, South Carolina. They are the parents of three sons, three daughters-in-love, five grandchildren, and five grand-dogs. You can visit her online at www.mykingdompearls.com or Dr. Peggie on all social media platforms.

Courageous to Live, Stand and Bridge the Gap of Two Worlds—the Deaf and the Hearing

By Jamie J. Brown

Being Deaf unlocked a whole different perspective on understanding the diversities within my Deaf community. It was more than just a condition of evolving into the person I was called to be; it was a greater understanding of my identity within the Deaf community, a sense of belonging. As I grew into the awareness that being Deaf was more than a condition I was born with. It allowed me to tap into which identities I resonated with. Throughout this chapter, you will see me use the terminology Deaf/deaf. The word deaf is used by healthcare professionals when identifying those with severe to profound hearing loss. The capital "D" in Deaf refers to people who are Deaf, are immersed in the culture, traditions, and values, as well as are involved in the Deaf community, and use American Sign Language. The term hard-of-hearing may identify with D/deaf culture, hearing culture, or somewhere in between. I identify with hard-of-hearing and the capital "D" because I am saturated with my Deaf culture and community.

As I reflect on this chapter, I am reminded of a favorite quote by Mahatma Gandhi, which states "Be the change that you wish to see in the world." That's how I would classify my mission and purpose in life. I learned this at a young age, watching my mother speak up and take a stand for justice for my education. She did not know the impact she would have, not only on me, but on others. You might ask, take a stand for justice? Let me share with you a glimpse of my journey through two worlds.

My mother discovered my hearing loss when I was 4. I recall her saying how she would call my name and I wouldn't respond. So she decided to do a little test to see if I could hear her calling my name. She called my name on my right side and I wouldn't respond but when she called my name again on my left side, I responded. She tried this same routine a few times to see if I would do the same thing and, indeed, I did. She got a little concerned and decided to take me to the doctor to get my hearing tested and the doctor rereferred her to an audiologist. After several hearing exams and multiple audiologist appointments, it was then she found out what my hearing loss results were. I was moderate to severe in my left ear and severe to profound in my right ear.

She was told by the healthcare professionals during that time, which was in the eighties, for my family not to learn sign language to communicate with me because I had some hearing. The healthcare professionals thought that if my family learned sign language I would not learn to speak well. (This is a myth that's still being told today.) My family did not learn American Sign Language (ASL). If they had learned ASL, the outcome would've been different to allow dual communication. There weren't as many resources back then as there are now that would explain the awareness of our culture and community.

Learning ASL and English early on for a deaf child of a hearing family encourages dual-language communication. Bilingual learners are most successful when having early access to incidental learning experiences in both languages. What is important is that children see parents and family members value both languages. This would allow access to language and literacy development. This would help to prevent language deprivation, delayed access to education, and misinformation from healthcare professionals.

Thinking back on this, I would have loved for my family to have learned ASL for us to have open lines of communication. Learning English and ASL at the same time would've created ACCESS to both worlds - meaningful conversations and creating a bond, a safe space for me to navigate my way into the deaf and hearing world at home and school. It frustrates me when individuals (parents and families of deaf members) are told not to learn ASL to communicate with their deaf children. It deprives them of the other piece of the missing puzzle, that they would later find in life at a point of questioning their identity of who they are.

But if it is instilled in them early on, they would have ACCESS to another world just like them, just like me.

I remember the day I was in elementary when I was mainstreamed with other hearing classmates and was set apart from my Deaf classmates. My daily routine would include my teacher meeting us at the bus stop to take us to our homeroom Deaf class. I enjoyed my homeroom class as that was a familiar space for me being with my Deaf friends. When in the homeroom class we would be so happy to see each other. This was a group that I felt like I belonged to, where I could be myself. I couldn't understand why I had to leave my Deaf class to go to my mainstream classes, but that was just the way it was set up. As I got older, I realized why I was set apart from the Deaf class and put in my mainstream classes. Although I was separated from the Deaf class for the majority of the day, eight hours a day, only six hours with my mainstream classes and two hours with my Deaf class. When I came back to homeroom, it was for a brief moment to swap out my school hearing aids for my home hearing aids, and then gone for the day.

There were many challenges I faced being in the mainstream classes. I'll share a few to give you an idea. For starters, I didn't have a choice of where I wanted to sit. Even if I wanted to sit in the back of the room, I would have a difficult time following along in class. It would always be an issue of students blocking my view. "My ears were my eyes, my eyes were my access through my interpreter, to the hearing world." The reason for my seating arrangement in "every hearing class" was to accommodate me to have access to my teacher and most importantly my ASL interpreter. This was one of the ways I had to adapt and adjust to the hearing world. Another challenge was teachers didn't like to wear the microphone FM system that was connected to my school hearing aids so I could have access and hear the voice of the teacher. They complained that they didn't like to wear it, sometimes they would forget to turn it on or off. The microphone would fall off or there would be some other technical difficulties. It was always a struggle to educate hearing people about Deaf culture, but I did my best every chance I got. I was always treated differently for needing accommodations. In the mainstream class, English was the primary language.

Now, let's switch worlds for a second. If I were in my Deaf class, it wouldn't have mattered where I sat because I would have access to everyone in that room. After all, they knew ASL. It was a sigh of relief to be in a group with students who were like me who knew ASL so that I could comprehend what everyone was saying. We always sat in a circle so we could all see everyone's hands and feel a part of the conversation. In the Deaf class, American Sign Language was the primary language.

Being that English was the primary language in my home growing up, I was exposed to English through reading, writing, listening, lip-reading, and being around my hearing family members. My strengths in reading and language comprehension were advanced and that is why I was mainstreamed with the hearing students. Even though I was comfortable being in my Deaf class, and missed my Deaf friends, when I went to mainstream classes, I knew my Deaf classmates understood that being in mainstream classes was beneficial for me. I now understand it was good for me to be exposed to both worlds.

The elementary school I attended wanted me to repeat the fifth grade because they didn't have a middle school for me to transition from the fifth grade to the sixth grade. One of the most admirable things about my mother that I remember as I stand in the gap to be a bridge of support for others, is how she fought for my disability advocacy rights as a Deaf individual. My mother used her voice to speak up for change in how the school board handled my educational and accessibility accommodations. There was no Exceptional Student Education (ESE) department established at the middle school level to receive any Deaf or hard of hearing students transitioning from elementary to middle school.

My mother was very determined to get me everything I needed as a Deaf individual. She wanted me to have a great educational experience that would meet my needs for accessibility and accommodations. Being my best supporter, my mother wanted the best for me and all I deserved! She made a case to the school board and fought hard with facts and heart. With her VOICE, she won the case. A school was founded and a Deaf department was established within the Exceptional Student Education department. The Deaf department consisted of staff with teachers for the Deaf, sign language interpreters, teacher's assistants, and other support workers within the department. Unknowingly, when she used her VOICE to stand in the gap for me, she stood in the gap for other Deaf and hard of hearing students coming after me and for generations to come. She had created a ripple effect that is still serving today.

There were moments when I learned to navigate my worlds and I remember the day I felt unstoppable. This experience changed the trajectory of how I saw myself and what others saw in me. This incident happened in my high school cafeteria where my Deaf friends and I were in line waiting to be served. Well, it was five of us in a group, three were Deaf and two of us were hard of hearing, including me. So, while in line, I overheard a group of hearing kids making fun of us Deaf kids saying "oh look at how they talk," "why do they make that sound when they talk," and "why do they do that hand thing?" They were just being outright RUDE! I was furious so I told my friend, who is also hard of hearing like me, to interpret for our Deaf friends what I was about to say. I told them that the group behind us was making fun of us and I am about to tell them off!

So I turned around with an attitude and said... "Excuse Me?"

"What did you say about us?" (mocking them back)

"Why do we talk with our hands?"

"The sounds we make?" I said I know you are not making fun of us.

"Who do you think you are?"

"You betta check yourself before you wreck yourself. You need to apologize to us. You don't know me or my friends like that, homey!"

So after saying all that and standing up to them, all they could say was...

"OMG! Oh my God, she can talk!" I said, "You're damn right I can talk and hear a little, too." We got our lunch and left them in the line looking stupid! After that day, they never messed with us again because they knew they had to deal with me! (LOL)

That was the day I became the champion, the ultimate supporter, the encourager!

My friends were happy and cheering me on for standing in the gap for them, for us! I am them and they are me! I was unstoppable then and I am unstoppable NOW! It was then that I knew I wanted to advocate for myself and my Deaf community on a different level.

I was bullied throughout my educational journey from elementary, middle school, high school, and even college. People would ask me "Why do you have to have all this help? - a Sign Language Interpreter, a team interpreter, a notetaker, sitting up front, the teacher wearing microphones, why do you need all that? Do you think you are better than us? Do you think you are special or something?" It was stressful and exhausting being me. Being Deaf! I was often misunderstood for being rude simply because I did not HEAR them. All of it was STRESSFUL! It was hard being in my shoes, growing up always having to explain myself. I had to work hard to do things over 200% more than the average hearing person. It was stressful having to pay attention in classes to make sure I didn't miss anything and I still missed a whole lot. It was hard to pay attention to the board, the teacher, and the interpreter and write notes all at the same time. I've had many difficulties. It was not easy, it was very frustrating. No one understands what we go through as Deaf children and adults except those who are immersed in the culture and community. I've always said "Try being deaf and then tell me how you feel? Put some cotton or earplugs in your ears, go 24 hours without sound, only closed captions on the T.V., lip-reading, doing routine errands. See how much you comprehend and you'll get a glimpse of what we go through daily."

I have always made myself available to assist in any way I can through teaching, tutoring, mentoring, interpreting, speaking, coaching, and more. Because of the values my mother instilled in me, I have grown up to be an assertive, compassionate, empathetic woman who stands up for what is right and speaks up for herself and others. I have over 30 years of experience in various capacities within the Deaf and hard-of-hearing communities. I have served and held positions as a Deaf Interpreter, Job Coach Developer, Deaf Ministry Leader, Deaf Mentor for families with Deaf children, Deaf Mentor for Interpreters, Teaching ASL for Deaf ministries, Deaf Consultant, and a Deaf Life Coach. It has allowed me the opportunity to support, serve and provide resources for the community.

One of the ways I've helped by being a support and resource was during the time of the pandemic. My Deaf and hard-of-hearing community suffered a great deal with lack of communication, including myself, being that we all had to wear masks which hindered the communication of lip-reading for us. Not having access to face-to-face contact limited our ability to communicate. We were already limited with resources and the pandemic made it worse. However, we rose to the challenge and became creative with ways to communicate. Many members of my Deaf community reached out to me asking for assistance and suggestions as to how we can rise to the occasion. I assisted them by sharing resources of information to bridge the communication gap. I served as a source of encouragement as a Life Coach and Encourager during this time through video support conversations, prayers of faith, devotionals, and encouragement for both my worlds.

Throughout my life's experiences, I've had to learn how to be a dynamic communicator. As an interpreter of visual language, I am grateful for my ability to grasp concepts that are in spoken language, to be able to convey my facial expressions, body language, and sign language, to create a visually expressive yet concise message, that the Deaf and hard-of-hearing can understand. I embrace my two worlds because I courageously live, stand and bridge the gap between my worlds. I've learned to accept myself for whom God created me to be, to embrace my deafness and continue to overcome obstacles that come my way. I want to encourage you, no matter what happens in life, to love yourself for who you are and believe in yourself! I am grateful for my tribe and village of supporters. I am grateful that my mother stood her ground and, in turn, taught me to do the same. Now it's my turn to continue carrying that mantle, to continue to be a pillar for change! I'm sharing my story in hopes that people will understand that everyone is different. We are still human beings in this world and we deserve the same respect as everyone else. My goal is to continue to be a resource for the community, a tower of support, and encouragement for change.

Wisdom for my two worlds:

Deaf

- Speak up, advocate for yourself and express what you need.
- Believe you are worth it and have what it takes despite your disability.
- Be willing to educate the hearing about our culture and community to bring more awareness.

Hearing

- Be sensitive to the needs for accessibility and accommodations. Grant us access when we request it. We deserve to have access and accommodations. (ex: interpreter, closed caption, assistive devices, etc.)
- Face us and make eye contact when speaking to us. We rely on facial expressions, lip-reading and non-verbal communication. If your hand is over your lips or if your back is turned away from us, we cannot understand you and you will automatically think we are rude for not responding.
- Learn sign language - at least the basics, to communicate with us in our language. We have to learn English and get adjusted to your language. Why not reciprocate the same for us?

Deaf and Hearing

- Don't assume anything, ask questions to gain clarity.
- Have patience with each other, we are learning each other's spaces as Deaf and hearing people.

"Deaf people can do anything except hear."
– I. King Jordan, former president
of Gallaudet University

Take a leap of faith in your abilities
to do amazing things.
You have a purpose in life. Live your life
with INTENTION and don't let anything
hold you back from being AMAZING!

* * *

Jamie J. Brown

Ms. Jamie J. Brown lives in two distinct worlds as she is hard-of-hearing. She is an amazing individual born to bridge the gap of communication with over 30 years of experience in various capacities within the deaf and hard-of-hearing community. She is passionate about helping the deaf and the hearing experience greatness within themselves by sharing tools and strategies to help them overcome adversity, build self-confidence, and achieve their goals. She is bilingual in English and American Sign Language. She mentors students to become confident, competent and effective communicators through interpreting within the deaf community.

Ms. Brown is the CEO/Founder of JBEMPOWERS COACHING & CONSULTING. She is also a Certified Professional Life Coach, Consultant, Author, Speaker, Deaf Interpreter and Encourager. She is the first deaf student to graduate from the International Coaching and Leadership Institute. She is an active member of several national and local organizations that have global impact, such as National Black Deaf Advocates, and the National Association of the Deaf. Ms. Brown's ultimate goal is to continue to serve as a passionate advocate by bridging the gap between the deaf and the hearing worlds through faith, empowerment, awareness, education, and encouragement.

Visit her at www.jamiejbrown.com

Uncharted Territory

By Candace Sewell

In Dedication. . .

I dedicate this chapter to my mommy (Durlyn S.). Mommy I shed tears for you often. The moment you physically left my world on Jan. 4th, my heart shattered into pieces. The very rhythm of my breath changed forever. One of the hardest things to work through is those days when I want to sneak into your room and just sit in the chair and watch you sleep. Words cannot express how grateful and honored I am to have been given the gift of taking care of you and being there for you.

There are days that I am still in disbelief, but I always feel your presence and can hear your voice telling me to follow my dreams. You have always encouraged me to keep moving and to keep my faith. You prepared me as much as you could, and I will now take those lessons and continue through life. I will forever remember your beautiful big smile, your unconditional love, your amazing hugs, and infamous eyerolls. As I now navigate through uncharted territory, I have gained another angel in heaven to watch over me. This goes to prove that your guidance will never stop, and I now find comfort in that.

I would like to invite you to take a journey with me. A journey that may consist of tears, smiles, and laughter. I encourage you to give yourself permission to go through all the emotions that may arise as I am doing the same. This story is about caregiving while grieving and loving your loved one. A story, in my opinion, not often told because grief can be difficult to maneuver. This is my story.

When I was a junior in high school, my mom picked me up from school and told me the dreadful news, she had been diagnosed with Diabetes. Shocked with the news, the journey of healing began, a changing of lifestyle and mindset, or so I thought. I can't recall any other emotions I felt from the initial news, other than mommy saying, "Y'all are killing me" in a joking way with a smile on her face. I gave her a quick glance as those words rang in my inner ear and traveled through my beating heart. It felt like my heart would beat with each word as they were repeated over and over in my head. Thoughts of confusion ran through my mind, but I sat quietly as she continued to share what the doctor had said. I couldn't understand why she thought this was funny. It is possible she was nervous about what the diagnosis meant for her life and the changes she would need to make.

I spent the rest of my high school and college years learning about the disease, sharing the information, as I learned it, with my mommy. Neither one of us knew that one must be prepared, emotionally and mentally, for such a lifestyle change. We would often get into debates and arguments because, ultimately, I wanted my mom to live a long life since I cared so much about her. Mommy lived her life on the go. She was not big on eating meals, rather than depending on snacks to get through her day. This is the moment when my journey as a caregiver began, more so than when I took on that role of a caregiver. I didn't go to many of the doctors' appointments at that time because of school, but I made sure I was in touch with all the doctors to gain a clear understanding of what was going on and how it could affect her life. Slowly but surely my life was revolving around my mom and all she had to do, as the nature of diabetes took its course. Loss of some of her eyesight, the onset of heart and kidney disease, were only the physical start. She began to lose some of that independence that the world knew her for. Anyone who knew her, knew how much she loved to work and get up and go as she pleased. Being forced into retirement and not being able to drive, I believe, pushed her into a spiraling downward depression. I became this mechanical machine, a robot existing among people who were living. I was listening to "turn right, now left," while losing my flexibility and zest for life. My life became work… school… mommy… on auto repeat, day in and day out.

In 2016, life as I knew it changed again. My heart, mommy, moved from Maryland to South Carolina. Strong minded, tough, independent, goal oriented, right? Right. All the things I would describe myself to be.

Mommy moving to South Carolina wasn't going to be an issue. After all, I loved to burn up the highway. It was a vacation for me. Nope, not what happened. I came to soon realize mommy not being five minutes away from me was going to be harder than I had originally thought. Dropping by on any given day now took planning and possibly, time off from work. It was no longer a quick and easy, "Okay mommy, I will see you later this week to run our weekly errands." I had laughed at my mom and her siblings for years for crying whenever they departed from one another. Now this became my "motto." I was becoming them. I now knew how it felt to leave someone you love, to not have daily access to them. Visitations became more and more precious and needed. They became those stolen moments, the little things we often talk about. I remember one visit; my momma didn't look the same. She had lost so much weight. She was almost unrecognizable. I pushed for her to go to the doctor. Not long after, I received a call with the horrid news that her kidneys were continuing to fail. She had to go on dialysis.

Mommy was turning into someone I didn't know. The woman I knew was a fighter, independent, and never gave up. Who was this person in front of me? It became increasingly apparent that she would soon need someone to take care of her full time. There were talks of a possible kidney transplant, but we were running into many roadblocks. There are numerous medical tests she would have to undergo (and, hopefully, her body would be able to sustain it), finding a donor, who, in my opinion, had to be in great health, and so much more. I tried to pray, keep the faith, and to remember God was in control. It seemed everything was going okay until mommy continued to lose weight and became more ill. There were many debates with the doctors, regardless if it was the kidney doctor, primary doctor, or heart doctor. No one knew why she would suddenly pass out and fall. No one could explain why she was vomiting constantly. No one could answer any of my questions with certainty, it was all probability. I finally came to my wit's end and did what I do best, which was research. I found out the doctors would pretty much gamble with your health because they feel you don't know anything. Here again, I found myself advocating for my mom. I picked up and moved to South Carolina, because the woman I knew had disappeared before my very eyes. I did not know her. She just went along with what the doctors said. It was like she had no fight left.

As I sit here and write this, I can hear her say "I am going to do better. I'm trying." Mommy would say to me, "I don't have long left." Who wants to hear that from their parent? Not me. Little did I know she was right. She was preparing me for the biggest challenge of my life. Throughout the next two years, I refused to ask for help from others. I was a superwoman. I was going to take care of my mommy. No one could do it like me. The caregivers we did hire either had an issue or did not listen. It caused me more heartache and a headache than doing it on my own. However, looking back, I realize that so many others in the family did offer help and I did not take their offers. I was feeling drained because I was lacking in the self-care department. The many headaches

I endured and feelings like I was going to pass out - was it all worth it? On one hand, I would say yes, because it was my mommy; however, on the other hand I would do it differently now.

Caregiving can be challenging and rewarding. Rewarding because you have the opportunity to spend so much time with your loved ones. It is a special time, one that shouldn't be taken for granted. It is an opportunity to learn about the person on a deeper level and have uninterrupted conversations. I learned so much about my mommy, simple things like the change in her favorite color. Challenges consist of not only taking care of yourself, but the other person as well. You are doing things the way the other person wants them done despite the level of difficulty it may be. My mom liked writing checks to pay her bills and I prefer hopping online to do so. Your loved one may want food cooked in a particular way, as I quickly found out with my mom. I grieved the person she was while loving and learning who she became. The more she lost her strength, the more I had to learn about the woman she was becoming and continue to love her for where she was in her journey.

I often fought with feelings of guilt because I felt I could do more, or I couldn't take away her pain. I often found myself feeling closed in because I felt as if I had no escape. I found myself being angry at certain people because they were not helping in the way I felt they should. I often felt depressed. Many nights I would cry myself to sleep because I felt helpless. It felt as if no matter where I turned, no one cared. One of the hardest parts was allowing her to complete her journey.

I mentioned earlier I would have done things differently. Let me tell you how.

One - I had to change my prayer. Most often we find ourselves bargaining with God to heal our loved ones. We hear of miracles all the time. Our family member could also be that story, that miracle, right? Well, my prayer was no longer to heal her for me, but for God to take her on the journey she needed to complete her journey in this world. So, it became easier to leave the hospital sometimes as opposed to staying all day. I knew He had her. "Lord whether You heal my mommy on this side of heaven or not, let Your Will be done." Second - I had many conversations with my mommy. I reminded her of her faith as she so many times before had reminded me of mine. I told her if she was tired, as I would often hear her say with tears running down her cheeks, she could go ahead and take her rest, I would be okay. I focused on the present and not the future or past. Thirdly - take time for YOU. You deserve it. You can't serve from an empty cup. Engage in **self-care**, whatever that means for you, such as getting your hair done, exercising, or going to the beach. My cup was fully depleted. I learned this lesson late in the journey, but nonetheless, it was learned.

Fourth - allow others to help. It is okay to receive help and to delegate tasks. We cannot make it through this journey called life on our own. Caregiving is no different. Don't get upset at how others help. I realized through this journey that some people are not equipped with the skills to help in certain situations. Some people can only show up with tending to the hygienic needs, while others may only be able to help with keeping the house clean.

Everyone is trying to cope with the circumstances. Fifth - give yourself the permission and space to grieve. It is part of the process. This is not an easy experience to go through. It is okay to tell people - you don't want to hear the cliches. Y'all know the ones, "The person will no longer suffer or be in pain." or "At least they're in a better place." Lastly, be grateful for the moments you do have. It is easy to focus on the negative and forget the positive. I did this exercise with my mommy. When she would be negative, I would immediately ask her what she was grateful for. I found this kept her present to being grateful, but also kept me grounded in gratitude. I was extremely fortunate that many people called and checked in on me. Many people respected my boundaries when I needed the space to be alone and didn't want to talk. When mommy transitioned on January 4th, life as I knew it changed. Even in her passing, she gifted me the space to grieve because she had her affairs in order. As I navigate this uncharted territory, I am continuing to learn more about myself.

I equipped myself with more than one coach because I knew I would need as much support as I could get. I didn't want a repeat of my grandmother's transition. Life consisted of work, classes, caregiving, and that's pretty much it. During this time, I went into a deep depression for months. I did a lot of retail therapy and went into debt. I isolated myself from the world and damaged a good friendship. I now find myself asking questions, like, what I am going to do now? Could I have done more? My sleep patterns are getting back on track, I'm worrying less, and I don't have to deal with ignorant doctors. What's next? What do you do when everyone looks to you for answers or solace? I never imagined my life without my mommy. I never thought about waking up to the day she was not going to be here. I never thought about not hearing her call my name or tell me happy birthday. I never thought about her not getting to know her grandkids, if I decide to have any. Even while taking care of her estate, so many emotions arise. I have many thoughts of it not being fair. She should be closing her accounts if she wants them closed. She should be the one to say this or that, not me. Going through these stages makes me realize it is final. My mommy is not coming back. She will no longer walk the face of this earth. I only have my memories left. It's like, on one hand I had a dream of being in a plane and I was flying first class. The front of the plane opened, and my mom and other family were there. She was waving at me goodbye with a smile on her face. However, we were also at a funeral. I believe she was telling me that my caregiving days are over while at the same time giving me permission to go live my life. On the other hand, I had another dream where she was calling me and I am in a full-blown panic because I can't get to her. I was screaming because my mommy needed me, and I could not help her. So confused on how to take these dreams.

This chapter of my life is most definitely about maneuvering uncharted territory; finding my path and peace; figuring out what I am to do and learning who I am as I remove the title of "caregiver of others" to "caregiver of myself." I find myself in this place of questions and seeking answers. This is a journey I didn't know I needed to embark upon until now. I find life is like a road. We must pay attention to what's in front of us, and, as we continue to drive the path, things will be revealed. Along the way there may be construction, an exit could be closed, a lane may be shut down, new lanes and bridges may be in the process of being built. Sometimes the ride seems slow, and the weather is unpredictable. The GPS could be malfunctioning. It all goes to show us that we must sometimes go through the trials and tribulations to get to the other side. Sometimes a detour will not be offered. Sometimes you must stay on the original path you are on.

My WISDOM G.I.F.T.S. are GRATITUDE for my journey and to continue SELF-LOVE!

✡ ✡ ✡

Candace Sewell

Candace Sewell was born in Baltimore, Maryland. She earned her Bachelor of Science in Psychology from Coppin State University and later her Master's in Clinical Counseling from Walden University. She was able to complete one of her life goals early on in life when she traveled abroad to Ghana, Africa, for six months and attended Cape Coast University. Candace has been a therapist for over five years and has experience in Substance Use and Mental Health Disorders. She also has experience in working with clients of all ages. In her spare time, she enjoys cooking and baking. Candace is a mommy of two boy dogs, Blackie and Chunkie. She also enjoys reading and going to the beach. Candace is a firm believer in "Life is about chances and choices. Everyday you wake, you have been given the chance to make a choice. What choices are you going to make with the chances given?" If you would like to connect with her, she can be reached at csewell.journeecounseling@gmail.com.

Secrets and Shame . . .

By Kathryn Washington, MPH

What goes on in this house, stays in this house.

"What goes on in this house, stays in this house" is a saying that is spoken in the African American community, and it means to keep your business to yourself and avoid discussing private affairs with the community. This is a principle some of my family members and I lived by, and still do. The damage this has done has led to a loss of trust and the covering up of lies. The opportunity to engage in authentic discussion fades, and the secrets either remain a painful reminder of the past or lead to self-discovery, clarity and gratitude.

This saying and train of thought has been passed down for generations. Instead of focusing on how to minimize shame, discuss mental health, mindset, and addiction, we lost the opportunity and the moment to heal. Denial and deception caused all communication efforts to fail. Having a discussion requires a level of vulnerability and authenticity. When dealing with someone experiencing addiction, it is difficult to discuss mindset or anything else during the moments they crave drugs and alcohol, and are controlled by the compulsion to use. My family and I kept similar secrets. They kept her addiction from me and I was ashamed of her.

My biological mother had an addiction to drugs and, despite my inquiry, I was never told who my father was. There has always been speculation about who he was, and whether or not he was still alive, but my mother never alluded to, or spoke of, any details about him. She never told me anything about what caused her addiction and I never got a chance to know much about her. My biological mother never had any true desire to be around me. She was not affectionate and when we did spend time together, it was brief. My family began to whisper about her actions with other family members but failed to have open constructive conversations with her. Often, because she wasn't ready to talk, she just avoided coming around. How do you fix something that is never discussed openly?

My family had good intentions to protect me from what they thought I was too young to understand. However, it turns out, avoiding talking about addiction, or the underlying causes of it, minimizes the opportunity for a discussion, and possible intervention.

"It's the shame that destroys, and the addiction that's blamed."
(Kathryn Washington)

When I started toward my downward spiral, everything began to change. I knew I was different from other families after I was adopted by my parents. My biological mother was unable to care for me, and her mother, my grandmother, was unable to raise me any further. My grandmother made arrangements with her cousin for me to stay with them. I was four when I began to live with them. I was adopted a few years later. For clarity, the family dynamics were good. My adoptive parents were protective and supportive. It was a home of love, laughter, understanding and forgiveness. I was happy with them.

My adoptive parents had an open-door policy and encouraged my biological mother to remain a part of my life, should she choose. However, as a result of my biological mother's addiction, I didn't see much of her, and that took a toll on me. I wasn't good at emotional regulation, and I began to treat myself poorly. I was insecure and felt abandoned. I struggled with it because my adoptive parents always invited her to come and visit, but she wouldn't. I wanted to know why she didn't want to be in my life, so I asked my parents the same questions for years: what did I do to her? Why didn't she love me? They were patient, and candid about the reasons why my biological mother never came for holidays or my birthdays, or why she only had a few minutes to talk to me on the phone. They explained "that she was doing her best," but her addiction to drugs kept her distant and unavailable. In contrast to my parents, who were forthcoming and transparent, the rest of the family, my aunts and uncles, kept her addiction hidden. They felt I wasn't able to understand, and they didn't know how to help her. I wasn't familiar with the dynamics of drugs and how they affected her mental health and decision-making at that time, until I became an adult.

At 27, I became a caretaker for my adoptive mom, who was at home, actively dying, in the home she and my father had raised me. My biological mother came to visit without advance notice. She didn't say anything to my mom, and I didn't think much of it. Everyone grieves differently. After retreating to the front room, my biological mother revealed her true feelings, sharing that "she wished she had never given birth to me, and she didn't want me. If it wasn't for my aunts and grandmother, I would not be where I am." I was devastated. For the first time, I finally received the truth from her and it made sense. I was nothing to her. She chose the most vulnerable moment in my life to tell me how she felt. I died inside that night.

The knowledge of my biological mother's addiction, our strained relationship, and my desire to be loved and accepted by her, was the beginning of my downward spiral; but my self-loathing began to surface shortly after her untimely revelation. The secret I kept was that I was depressed, ashamed and willing to do anything for love, and that came with a price. I didn't know how to love myself. I would look in the mirror, and I didn't know who I really was; and I couldn't put all the pieces together to find the answers. I felt worthless. I was in crisis, and I contemplated suicide. My self-esteem was destroyed and I began to drink. I gave up. I was broken. I had tunnel vision and such pain that my inner judgment to live became distorted. I finally followed through with my suicide attempt. I cut my wrist with a straight razor. It was in my worst moment, alone, burdened, exhausted, that I was given a second chance at life. It was then that I knew something shifted. I acquired a new-found appreciation and gratitude for life.

At that moment, I realized my adoptive parents had given me everything I needed and wanted. Although I was still longing for the love from my birth mother, I had to let her go. Through gratitude, I realized that I had all the love and affection from my adoptive parents all along, and I didn't need my biological mother to fulfill those requirements. Once I recognized the blessings of having loving parents, I was able to move forward to continue my life's journey and seek higher levels of ascension through being grateful for what I already had.

"The trouble is, you think you have time."
(Buddha).

I made it through the tough times, and you can, too.

There were consequences to my actions. The consequences were, I took my life for granted, I didn't see my life as a gift. I did not appreciate that I had people who loved me, instead, I expected for them to. I wasn't humble enough, and I finally realized no one owes me anything. By recognizing humility, I found gratitude. Living in the past cost me time, a delay in reaching my purpose, and almost my life. An example of time wasted was I didn't deal with my problems. I ignored them and stayed busy as a way to avoid working on myself. I just wasn't ready to deal with the reality of my failed relationships. I overcame that obstacle by leaning in with gratitude and knowing that everything happened as it was meant to. Had I stayed with my biological mother, I may have traveled down the road of addiction, living my life in shame or even worse, died from it. Another example of wasting time is, I learned to self-sabotage, and I would do it by starting my day out revisiting unforgiving thoughts of pain. The underlying root cause was, I didn't know how to be enough and deal with feelings of inadequacy. I overcame those feelings by seeking professional therapy. After becoming aware of my behaviors, I changed them by being mindful of my thoughts, and not allowing my negative thoughts or anyone else's opinion of me to damage my self-esteem.

Now that I am aware of the consequence of losing time, today my journey continues as I work to move closer to the vision in my mind's eye. Some of the most profound words of inspiration came from the legendary Les Brown, when he said, "The graveyard is the richest place on earth, because it is here that you will find all the hopes and dreams that were never fulfilled, the books that were never written, the songs that were never sung, the inventions that were never discovered, all because someone was too afraid to take the first step, keep with the problem, or not determined to carry out their dream."

Here's 5 things I've learned about myself that I want to share with you.

1. Time is valuable, cannot be recovered, and must be used/spent with wisdom.
2. Purpose is spiritual alignment with our God energy. It connects us with our true essence, and guides us to reach our highest, best version of ourselves.

3. Hindsight is a gift of reflection, the basis for clarity, an expression of gratitude.
4. Mindfulness is letting go, striving for self-awareness, and compassionate awakening.
5. Appreciation is a spiritual celebration, a prerequisite for gratitude, a vehicle for acceptance.

My life took shape through events, some in my control and many out of my control. I chose to improve and adapt while embracing all of who I am, and by being grateful for what I have.

I made a conscious decision to be honest with myself, recognize who I am, and who I was becoming. I began to acknowledge what mattered most - my feelings! I had lived in a state of denial and I refused to accept the truth about the state of my life. I allowed people to take advantage of me, and I accepted their abuse to avoid being alone. I overcame that state by taking a more rational approach to problem solving. Instead of ignoring my feelings, I removed those people from my life. I made a choice to feed my soul words of encouragement so that I could become more confident and I was grateful for each step I took in the right direction.

I had to choose love over fear, and select my words in a way where they wouldn't hinder my progress. I feared hurting people the way I had been. I knew what that felt like. I never wanted to show up and behave like my biological mother, someone who could say hurtful, unkind words, like she said to me. I overcame the challenge of being heartbroken by meeting people where they were. I am kind to people. I give compliments, and I enjoy being of service to others. It's easy and rewarding. I had to focus on what I told myself so that I could lose the limiting beliefs that kept me from believing that I was enough. I chose to be grateful for each moment. When the unexpected happened, I expected the best. I chose not to live in fear, but to live fully and deliberately. I accomplished this through gratitude.

Every day I was changing, and I still am. I look back, and I see so clearly the events that made me who I am today.

I have chosen to no longer close myself off to the possibilities that await me. I have done this through gratitude. Gratitude has been the key to my overall success, and through gratitude, I have an undeniable connection with the universe. I have appreciation in knowing that life happened for me, and that I am in a constant state of allowing. I received a second chance to live life and experience all I've ever dreamed of. I am grateful for the gift of hindsight. Knowing that I was where I was supposed to be and that I was never alone on this journey, is a moment of solace.

Here are 11-lessons I've learned based on applying or implementing gratitude in my life. I'd like to share them with you.

1. Through gratitude, clarity and discernment, the path to enlightenment unfolds.
2. Never be ashamed because of someone else's choices.
3. Live from a place of love, service and expectation.

4. The practice of self-love maintains the connection between Source energy and me.
5. The sacred bond of family can restore the light, even during the darkest hour.
6. The journey toward healing and self-worth is not linear.
7. Establishing positive therapeutic strategies promotes strong mental health and well-being.
8. What we speak is a direct reflection of our beliefs and mindset.
9. Embrace each spiritual transformation through the lens of love.
10. Letting go is spiritual resolve.
11. Gratitude is key to unlocking grace, hindsight, infinite truth and understanding.

"The wound is the place the Light enters you."
Rumi.

Through the awareness of my experiences, I had to choose to heal and use my pain as my strength. In doing so, whatever I thought my vulnerabilities were, have naturally become my greatest assets.

Each moment, and experience, has been for my greatest benefit. The event where my biological mother shared her true feelings was what I needed to understand the difference between receiving love from my adoptive parents, and feeling shame from my biological mother. My experience with suicide allowed me to see the importance of my existence and how blessed I am to be here today. What I learned through gratitude is clarity. I learned that I am enough and that trusting myself is the key to happiness.

The picture can become obscured, unclean and the message unattainable. That is, until we look back. It is often in hindsight where the pieces align, messages appear and the truth is discovered.

Gratitude is my birthright; pain is meant to grow from, but not to live in; and I will always be grateful for life and each experience. I know that the Universe made no mistakes. Gratitude taught me that nothing is by default in this life, and knowing that early on helped me get out of my own way. Shame can be dissolved, and once it was, I no longer needed to hide and be in fear. I can live, and love, as I was meant to.

The journey led me to where I am now. It was a necessary step in making me resilient, strong, brilliant, and perfect, just as I am. This journey has been my opportunity to learn. I will use it wisely. It is here and now. I can use each experience to leap forward and face each challenge that awaits me. I have become well-equipped to handle what I once feared, and that is one of the greatest achievements ever.

As a result of the distant relationship with my biological mother, attempting suicide and the self-sabotage, I've learned how to better care for myself. I overcame obstacles by repeating affirmations of gratitude twice a day while standing in front of the mirror. I journaled to get a different perspective about my situation. I began to practice mindfulness and deep breathing techniques. I learned to be gentle, show compassion and have gratitude toward myself and others. Most importantly, I had to give myself permission to talk about it, and learn to let it go. I am resilient and grateful and can make it through any challenge that comes my way. I am the key to unlocking all of my desires. I am bountiful, worthy of love and I am enough. Shame didn't serve me, and neither have any of the secrets I've held onto.

During episodes of depression, I began to use affirmations as a source of relief. I implemented affirmations as a part of my daily routine, and I have become more in tune with myself. I found peace, comfort, and optimism.

I will explain the steps I use to prepare each day for my affirmation session. I will explain what affirmations are, why they are helpful, why I use them, and the feeling or end result from using them. Affirmations are positive sayings or statements that can be helpful for overcoming negative thoughts. I repeat them in front of a mirror when I first wake up in the morning and right before bedtime. I do my affirmations two times a day. The purpose of repeating affirmations is to replace any negative thought patterns with positive thoughts. The results have been good. I feel positive and motivated. I've released critical levels of self-judgment and I've gained more confidence.

Here are the steps I use to help me focus and prepare for my day.

I first begin by thanking the Universe for all that I have, for all that I am, and for all that I'm becoming.

Second, I show my gratitude out loud by repeating:

- Thank you for the perfection of this day.
- Thank you for allowing me to awaken this morning.

- Thank you for allowing pure positive energy to surround and protect me.
- Thank you for my perfect health, wealth and prosperity

I am clear on my intentions and I only expect what's best for me to show up. I trust the Divine, the higher power, the Universe, Source and God's energy to surround me. I visualize being surrounded by this pure, positive energy and I quietly sit with it.

What I was looking for, I found, and the path to my healing was through GRATITUDE!

✡ ✡ ✡

Kathryn Washington, MPH

Kathryn Washington is the creator and host of SOS-Strategies Of Success podcast, where she examines mental health, wealth and mindset strategies that lead to empowering transformation, healing and wellness.

Kathryn is passionate about science, and uses it to improve the lives of those around her. By combining this passion with her expertise as an Army veteran, a public health professional and consultant, she advocates for and works with underserved communities through grassroots efforts.

She serves on healthcare panels for veterans and facilitates peer-led veteran groups and even makes appearances at the local barber shop, all while focusing on well-being and whole health. She also incorporates and teaches healing arts, energy, vibration and manifestation.

Kathryn received her Bachelors of Science in Biology from the University of Colorado, Denver, and her Master's in Public Health from Kaplan University, Fort Lauderdale, Florida.

Kathryn believes in the power of gratitude. She fully understands the transformation, expansion and perspective that comes from being grateful.

She trades in the stock market, adores butterflies, and enjoys thrill-seeking activities through free falling and tandem skydiving.

You can visit her online at: admin@sos-strategiesofsuccess.com

Be Intentional In All You Do

By Keke Andrews

What happens does not make you, it
will only break you if you let it.
Your choices decide your life.

I am the youngest of eight children. Prior to marrying, my father had two adult children and my mother had four children. By the time my youngest brother and I were born, all of our other siblings were grown. By the time I was four years old, my parents decided to return to Atlanta, Georgia, to live. Prior to the return, we lived in Los Angeles, California. There my parents owned a juke joint named The Psychedelic Shack, with pool tables, a long bar and televisions. We were able to visit the juke joint before the opening hours. During open hours was what my parents called 'grown folks' time.' I was born in California so when my parents told my brother and I that we were moving, I was not very happy. My parents began to tell us how we would get to see almost all of our family, especially those I had not met. My brother was born in Atlanta, Georgia, but did not remember much.

It seemed like forever, but we finally made it to Atlanta, Georgia. The first person I met was my father's mother and her name was Nana. She gave big hugs and lots of kisses. She lived alone in a small three-bedroom home. From day one my brother claimed the back bedroom as his. My brother was quiet and laid back. He would practice basketball by himself and sometimes would sit in a corner with a book. He made friends easily and everyone he met seemed to love him. He became the neighborhood 'son.' We spent time together. He would teach me how to read and would say you can watch television with me, but you cannot talk.

My parents and grandparents were influencers in my life. Nana was my father's mother who lived three houses up from our new home on the opposite side of the street. She was a slender, petite, soft-spoken woman who was very independent and wise. She had quotes for almost everything and would make you repeat them until you knew them by heart. Her quotes were life lessons that I later understood. One of my not-so-favorite quotes was "A job half done may as well not be done because it has to be done all over again." That meant whatever task you were given you were about to experience doing it all over again. Nana believed in hard work and dedication. Whatever you do, you do it to the best of your ability. She retired from a lighter company after thirty years of service. She was very proud of her accomplishments. As for my father's father, I never met him and don't remember anyone ever mentioning him.

My mother's parents lived about ninety to a hundred miles away from Atlanta in Crawfordville, Georgia. My very first visit was shocking. I remember us pulling in the driveway and seeing chickens running around. I asked my mother why the birds were not in the sky. She replied that these are yard birds. I did not want to get out of the car, so my father picked me up. Inside I was greeted by my grandfather, a tall man, and my grandmother, a very short woman. There were also other family members in the house visiting. I was beginning to wonder where all these people came from. I met my brothers and sister. All I remember was thinking that they were old. It was fun, we played and enjoyed ourselves. The next day we headed back home.

My father was a mild-mannered man. He would come home from work, take a bath and jump into his pajamas (he would call them house clothes). Then he would find something on tv and tell me to come watch with him. Most of the time I would fall asleep. By now, my mother would be cleaning the kitchen and my brother was at Nana's house. He worked as a mechanic at his job and even worked on cars for individuals on the weekends. He loved cars and working on them. When he was not under the hood of a car you would probably find him somewhere fishing.

My mother was totally opposite of my father. She spoke her mind without a second thought. She worked part time outside the home a few days a week and she was a hairstylist. She was particular about how the house was kept and reminded you to put things back where they belonged. Her hobby was sewing and she loved to make clothes and blankets. Every time there was an event to attend, she would make outfits. She also would cook on weekends and many people would stop by to purchase plates.

Our household was like the average, good and bad. If my parents stayed busy and kept moving, everything would be alright. The moment they had nothing to keep them occupied, the arguing would begin. My parents were functioning alcoholics. I often wondered if they drank out of boredom or would true alcoholic tendencies start them on a drinking binge. This was not everyday, sometimes it would not happen for weeks. But when it happened, you knew it was happening. It first started with some petty argument and exploded from there to something outrageous. Of course, it was time for me to go to my room when it started to get heated. You did not have to tell me twice. Doors would be slamming, there was screaming back and forth, even glass breaking as someone was throwing something against the wall. I would lie in my bed with the pillow over my head trying to block out the noise, fussing and sometimes fighting, until they became too tired and worn out.

This went on for years and I became numb to the situation. It did not bother me. I had gotten used to it and assumed that it was what all parents did. As the time passed, I realized that not all households were the same. I would talk to Nana about the fighting and fussing my parents would do regularly. I remember her saying it is not good and it is surely not right. She explained that all grown people don't fuss and fight like they did and when I got older, I would have to make the decision to not do the same things that they were doing. She always ended with "you know they love you don't you? They just have problems." Around the time I turned 12 my parents separated. My mother, brother and I moved to the country where her parents lived and my father stayed in Atlanta, Georgia.

Me being the daddy's baby that I was, I did not want to go. My brother being himself, he could adjust to any situation. My brother made friends quickly and was always gone. Like most, when you don't like something you can never see the good in the situation. I did not make friends and I didn't like people, because I was mad. I was not able to talk to my father and that was awful. The second year we were there, on February 13, a Friday night, the police showed up at my grandparents' home and told us that my brother was in a car accident and did not make it. My mother was screaming and everyone was crying. I was standing there looking at them. After a while I blamed my mom. I told her if she did not make us come here that he would still be alive. I just knew I was going to get knocked out. But she agreed and said I was right. When reality hit, I felt as if I had no one.

I talked to my father and Nana and explained that I could not stay there anymore. After a few weeks, my mother agreed that I could move back to Atlanta. My father was living with his girlfriend, and she had three boys, so I was not able to live with him. So, I was to stay at Nana's house. Wow, I thought. I will get the same treatment as my brother did. My mom would tell her that she was spoiling him. After the first couple of weeks, I was shocked. My brother did not have to do anything. I had a list of chores. I had to learn to cook because one day I may have a family. We would eat supper at the kitchen table and talk about our day. I was in school across town and had to catch public transportation to and from. My Nana would say school is out at this time and you get out there and catch this bus so you can meet the next bus and not have to wait for a long period of time.

As time passed, I met some friends and wanted to start hanging out with them on the weekends. In Nana's words "It is not a nice look for young ladies to hang out." We were just going to go places and grab something to eat. "Not in this house. My house, my rules, end of discussion!" So, I was not liking that and started thinking about what I could do. A month or two later I moved out and she asked where I was going. I said out of your house with your rules.

I moved in with my brother and his girlfriend at the time. I was enjoying life. My godparents gave me an allowance every week. I then staredt hanging out with friends and family members. I stayed up all night and slept all day. In my soul I knew it was wrong, but the flesh was loving every moment. We partied day and night, just having fun. I would occasionally call and check on Nana. She would give me her advice and I would listen, taking it all in and sometimes feeling guilty. When it was time to party, the guilt went away.

At sixteen, I was not feeling well. My niece had a doctor appointment and I called to see if I could be seen. I was told to come on in and they would see me. Me and my niece are at the appointment and they ask what is going on. I say, "Well I have a pain in my side." My niece was seen first. I was sitting waiting and the nurse said they needed to draw blood and get a urine sample from me. About twenty minutes later he comes in and says it is triplets. I say "wrong room." He laughed and said "I don't know how many, but the test is positive." My facial expression must have been very serious. He asked "are you ok?" Not unless he was joking. He then proceeded to tell me he would give me some time to digest the news. We left and I did not have much to say on the ride home. My mind was racing. What am I going to do? This was not planned, and I was not sure that I was ready. After arriving home, I had to do some soul searching. After several days, I decided that I was going to be a mother. I started collecting books and information from all the sources I could. After telling my Godparents, they decided that I should move in with them and begin to focus on our future. I moved in and started reading, praying, making plans and setting goals. I spent many nights asking God what I should do. I began to revert to the ways of my raising. I spent more time reading the Bible, refreshing my memory. Nine months later I was the proud mother of a nine-pound baby boy. Those big bright eyes inspired me to grow. We were a family of three.

I started school to get a certification. I begin working on building my skill set and working towards promotions and growth. Life was good. I had a family, was working and taking classes. I worked at a daycare for a while but realized that I needed more. So, I decided that I needed to get more training. So, I started to question people about their line of work. What made them choose that job, what skills were required and where did they receive their training. Many stated they knew someone who helped them get the job. I remember asking a family friend, who was an attorney, how and when did he know he wanted to be an attorney. He said during high school he looked at the job market and realized that there were two employment fields in life that will always be necessary - Law and Medicine. He chose law because he did not like the sight of blood.

By now my family is growing. I have a bouncing baby girl. I continue to take classes and look for ways to grow and better myself. I knew that I had to keep setting goals and growing. A friend introduced me to temporary staffing, it was the breakthrough that I needed. I joined the ranks of Corporate America. It became a lot easier for me to be promoted and provide for my family. We separated and stayed cordial. He would continue to pick up the children and do whatever was needed. Life was moving on and I was thanking God everyday that my children never lived in the type of atmosphere that I grew up with.

Philippians 4:13

I continue to thank God for everything and ask that he make me a better person. I went back to school. Computer Information Systems was the hottest educational topic. That did not last very long. Now I have two more bundles of joy, a boy and a girl. They are three years apart. Four children have me on my toes, but I enjoy it. Not long after I became a single mother of four, Philippians 4:13 became my mantra.

I am working it out. I drop the youngest two at daycare and then the older ones at school or at my friend's house so they can catch the school bus with her children.

It was hard sometimes, but I did not have a choice. My friend asked how I did it. My answer was how could I not do it. I continued to pray and kept my faith. Later I was able to put all four of my children into private school with aftercare that allowed me to not have to rush each day.

Now, everyone is growing and picking up extra curricular activities. I adjusted things to make it work. I cooked three days a week, preparing two meals each day. Through the school year and summer, we had basketball, football, soccer, band, student government, dance, algebra camp, and Upward Bound Program, just to name a few. I would not change a thing. It was a lot, but you can do anything if you believe in yourself and keep the faith. People will be themselves and they will show you who they are, just pay attention. Doing you is just that! Do what is best for your situation. Everything does not work for everyone. Find your path and follow it. There is nothing wrong with being different.

To the person reading this WISDOM G.I.F.T.S., stay INTENTIONAL. Whatever or whoever is your source or higher power, keep the faith and remain grateful as you grow.

To the co-authors and Queen Kim Coles and King Dr. E. Jaye Johnson, I am forever grateful for your service and inspiration. My battles hit hard during this project, but I had to stay faithful, and to each of you I say, thank you.

✲ ✲ ✲

Keke Andrews

Keke Andrews is the co-founder of Gifts 2 You, Inc., a nonprofit organization that assists disadvantaged youth. Gifts 2 You offers hands-on training and development in different career fields, workshops, volunteering services, and feeding those in need. She is also the owner of Business Credit and Services which offers entrepreneurs and established companies assistance in obtaining credit lines and growing their business. Later this year BCS will launch publicly. She received her Associate's of Applied Science Degree in Paralegal studies. During this time she received A

Resolution from the Georgia House of Representatives. Later she returned to obtain her Bachelor of Applied Science Degree in Business specializing in Management. Keke is a benevolent, self-motivated individual who takes pride in her community and gives back to those in need. She believes in continuing education through traditional schools and the knowledge industry. She is currently in a program studying to be a Life Coach. You can connect with her at www.g2yinc.org.

Is What You See, What You Get?

By Linda Fegins

I walked to the bathroom and looked straight in the mirror at my face. Reflecting back to me in the mirror was a black raised non-smooth birthmark plastered on the left side of my mouth, on the left side near my hairline, and around the neck. Further, tiny tumors are raised on my skin around my nose, my eyes, and lips because of the neurofibromas. Multiple tiny ones cropped up around my nostrils. How many had been surgically removed through the years to reduce the ugly impact on my face that were now growing back? There are a few new tumors.

The good thing is that I looked straight ahead without trepidation and with acceptance. I smiled. I can see the gems of my face that have been hidden by a birthmark and marred and overwhelmed by tumors. These skin conditions, in my youth and as an adult woman, in times past, impacted my self-confidence, influenced my interactions with people, and how I handled some social situations. No longer did the skin condition cause me concern.

I need to have some more surgery on my face to reduce the tumors, one more time, I thought. I care about my appearance, and it is my desire and right to look the best I can.

Scarface

My mind recalled the painful words that bruised and punctured the heart of an 11- or 12-year-old girl. "Scarface, scarface" my friend's brother yelled as I walked down the street. I was taken aback. I said nothing. Boys laughed. It happened more than once.

I told no one. Not even my dear mother, who had raised me to be proud, happy, loving and to live the best life I can. This was the one who always said I could do anything, and at 10 years of age showed me a picture in Ebony Magazine where Constance Baker Motley, the first Black woman appointed a federal judge, graced the pages. Former Judge Motley had served as an attorney for the NAACP and won nine out of the 10 cases she argued before the Supreme Court. The thought of becoming a lawyer to be a voice to help others was etched in my heart.

The smart and happy girl, who talked a lot, had great grades, and was recognized as smart by teachers, became sensitive about possible ugly comments about her face and sometimes limited her face-to-face contact. The girl who loved school, loved to dance and to give speeches, was hurt. The one who loved Shirley Temple and thought she would love to be in the movies, now knew she would never be considered to act in the movies.

Is Beauty Only Skin Deep?

My birthmark is not the cute little flat smooth birthmark people think is cute on baby bottoms. My birthmark is jet black, slightly raised, embedded on the left side of my mouth like a sea to me. It is also on the left side of my face in the hair line, shaped like a peninsula, where my hair does not grow well. The birthmark lies at the front of my neck shaped like a country and is thickly plastered on the back of my neck. The skin on my body has various café-au-lait patches and my left hand and left side is peppered with black moles that appear as freckles.

My skin condition was compounded by a more overwhelming skin disease that did not become visible until age 12 or so. Small raises or "hills" began to develop on the left side of my face. This became more of an issue than the birthmark because the left side of my face looked like I was covered with small hills.

One of the problems about skin conditions is getting the right diagnosis and the right treatment. Most of the various doctors I visited for diagnosis and treatment treated my condition like it was some form of acne. You see, the right side of my face was largely clear. I had nice skin, a keen nose that comes from my father's side and nice eyes. If one could sweep my face with a paint brush to remove the defects on the left, you could find an attractive face underneath the surface.

Finally, I learned the nature of my skin condition . The University of Michigan diagnosed my skin disease as neurofibromatosis. Neurofibromatosis I (NFI), also called von Recklinghausen's disease, is a genetic disorder characterized by the development of multiple non-cancerous (benign) tumors of nerves and skin (neurofibromas) and areas of abnormal skin color (pigmentation). One aspect of the condition is that café-au-lait patches arise all over the skin in various areas. That explained the 'hills' and now some 'mountains' on my face, and the café-au-lait patches on parts of my body and several moles, all largely on the left side. The tumors can grow anywhere in the body, but they grew on my face. They became more prominent and of more concern than the birthmark.

The combination of the two, but more so the neurofibromas, caused people, especially children, to stare. One or two people, thinking it was an extreme form of acne, told me, "I know a doctor who could get rid of your skin condition." Others asked, "Were you burned in a fire?" The look, stare and/or reaction on a few people's faces reflected that they wondered what had happened to my face. I heard a man, who pretended to be a friend, say to another, "Her face is messed up, but she has nice eyes."

I remember getting into an argument with one of my cousins. She reminded me, "You have that ugly birthmark on your face." A so-called friend needed a ride and asked me to pick her up. I agreed. I was always a good, reliable friend. Somehow, she did not hang up the phone right away and I heard her tell another person that I had a big black ugly birthmark on my face. I was a Juvenile Defender representing a young juvenile allegedly involved in a gang shooting in a jury trial, and one of the gang members said, "Baby, what happened to you?"

Accordingly, my skin condition sometimes affected my interactions and relationships with some people. I would hold my hand to cover the side of my face. Sometimes, I did not look people straight in the face or I talked to them from the side that did not have the birthmark on it. While my hair was well groomed as a teen and young adult, (I dressed well and later was armed with degrees), on a few occasions I could quickly walk into a room filled with a group of people and look straight ahead as if I saw no one, then I could be invisible. This bad habit of walking straight ahead, sometimes without speaking, focused only on my destination or purpose, made no sense, and could be perceived as mean or haughty. But in the early years, I still had the foolish thought that no one could see my face if I moved quickly straight ahead. It was a poor automatic form of self-protection from someone not saying, "scar face." What they didn't know was that I did not really "see" them because I was focusing on getting to my destination before they could see that side of my face. Those actions brought greater attention to me.

One Sunday morning, walking into church, a member let me know I had walked past her and did not speak, which is a "no, no" in the Black church. I stopped and apologized and told her I had a bad habit of focusing on where I am going which my Mother would chastise me about. Another church member who observed the scene came up to me and said, "I am so glad I heard you say that." That church member became a very good friend to this day .

When people got to know me, they could not believe how encouraging, helpful, reliable, kind with a servant mindset, and loyal friend I was. While I did not speak up for myself all the time, I disliked bullies and would speak up for somebody else.

Cover Girl

In my teenage years and young adult life, Mom hunted for makeup and facial items or accessories that would enhance my face so as not to focus on the blemishes. She was excited when she found Covermark in the late 60's and early 70's. Covermark was a makeup used to cover up birthmarks and other skin conditions and was really made for Caucasians. Mom mixed colors to find the right color for me. It was not made with Black skin in mind or the best match for my skin, but it was better than nothing and we worked with it.

My hair was very thin on the left side of my face where the birthmark lay. Mom discovered a male beautician who knew how to sew hair pieces in your hair in the early 70's. While in high school, I wore a piece on that side so that the hair would come down to my cheek to cover the left side and perhaps try to camouflage the dark sea around my mouth .

Keep Pressing On

In high school I was in the National Honor Society and took honors classes. Loving the arts and wanting to be a lawyer, I took a Debate class and was on the Debate Team. I was in the Thespian Society and tried out for school plays but never got a lead part. My Speech and Debate

Instructor did not know what to expect from me because I was very quiet in his class. However, when I stood to give my first practice debate speech, he was floored. He could not believe the voice and the presence that I had.

Outgoing yet anxious, I would still try out for activities in high school and college. In college I took theatre classes. I even auditioned for plays and was selected as an understudy once. I would help backstage. I would wonder if I did not get the part because I was not a good fit or was it because of my appearance. I went to some dances at college. A good dancer, I would shine on the floor. When my sorority performed, I would either lead in or be up front. On stages like that I shined.

An Answer?

Thank God that, in 1981, American dermatologist, Dr. Craig Roberts, in partnership with his makeup artist wife, Flori Roberts, created Dermablend. Dermablend's mission was to improve the quality of life for people with visible skin problems through high performance makeup. They recognized that skin care was not going to fully heal some patients. Some patients also needed special makeup to solve the problem. It was made for Black skin. Dermablend is a camouflaging makeup that contains high-performance pigments formulated to conceal the most difficult skin conditions or concerns, such as vitiligo, rosacea, hyperpigmentation, birthmarks, burns, scars, bruising, tattoos, and spider veins.

Around the age of 28, I learned of a surgeon who performed surgery on children with severe deformities.

I visited the surgeon's office for an appointment. Over the years, the doctor performed about five surgical procedures on me. It called for him to determine where the incisions would be made in my face and be in a location that would not leave a worse looking scar than the tumors on my face or result in a keloid on my face.

I would joke that it was like I was having a face lift. Initially, you could tell a difference. While nothing went away, some of the "hills" were reduced and were not as visible, and my face appeared smoother for a while. Excitedly, a few of the hills even miraculously appeared to have been removed.

Years later I discovered there was a gorgeous Black surgeon from Harvard University in the area and later he performed some work on my face.

Press Toward The Mark to Triumph.

These days, I am comfortable in my skin and less conscious about my face. I share my beautiful smile more. I am a bold encourager.

My love for the arts never waned and I have taken several (probably more than anyone) Detroit Repertory Theatre Workshops. I auditioned for a short showcase and nailed the part. I tried out for another short play written by university students and got a part. However, Covid 19 stopped the rehearsals.

Teaching Sunday school is a delight. Formerly, leading prayer boot camps for the Lydia Circle of Christian Business and Professional Women in Detroit and teaching prayer in the Bahamas for an International

Women's Conference was my passion. I've traveled to South Africa and Jamaica for missionary work and prayer work, under the leadership of the visionary for the Lydia Circle. I even campaigned for a judicial position and lost.

Yes, I may have gone through hell, but not as much as others with more severe forms of neurofibromatosis, which can cause learning disabilities, or others with severe conditions that affect their body or skin or challenge their health. Paul, the great apostle of the Bible, had some "condition" that he was not delivered from. When he asked the Lord three times to deliver him, God said, "My grace is sufficient for you." Whatever the condition, Paul made an impact on the world and triumphed over many enemies and much adversity to the glory of God.

In my forties, a large neurofibroma grew over my eyelid and I needed to have it surgically removed. As a result of the five surgical procedures I had earlier, my face was used in a presentation to show the various forms of neurofibromas.

No matter your skin condition or challenge, know that God has a purpose for your life, and you matter. You can overcome challenges. With faith, belief in God and commitment, you can triumph over adversity, heartache, and rejection. Didn't say it would be easy, but it's possible.

Challenge yourself to go after your dreams. You must learn to like yourself even with your flaws. It is important for you never to allow anyone to make you feel unworthy of kindness, love, and respect. Please don't compare yourself with anyone or try to be someone you are not. Making a comparison with others doesn't help with self-esteem and can lead to envy and unhealthy thoughts. Work on perfecting the good things about you. Take the time to discover and know your gifts and talents that can bless others.

Are you thinking or saying aloud, "My skin is ugly or awful. No one will love me," or "My skin is hideous. I hate myself," or "My skin is horrible, and the challenge or condition is tough to overcome. My life is hopeless." If you have experienced any of these thoughts or similar ones, reach out for professional help from a psychologist or therapist. Also reach out to someone you can trust who can help you. First, please know you are not alone in having negative feelings. I never said, "I hate myself," however, I know how one can feel hurt and long for the right treatment. Second, you can have hope that the God of hope will fill you with peace to know that things can get better.

Psychologists are recognizing that many patients with dermatological problems, especially disfiguring skin disorders, have psychological, mental and emotional problems. Psychological studies recognize that different skin problems can cause intense distress, lower self-esteem, cause lack of self-confidence, anxiety, depression, the desire to avoid face-to-face contact and physical isolation. Youth and adults who feel self-conscious, need to learn coping strategies, how to overcome negative thoughts about their appearance, how to handle social situations such as answering questions about their condition and how to cope with teasing and bullying.

You aren't alone. Seek the Lord and pray daily. No, not every challenge will be magically or easily wiped away. But you, too, can triumph over your circumstances.

You can take brave faith action steps to help yourself and to seek out the help you need for the healing you need inwardly and outwardly. Courage doesn't mean you aren't afraid of bullying, stares, and rejection, but that in the face of adversity you are willing to take faith action steps and press forward to triumph over the circumstances, to a better you and a better life.

And yes, it takes work. Yes, it hurts. Some days it may be tough, and you may be tired of going from doctor to doctor or feeling down. Holler. Sit down for a moment then get back up and take another step forward. Say "Lord, I can't do it by myself. Only through your strength can I take this step. Only with your help can I be triumphant over this condition."

Faith Steps

Pray, without ceasing, for strength, wisdom, favor, and resources. Develop a personal relationship with the Lord. Know that He specializes in things that seem impossible.

Learn to accept your skin condition, but take action to see what can be done to improve it.

Do not compare yourself to others. It can lead to envy and more negative thoughts.

Find sincere, positive friends who can accept you as you are.

Be kind to yourself and practice positive self-talk.

With SELF-LOVE you can have an
amazing, fulfilling, happy life.

Go for it, you are worth it.

✡ ✡ ✡

Linda Fegins

"More things are wrought by prayer than this world dreams of." is a favorite quote by a prayer warrior. Prayer, acting, writing, and teaching the Word of God and strategic life skills ignite her passion to serve and inspire others. Traveling to South Africa and Jamaica with a team doing missionary work was a challenging joy to Linda. At an International Women's Conference in the Bahamas, Linda taught a workshop on prayer and she has led many prayer bootcamps in the City of Detroit.

An attorney, Linda loves the challenge of oral argument in state and federal appellate courts. Linda's book, "The Courage To Be First," will be released this summer.

The Deborah Woman of Faith Award was presented to Linda from the Lydia Circle of Christian and Business and Professional Women. She also received an award from the American Business Women's Association for her service in the community.

Such real-life characters as "Eve" and "Sojourner Truth" have been brought to life by Linda in her love for the arts. A life-long learner, Linda loves to read, to dance, and to empower women to take courageous faith action steps to achieve their dreams.

Caught in the Middle

By Lana D. Tucker

"You don't have to pursue what you attract by the person you've become. Maturity, decisiveness, consistency, and strength are in the heart and mind."
—Alfonso R. Bernard, Sr.

Many people have pondered the question, "How in the world did I get here?" After I hit a low point in my life, I asked myself the same thing. At 51, I found myself in an all-too-familiar place. I was broken-hearted because of another failed relationship with a man who had said he loved me and would never leave me. I looked inwardly at myself and tried to figure out what happened, because as an engineer, that is what I do. I solve problems. After praying and reading a few more self-help books, I figured I would be able to open my heart again.

After a year passed, I was still hurting. So, this time, I wasn't sure if I was going to be able to bounce back and open my heart again. The decade of brokenness, unfulfilled promises, depression, and obsession to please or meet men's expectations had taken a deep dark turn. If the pain of feeling unwanted and unloved from every man I dated wouldn't stop, then I wanted to quietly depart the life that beat my hope of finding love to smithereens. I was so plagued with suicidal thoughts that I found myself looking on the internet to find ways to quietly end my excruciating pain, because my hope of finding love had dwindled. I kept questioning myself. Will I be able to love and trust anyone ever again? Was it not my purpose to be loved and get married again? Why was finding a partner, best friend, and soulmate so hard to do? How long will I mourn the 'one' that got away? How many years of my life do I keep repeating the cycle of meeting a man, getting to know him, and falling in love? My repeated rejections hurt too much; I wanted the pain of not being good enough to go away.

In order to understand and relate to the anguish I felt, it's important to know that I am driven by relationships. Therefore, my failures to find a rock-solid relationship with a man made me label myself as a complete disappointment. It didn't matter what I did for a living or how much I had, without the love and acceptance of the people around me, or better yet, one man, I saw myself as nothing, not worthy of love.

To heal and move forward, I decided to make a conscious choice to assess my past. Part of the reason I felt unwanted was due to my environment, not seeing many people celebrated, that looked like me. I live in a predominantly White city, Knoxville, Tennessee. When you see me, you would think I am a Black woman living a successful middle-class life. I thank God that I am blessed to have a family, my best friend, Robin, and many multicultural women around me who genuinely accept me. However, as a Black woman, there is an added pressure to daily prove my worth to others, which can be trying, painful, or exhausting.

Looking at my dating life from high school and over the last decade, I realized that in my hometown, most of the men I lived, worked, and went to church with, had only tolerated my existence, where I thought things should be different. No matter what color the men were, I was equally dismissed by them, as someone they could not see themselves loving long-term. I was around people who purposefully did not bring me into their inner world, they were only tolerating my existence in their space.

I naturally gravitated to dating White or Black men outside of Knoxville. There were some awkward situations with them. I had White men claim to love me yet avoided being seen out in public with me. One frequently took me to a bar that had confederate flags displayed inside. One said because his family would never accept me, what was the point of loving me?

Dating Black men was uncomfortable at times, too. Some of them said I was whitewashed, as in not Black enough, or an 'Oreo' (white on the inside and black on the outside). This was partly because in politics, I considered myself to be Ultra-conservative. They hounded me to vote the way they thought most of the Black community was voting on any issue. I call this 'blackwashing;' which is when you are Black, and another Black person tries to endlessly shame and bully you into fighting for every perceived belief and cause of the entire Black community. I did not relate to most blanket statements about what Black was supposed to be in America. I held the stance that one Black person's experience, although valid, is not the experience of the entire Black population.

From my dating experiences, I had to take ownership of being disgruntled about how I was perceived as a Black woman in America. I did not want to focus my identity solely on my skin color. The 'one drop rule,' which was one of the laws of some states in the South, said that if you had any African Black ancestry, or one drop of color, you were Black. I wanted to identify exclusively as an American woman. Much of my DNA is from people in Scotland, England, Denmark, Nigeria, and Southwest Africa. I didn't want to water down any of it. The poet, Langston Hughes, mentioned in *The Big Sea, An Autobiography,* that he was not Black because there were different kinds of blood in his family; he said he was brown.[1]

Much self-reflection showed me that the world of dating had been difficult, and at times, painful, because I felt like a social misfit that had difficulty completely connecting with the Black or White men I dated. I felt 'caught in the middle' of what I was supposed to be in the White world versus the Black world. I am not considered to be biracial, but in terms of my community experience as a Black woman in a White world, I was torn and pressured by the men I dated to make a choice, pick a side. Are you on the White side or the Black side? I didn't want to do that. I should have stood up for my life experiences, regardless of my skin color.

I decided to process and take ownership of where I was in the dating process and the many mistakes that I had made. Why was I feeling detached from the men I dated? How long had I been this way? I was certain of one thing. I was a spirit-filled Christian. Being a Black woman, mother, daughter, sister, friend, and professional were great, but those parts of me did not completely define what I most valued, my Christianity. Although proud of my faith, I downplayed this side of me sometimes when dating. I would not talk about my prayer life or the fact that I prayed in tongues. I would not talk about my favorite televangelists or striving to walk in love with everyone I met. I did not often ask the men I dated to come into my spiritual world. Although the words and actions of my parents and other strong Christians had directly shaped me, I let society and the men I dated tell me who I was supposed to be in their world to gain their love and respect. I didn't correct them when they were wrong. This was something that only I should have had the courage to do. I sacrificed the very essence of who I was by failing to end relationships where someone did not celebrate all the different parts of me.

While dating, I did not always choose men of character because of my low self-esteem. Many of them only focused on my outward appearance. Physically, I have never felt attractive in my White community. There were not any public images celebrating voluptuous Black women in my hometown. So, I spent thousands of dollars on my appearance to gain acceptance. But because it was not coming from the right place in my heart, I still felt unattractive and insecure. That was my mistake.

Another piece of the puzzle for my failed relationships was that I had unrealistic expectations. My number one criterion for dating someone was that they had to be a Christian. I could not have cared less what color they were. However, I demanded the label of being a Christian man to mean perfection. In the end, their unfulfilled promises were crushing. But, as humans, all of us sometimes fail to meet each other's expectations, no matter what our faith is.

As I reflected on the different pieces that shaped the happy person I am today, I looked back. My college years were when I came to understand myself. I went to Georgia Tech, where my friends were Black, White, and genuine. I later received a Bachelor of Science in Civil Engineering degree from the University of Tennessee, Knoxville. This is where I got to know love, and understand myself as a Black woman. While the people in my White world were watching "Friends" on television, I was watching "Living Single," "A Different World," and "Martin" instead. I discovered that I did relate to many Black women and men. I joined a historically Black sorority, Sigma Gamma Rho, Incorporated. Despite being on a predominantly White campus, this experience was a beautiful multi-cultural experience for me. The ladies I was inducted with were not only Black, but White, Brown, and from other countries and backgrounds. They embraced me! We embraced each other. Because of my newfound Sorors, I found out that there were a lot of beautiful colorful girls who grew up like me and many who did not, but our differences weren't our focus. It was a beautiful time in my life.

As I continued to look back at all the people and events that shaped me, I realized that I was no longer going to accept my low self-esteem and was going to speak up about my beliefs and faith. In the Christian world, I feel that over the last several decades in the United States, most of us have been quiet about our beliefs and our faith. We have not stood up for our principles for fear of being misunderstood, or even worse, labeled haters from the people on the outside looking in, who do not understand our beliefs.

Although the recent inhumane killings of Black women and men that I witnessed completely shattered and broke my heart, it made me face the fact that I had been sheltered in a predominantly White community all my life, whether I was dating or not. I had held my head down. I could have experienced racial, gender or other discrimination daily from others I was around, but I kept to myself and didn't look people in the eye or question their motives. I now have the courage to stop sitting quietly in the corner, making excuses for the community I live in, and instead, open my eyes to ways that I am likely not accepted. I have an overwhelming strength and courage to speak out when people say things that are not true about my God, my life, and my beliefs, whether I am dating them or not.

Through it all, despite the poor dating experiences I have had in my life, I appreciate the fact that my parents have affirmed me. They encouraged me to live my life to the fullest. My mom was an amazing homemaker. My Dad is still a phenomenal Chemist. My parents chose not to continuously play the race card in my formative years. They rarely made blanket statements like, "White people" this or "Black people" that. They talked about the good and the bad in all people. My mother said, "I have never doubted the greatness of Black people. But know this. There is a difference between knowing your heritage versus carrying the weight of it. If you are in

Christ Jesus, you know that we weren't meant to carry the weight of the sorrows of your ancestors...the anger and pain destroys you mentally, physically, and spiritually." This helped me go beyond the pain of discrimination and hatred towards focusing on the good in all people.

My grandmothers and aunts told me to put God first, and that is who I am. My place of worship, Redemption Church, taught me that I am a child of the highest God, and that this identity trumps everything. My non-denominational faith taught me that God is no respecter of persons. There is nothing I can do or not do to change his love for me. I was taught that I must have a relationship with God. This means reading the Bible, praying, worshiping, being thankful, and showing the light of Jesus Christ that is in me by being kind to others no matter who they are or what they have done.

After sitting back, and looking into my past, I am in a good place. I am more vocal. I do not hide the fact that I choose first to be identified as a Christian, always. I want all my actions and words to validate this. As I have not given up on finding a mate, I have determined if someone I am dating is only tolerating who I am, instead of celebrating my quirky and unique ways, then we can part as friends. I vow to do the same for them. I will remember that celebrating someone and their excellence doesn't mean they are perfect. Authenticity is powerful. As I have grown to love who I am, I try to surround myself with people who embrace me, Lana. I am an American, Christian, and beautiful woman of color. I would be happy to tell you all about myself, if you would just ask, and invite me into your world. All I have ever wanted is to be accepted and loved. Whether I am blessed to find the man for me or not, my God offers acceptance and love to me. He offers it to you, too, as he is no respecter of persons. You can't earn it, you deserve it!

Whether you choose to identify by the color of your skin as a source of pride or not, remember it can't entirely explain the beautiful pieces that make up who you are and your life's story. Approach one another daily with a clean slate. Your name is the starting point that represents who you are. Introduce yourself with the intention of helping the other person know what you want them to know about yourself. Be intentional and respectful when sharing your views. When someone misunderstands who you are, gently correct them. Openly share what makes you interesting and worthy for anyone to get to know. When people ask you specific questions about yourself, choose not to be offended. Be purposeful in getting to know people different from yourself. They just might bring kindness, laughter, caring, and more importantly, love into your life.

This statement from A.R. Bernard, Sr., "You don't have to pursue what you attract by the person you've become. Maturity, decisiveness, consistency, and strength is in the heart and mind," has helped me to take ownership of where I am in life and how I see myself. I have learned not to be afraid of being genuine. I became intentional to heal my heart. It was through self-reflection, prayer, Christian-based counseling, mental health awareness, and confiding in my mother, women of faith, and my best friend, that I got back on the right path for me. Before this, I didn't know, understand, or fully value who I was. It's ok to realize that you are different amongst the people you are around. Dig deep inside of yourself and note the things that drive you, that make you want to get up each morning and do the things you do. Operate in your own belief system, respectfully. Make a note of your painful experiences and find a support system to work through them, so that you can move forward and help other people who may have had similar challenges. This system can be your family, friends, social clubs, wellness programs, counselors, or a good church.

We all bring a different spice to the table. I now refuse to let someone, something, or society limit how I bring it. I am not average or mediocre. My worth is not measured in someone else's timeline, their system, their favors, their politics, or their unwillingness to give me opportunities to utilize my brain and knowledge to bring kindness to the people I meet. I will not be held back by someone's lack of respect or understanding of who I am, in Jesus Christ, and what I am called to do for God, either. I choose to simply humble myself, love, and serve.

Finding SELF-LOVE has made me blessed and fabulous! Bless others by telling the world who and how lovely you are, because nobody can do it better than you!
~ Lana Tucker

Citations

I. Langston Hughes, *The Big Sea, an Autobiography* (New York: Knopf, 1940).

* * *

Lana D. Tucker

Lana D. Tucker graduated from the University of Tennessee, Knoxville, with a Bachelor of Science degree in Civil Engineering. After cultivating the desire to be a writer, she wrote her first book, "Releasing Your Life," which has helped those looking to simplify their lives, while focusing on what matters to them the most. Her personal ministry mission is to focus on broken-hearted people who feel stuck in their lives. She has a compassionate heart and desires to help Christians reveal Jesus Christ, who is the light within them, to others they interact with in their everyday lives.

Currently, she is a manager at a utility company where she has been employed for 30 years. In her spare time, she likes to watch movies, eat out, go to concerts, immerse herself in Bible study and self-help books, travel, and hang out with friends and family. She grew up, and still resides, in Knoxville, Tennessee. You can visit her online at www.EmbracingLight.com.

The Sixty-Year Triumph

By Debra Bonaparte

Personalities and behaviors of mistrust, rage, challenges to authority, very few boundaries, low self-esteem, bad money management, self-sabotage, and more came out over my lifetime. I'll start at the foundation of where this started with me.

My younger sister and I would play while getting her diaper changed. We're 1½ years apart. She'd be chewing her hair and thumb-sucking. One day something fell; I bent down and saw a bird underneath the chair. I reached for the bird, but it pecked and jumped away from me. I stood up excitedly, "It's a bird under there!" Dad's mother, Mama Elli, said, "There's no birds in this house." I said, "Yes, it is," pointing in the direction of the area. Mama Elli sternly said, "No, there are no birds in this house!" My parents owned the house, and Mama Elli was just a guest at that time.

In her uniform as a registered nurse, Tee, my biological mother, was sitting across from the front door, on the steps, ready to go to work. Her name (short for Tabinique) came from my brother who picked it up from one of our uncles while visiting. It stuck. She saw

Mama Elli accusing me. She glanced at me but didn't say anything.

Tee often said, "Don't open the windows," while she was gone. Maybe because it was the first level, and someone could've come in and attacked the family. Or, maybe because there were no screens on the windows and critters could've come in. However, Tee said we could go outside, possibly encouraging Mama Elli to get out to sunlight and fresh air. Instead, Mama Elli would open the windows to get us 'fresh air' because she didn't want to go outside. I believe that was the issue with the bird in the house. It would've shown that she had disobeyed, jeopardizing her welcomed status.

In front of Tee, Mama Elli gave a snickering laugh and called me a storyteller. That was a close way of calling someone a liar in our household. I looked at Tee for support and reassurance, but she didn't give it to me. After giving Tee a work hug, I looked out the window, thinking she would turn around and give me a wink, a nod, or some validation when she left, but she didn't. My foundation shifted. That was the first time I felt an emotional separation from Tee, but it wouldn't be the last time Mama Elli called me a storyteller.

We lived on the west side, and my younger sister and I ran in and out of our small 2-story house. I'm sure we were probably dirtying up the floor, making a lot of noise, laughing, and having fun. Mama Elli didn't want to clean up after us and told us to stop, but we didn't. She told me to tie my shoe, but I didn't know how; I was only three or four years old and hadn't been taught yet. She yelled again, "Debra, come here and tie your shoe."

My sister and I went into the kitchen and sat down on the floor.

While we were looking at my shoestring, Mama Elli, mumbling, "I'll bet you gon' tie that…," went into the kitchen utensil drawer and returned. I looked up at a knife with jagged edges. She said, "I'll cut your throat if you don't tie your shoes. Now!" pushing the knife towards my face. Terrified, I screamed, cried, and froze. My sister hollered, "Ooh. I'm going to tell Tee!" Mama Elli quickly returned the knife to the drawer. My sister helped me tuck my shoestrings into the side of my shoe. I was shaking by then. The days after that incident, Mama Elli would tell Tee that I was telling stories, making up stuff. I told Tee that I didn't trust Mama Elli. Tee was very ambivalent and shrugged it off, not doing anything about it.

I found out decades later that my sister never said anything to Tee about the incident. Initially, she said it wasn't necessary, that was how Mama Elli was. Ten years after that, my sister admitted she was scared to say anything because she may not have gotten fed by Mama Elli, who was our full-time nanny while Tee and Dad worked their businesses.

Months after the knife threat, we moved into our next home. My oldest sister, younger sister, and I shared a room in that house. Altogether, there are six siblings, plus Tee, Dad, and Mama Elli. Mama Elli started coming into our room, supposedly to read bedtime stories to the 'babies.' Except, when she got to my bed, I heard about lying, the boogieman, imagining things and making 'mountains out of a molehill' while I was trying to go to sleep. More accusations and undermining of my character would go on for years from Mama Elli and, eventually, Dad.

Because of Tee's schedule, Dad became responsible for potty training and bathing my younger sister and me when we were around age four to five. Initially, when I went to the toilet, he'd cut the lights on, which would make me grumpy. They were bright, so he'd turn the light off, leaving the door cracked open, to get light in. One night, I overheard Mama Elli tell him, "Don't believe Debra. She's making up stuff." Dad asked what she meant. "She's telling stories. Don't believe her." I don't recall Dad saying anything after that comment. He came back into the bathroom to get me off the toilet.

Shortly after that, during one particular bath, Dad told me to stand up so he could bathe me. I would've been four or five before starting kindergarten. After standing up in the tub, Dad washed me gently in the front, then told me to turn around and bend over a little. Next thing, he was digging and scratching me with jagged nails in an area that I was not familiar with. I screamed, saying, Dad, that hurts. He said, "I'm just trying to make sure you're clean down here." When I turned back around, his averted eyes looked weird. I thought, "Okay, what did I do to be cleaned like that?" I sat back in the bathtub. My younger sister, who was there, excitedly jumped up thinking it was pleasant and said, "Dad, do me." He started laughing. "You're not that dirty back there." I remember sitting in the bathtub looking at them, puzzled, "What made me so dirty?"

I refused to stand up whenever Dad told me to. I sat there with my back on the bottom of the tub. He tried to pull me up a few times. Each time he would get me up, I would slide back down. Tee worked the third shift. Often for more than eight hours.

She got home from work in the morning, saying she was tired. Dad told her. She came to me and asked, "How come you won't let your Dad give you a bath?" I said he hurt me down there. She asked what I meant. I whined, "I don't want to because he hurt me down there." She looked at me quizzically and said, "Okay, I'll bathe you, but you have to stand up in the sink because my back hurts." I started smiling.

She bathed me in the bathroom sink. We had a 60's style mirror chest with a half-moon on top (my sister and I called it 'The bologna'). Still playing with my younger sister, I couldn't reach the bologna while standing in the sink. So I grabbed a hold of the light to reach it. It shocked me. Tee immediately said, "Your hands are wet, leave that alone!" We were connected, and I'm sure she got shocked, too. That was the last time I spoke about the bologna.

Another time, for reasons I don't remember, Dad gave me a spanking while I was sitting on the kitchen floor. This spanking was different. Usually, our spankings would be 3-5 hits. He hit me almost ten times, but his eyes were so distant, like he wasn't there. A similar appearance as that invasive bath. I kept yelling, "Dad, stop!" but it only seemed to fuel him more. The swinging door behind me opened as I was scooting away from him, and he lost his balance. I crawled and then ran from Dad around the dining room table. He couldn't catch me.

When Tee got home from work, I didn't run to give her a welcome home hug. Dad told her he had spanked me. She came and asked me what was wrong. I told her, and she said, "let me see." I showed her. She examined the bruises, nodded, and went into the kitchen, closing the door behind her. I heard Tee tell Dad, "Never touch Debra again." He had spanked me in between my legs.

I didn't tell Tee I was eavesdropping, but 'never'? Will he hold my hand again? Will he play piggyback or carry me upstairs again? When I went to school the next day, I thought I would come home from school, and he would be gone so that he wouldn't hurt me again like that. When I got home, he was there. My heart sank. How long was he going to be there? Who could I trust now? I started talking to our dogs and God.

Over the years, Dad rarely healthily touched me. Sometimes my siblings and others would be there. Was this a secret game everyone was playing? Was nobody talking about it? It didn't make sense to me. Why didn't my sisters get touched the way I did?

Other people thought my parents were these great, upstanding people with their businesses. They had adult foster care homes, restaurants, a small motel, and a farm during their lives. The companies had good cash flow, meaning they could pull enough cash off to pay for other stuff. Tee's other passion was cooking, and the businesses allowed her to embellish that, so my siblings and I always had provisions, physically. I witnessed their support and encouragement to my siblings. I thought I was adopted and only getting taken care of by osmosis because my siblings lived there. Thank goodness for their presence. But emotional support for me? I lived in the darkness of their shadow personalities with the residual effects.

Dad went into voyeurism and inappropriate touching, for over ten years, with me in our next two living places with all the different spaces. At the next house, there were plumbing problems. Dad would come into the bathroom unannounced to check and ensure the 'plumbing and water were draining properly' while I was getting out of the bathtub or shower naked. By then, I was having issues at school with boys inappropriately touching me and trying to figure out what was happening with all this irregular bleeding (menses) from my private parts.

One day, when I was 11 or 12, Tee was hot pressing my hair. By then, she had started repeating what Mama Elli had implanted in her head about me. I matter-of-factly asked, "How do you know when somebody's lying or telling the truth?" It was a question she didn't want to hear, let alone answer. Tee burnt my scalp from either the heat from the comb or hot oil while she yanked my hair, growling—no more hot presses. A few days later, I decided I would never speak to Tee again about Dad, boys, or anything about my body that she didn't ask me about. Fifty years later, I can still feel that scar.

I was 13 when our adopted cousin came to live with us. He was Cinderfella at his house. By then, trust with my authority figures was virtually gone. Tee and Dad quickly validated him. At first, I was like, "Ain't this some shit." But he boldly supported my interests, encouraged and listened to me, thereby becoming another shield for me. Mama Elli despised him for that.

When I turned eighteen, at Tee's behest, I applied, got accepted, and went away to college. Whimsically, before I left, I decided to confront Mama Elli while she, Tee, and I were sitting together in the front room. Wherever the chips fell, oh well. I had been depressed and contemplating suicide for a while, years. For 14 years, Tee had treated me like a liar.

We started talking. Mama Elli spoke about telling somebody something, and I asked, "Why should anybody believe you?" She looked at me and smirked. "When you pulled a knife on me and threatened to cut me about tying my shoestrings, you said I was a storyteller? Why would anybody believe what you say?" Mama Elli responded, "Oh, you know, I was just joking." I looked at Tee. Her eyes got as big as silver dollars. Tee looked at Mama Elli, then me, and back at Mama Elli and said, "You mean to tell me that was true?!" Mama Elli said, "Oh, you know how kids exaggerate. It wasn't that bad. It was just a little ole butter knife." I went to the toilet to break the tension from the flabbergasted look on Tee's face. When I came out of the bathroom, Tee glanced my way but stayed sitting in her seat. I went upstairs to my room and shut the door. I lay down, crying. Tee never came to apologize.

Twelve years later, after I got married, had my only child, and divorced, Tee, finding out she had organ cancer, came to visit Atlanta where we were living. Tee explained that she knew Mama Elli was being mean to us, and Dad wasn't 'right.' But she was scared. She didn't press issues because Tee didn't want to be a single Black mother with six children. She was afraid Dad would leave, and Mama Elli would also leave. What did she mean by 'right?' I was silent, but the look on my face! I was livid! Hours later, I thought, "If that is what money will make you do, I don't want it!"

She could've whispered, I believe you or somehow validated me. When she died, I was angry. I never heard her say, "I'm sorry." Years later, I started therapy twice a week for almost ten years. Most of my relationships were toxic and disrespectful. I needed to figure out how to fix them and me.

However, Dad never crossed those boundaries again once I got married, even when I divorced and eventually moved back home with him being a widower. In time, Dad's apology would be helping me raise my son to be the well-rounded, caring, creative genius he is today. Dad didn't abuse any of his grandchildren. Before he transitioned, I told him I was in therapy. He simply replied, "Good."

Common to many abuse victims, I didn't realize I'd been mistreated by all my authority figures until after Dad passed away, the last one of them.

I exhibited a shortlist of common behaviors as a sexually abused child.

- Excessive shame by holding my head and eyes down
- No age-appropriate boundaries around private parts of the body
- Bullying
- Crying excessively
- Clingingness
- Long periods of being down

- Terrified to be around certain 'acceptable' people
- Second-guessing my decisions
- Extreme personality changes

Solutions, for those with similar issues, can consist of:

- Remove the child away from the threat as soon as you realize it.
- Often, the child will tell you, even though they may not know the right words.
- Make counseling or therapy with the child a priority. They need you.
- Put your own needs/desires on hold temporarily to protect your child. A few months or years is temporary compared to decades of bad relations or the guilt of your child trying to commit or committing suicide because of your inability or unwillingness to support them while in your care.

I am grateful for:

- Access to abundance
    - The galleries, museums, or public libraries to get absorbed in the art or books, where I would stay until closing. (Often, they would put me out.)
    - Free art classes. Most of the time I got my parents' permission.
    - I could go to my parents' business, not far to walk.

    - I usually had bus fare to get from/to home.
- Provision and physical support; even abusers aren't 100% bad.
- I didn't get put out on the streets.
- Even though they didn't realize it, my siblings were a profound lifeline.

What I've learned from therapy, wise folks, and meditation are:

- To channel my emotions into creative outlets of art.
- To refrain from giving away my power because of someone's position or title; observe their heart and how they treat others and me.
- I have the right to defend myself in whatever form it takes.
- All children have varying and different needs. My parents couldn't figure out the validation for me.
- Money is a tool.
    - It can be used properly or be abused.
    - There are (or should be) ethical responsibilities with abundance.
- I can find mothers in many different women.
- I did have a few good teachings from my authority figures.
- I'm here for a purpose, ordained by the Creator, higher than my parents.

- Dad could be a good father figure because I had seen it exhibited with others.
- Prayer is personal. How I communicate with the Creator is my business.
    - I can be shy, even confused.
    - Or very loud, vocal, and, yes, cursing. I won't knock God off the Throne.
    - Don't limit what or how the answer will come; I'm not that big.
    - God answers me through: interfering in situations, random people, dogs, birds, insects, plants, and even the wind.
    - Some of my most potent prayers have been, "Help."
- Radically, I am learning to
    - Trust
    - Remain calm
    - Be righteously obedient
    - Create or maintain boundaries
    - Be self-confident
    - Be fiscally responsible
    - Value my self-acceptance
- I am one of the infinite Universe's creations: one in several billion egg/sperm possible combinations. Resilience is my inheritance.

We are spiritual beings having a human experience.
Pierre Teilhard de Chardin, 2015

* * *

Debra Bonaparte

Born and raised in Detroit, Michigan, during the Civil Rights Era, Debra Bonaparte, with her family of eight, spent many summers in western Michigan. The author's siblings, their pets and art provided grounding.

Following high school graduation, she enrolled at Western Michigan University (WMU). Following traumatic incidents there, she left to redirect her focus. While refocusing, Ms. Deb fell in love, got married and had her son. Post-marriage, she raised her son with a hawk-style demeanor to minimize his exposure to inhumanity. Being outspoken, corporate work life was not for Ms. Deb. Accepting jobs for easier access to her son, she included work as: farm manager, substitute teacher, server, cashier, and restaurant owner; while catering to her free spirit.

After induction into Phi Theta Kappa and The National Dean's List, Debra re-enrolled at WMU, and 18 years after first stepping onto the campus, graduated with a Bachelor of Science degree.

Other accomplishments include a Board of Directors executive position as Training Committee Chairperson for a local cooperative, and a Paralegal Certification from Emory University.

She lives in Georgia and enjoys art, travel, tinkering, and Pickleball.

Visit RadicalHealthSeries.com. Need a speaker? Send request to dblmrllc@gmail.com, subject 'Speaking Request'

Tell Your Story With Intention and Style

By Zayna Rose

What do you do when the world doesn't see you the way you see yourself?

So often, there's a significant difference between who we are and who others think we are. There is a difference between how we're known and what we know we can do and be. When we begin to tell our story in new ways, this gap starts closing.

We present ourselves to the world through our voices and words and through actions, body language, clothing style, social media content, and much more. It feels obvious that impressions of us are being formulated while we are interacting in person. Still, it's also potentially happening at any time because most of us have left representations of ourselves online in the form of photos, videos and written content. These pieces are signaling people and speaking on our behalf, even when we're offline, at the theater, snacking, or napping!

It's much easier when people see us for who we know ourselves to be. It's certainly good for business, and helps us live with more fulfillment, confidence, and joy. I've lived on both sides and everywhere in between. I know how it feels to be misunderstood, overlooked, and misjudged. I know what it feels like to be recognized, accepted, and celebrated for my true self. I'll tell you more about that in a few minutes.

If we take our place as the narrator of our story, we have an opportunity to tell it over time, with intention. I'm advocating for this here. Working on how you present yourself to the world is an act of leadership and self-love. It's our best chance to be seen the way we see ourselves, and the benefits are unlimited.

What I'm sharing in this chapter comes from my experience and is for anyone, regardless of their background, or the culture with which they identify. When I write about confidence, style, and beauty, it's with a global perspective, an open mind, and an open heart. Beauty begins on the inside, and style is rooted in one's unique essence and point of view.

My Favorite Magic Trick

"Zayna, what did you do?" I thought I heard panic in his voice. This was the headline of the voicemail left by one of my favorite early clients. I'm paraphrasing, and it went something like this: "Zayna, I need to talk to you; what did you do? Please give me a call back."

I had helped him by designing and facilitating a personal style makeover. We'd been shopping for new clothes, we'd visited the hairstylist, and had some extensive discussions. I got nervous when I first heard the message and quickly realized the chances of a post-makeover emergency are low. (On the other hand, pre-makeover emergencies are surprisingly common. Think, last-minute job interview, last-minute media appearance, hot date with dream person, and only hours to get ready.)

Anyway, back to that message. I laughed with relief after giving him a call. The next part of the conversation was spoken politely and with respect but much funnier than the way I'm paraphrasing it here. Let's just say, he said: "Women are giving me so much attention! What did you do?" My reply? "You love the way you look now, and I'm guessing you're giving off a different energy that's pulling people in!"

I'll tell you how I think it works based on my twenty years of experience in this area. It's something that has been determined by many, in different ways. I've learned a lot about psychology, communications, personal development, sales, negotiation, relationship-building, digital marketing, etc. All of that helps me to get results for people, and there's something else that's more important.

When you change the way you see yourself, you change the way others see you. In this context, change is simply growth, and it can be a small tweak or a big shift. Personal life and business move forward. Who we are and what we want for ourselves evolves, and so must our self-expression.

When you love the way you look, the way you move, the way you talk, the way you walk, etc., it activates something in your energy that, when amplified, can make you unstoppable and radiant. The confidence, comfort and happiness that can come with this are not to be underestimated. That's the magic.

Intentional Authenticity

There's a lot of talk about being authentic. I've often been asked how someone's brand or image can be authentic if it's carefully crafted. To me, crafting your image is about making sure that the messages being communicated by conversation, body language, relationship building, style, videos, photos, etc., align with the person's personality, values, purpose, and who they are growing to become. It can be done relatively quickly, but it's deep work.

You don't need to figure out the perfect way to be or the perfect way to look. You just need to give yourself attention, ask questions and try new things to figure out what feels good and what works. I see it as self-nurturing.

Science shows us that first impressions matter and that how we put ourselves together can influence our success because of the mechanics of perception. *You* are your most important audience member. You don't need to turn it on every day, but when you know how to be at your best, you carry that confidence in your raggedy sweats with the holes (that you should probably recycle, but they're too soft to give up), as well as, in your loveliest ensemble. Suddenly, and maybe strangely, it doesn't matter how you look because you can turn on the inner light and do what you need to do! That's the place to be.

It may not be an easy road. Underneath the portrayal of ourselves to the outside world lie the feelings that are closest to our hearts. Do we feel accepted, beautiful, or attractive? Do we feel as though we're enough?

I won't say we *should* feel these things because we all have different priorities and experiences. I will say that working on feeling more accepted, beautiful and, as if I'm enough, has helped me to be the happier, more productive, more powerful person I needed to be. My ambitions are big. I want to help many more people, and my previous state wasn't going to get me there. Changing the way I saw myself made everything move.

Feeling Beautiful Is Complicated

Is it important to feel beautiful? For me, it is. In my experience, there's an extra layer of complication if the way you look isn't lined up with the most commonly accepted standards of beauty.

As a person of color, I've been quietly battling against misconceptions, stereotypes, and assumptions for as long as I can remember. These things hit very close to the heart because it's judgment about something I can't change, and so often judgment about something that isn't even true. I'm Canadian, with parents originally from South Africa who met each other in Canada. I love to travel, so I feel comfortable in many places, and I've got relatives in spots around the world, including Ireland, the United States and South Africa.

I love being Canadian! By the way, you can thank us for the telephone, peanut butter, time zones, Ryan Gosling, basketball, and the Wonder Bra. If you're familiar, you'll know we're extremely considerate and we live in a truly multicultural country.

We still live in a time where discussion around the color of one's skin is raised and judged by familiar people and strangers alike. My frustration isn't about not looking

Canadian in the way some expect. That's easy to brush off. It's about the unwanted assumptions and questions that come when people focus on my complexion so they can figure me out. I do have to say there are many people I meet who are simply curious about me and want to relate to me. The tone of voice, language, and facial expressions in conversation tell you what you need to know.

It's tough, because you're rarely told outright that you're not being accepted because of the way you look when that's the case. People often have just enough sense to talk in code about why you're not right for them or for the opportunity. You can't prove it but you know it and it hurts. Of course, what I'm talking about also applies to those not accepted for *anything* they can't change or choose not to change.

If you've ever been at a disadvantage because you didn't fit someone's vision of an ideal mate, friend, or collaborator, then you may have developed emotional armor, fascinating coping strategies, and self-doubt. I did. I used to have moments where I wished to have skin one shade lighter or to have green eyes, just something to make me look slightly more acceptable. I just wanted people to see me the way I saw myself and to have them focus on my personality, because it's rare and incredible!

I've taught myself to feel beautiful, and it was a lot of hard work. I no longer wish to have different features. I still wish I were two inches taller, but that's a hurdle for another day! It feels strange to write about this, but I've come to a place where I can discuss it without discomfort and with the intention that someone out there will relate and know they're not alone. My experiences made me careful, watchful, and sensitive. They also informed my wit, creativity, and my, sometimes dark, sense of humor.

I've experienced things slowly changing. We have an expanding global sensibility when it comes to beauty. Many thanks to activists, publishers, entrepreneurs and artists, to name only a few. In some situations it's less of a roadblock to have a complexion that isn't fair and that's a big deal.

If you haven't experienced what I've described, I'm sure you know someone who has. More than ever before, I'm seeing people accept each other first and ask questions later out of genuine interest rather than judgment. There are more than enough people out there who think and see with their hearts first. When we see ourselves and treat ourselves as beautiful and stunning, those wonderful people come running. See others and yourself inside-out and keep that going!

Who Let Me Wear That?

I've watched many people cope with the stress that comes with taking last-minute guesses on how to dress for a big interview, pitch, or important photoshoot. While I'm happy to come to the rescue, I may not be there to take the call you're making from the dressing room at the mall because you stopped to buy your outfit on the way to the big gig. This happens more than you'd think. I get it. It's important to handle logistics, content, and strategy first. How we're going to present ourselves is often an afterthought, but it's actually a critical part of the content.

If it works for you, share my approach of meticulous planning for important moments (when possible) while not taking it all too seriously at the end of the day.

Although style is one of my areas of expertise, I've often regretted outfits I've worn. I probably should have been embarrassed, but I've found it funny instead.

I took two excellent dresses to my TEDx Talk and managed to wear the less flattering one. I found myself at a prestigious gala in a casual denim dress (that one wasn't my fault). While seated, the waist-up view of that outfit was just silly beside all the gowns at the table. Thank goodness for the emergency red lipstick I carry when I travel. It helped me keep the attention on my face. I've also been comically overdressed at a special event that sounded formal and featured more shorts and flip flops than anything else. That's the last time I let a Carrie Bradshaw outfit from an episode of Sex And The City show me what to wear instead of just asking.

Having an imperfect approach and a sense of humor about your style is helpful. There may be regrets but, in the long run, it's a much less stressful way to go. On certain days, you'll need one of your best looks, with each detail carefully planned. On other days, a clean t-shirt, some decent natural light, and the digital lipstick in your Zoom settings will do the trick better than you might believe. My friend, Haley, and I must have amused ourselves for thirty minutes while trying out each color and asking each other which looked best.

I love helping people to create authentic looks they love. I enjoy and respect the art of fashion, yet I'm not a fashionista. You don't need to spend a lot of time, energy, or money to love the way you look and feel good in your outfits. A level of dedication to discovering what you love and what works well, strategically, is what matters. This will change over time as you, your preferences, and priorities change.

What was *your* best worst outfit? Plan ahead when you can, and don't feel that you always have to look your very best. It's exhausting! I prefer not to cringe looking back at photos and videos, but it's hard to avoid that all together. Usually, it's not as bad as we think. The most critical eye is often our own. Try things out, stretch your style, make mistakes and enjoy!

Prioritize Naps and Snacks

This is the second time I'm mentioning snacks and naps in this short chapter. You can switch these out for cross-fit and making healthy smoothies from scratch, if you like. Team nap, team workout...you decide. The point is, you'll have more time for whatever you love to do when you spend less time getting ready to go to parties, meetings, go on camera, or to just look like a grown-up who leaves the house sometimes. When you've got a styling system in place, you'll save 15 minutes here and there. You can use that time to catch up on a task or to sit on the couch watching half an episode of a sitcom you've seen twenty times. You know the dialogue by heart and still laugh out loud? Worth it.

When people take a long time to get dressed and groomed or worry about what they'll say, it's usually because they want to look and feel good. That's a wonderful thing, and it can be much quicker. You've got gold when you've figured out what supports your true personality style and your goals. . Experimenting with different looks, different conversation styles, and different ways to market business projects is a way to determine what works best. We often act out of habit without considering what's most natural and powerful for us. Let it be easy.

Lead From Your Heart and Soul

Most of the people I work with arrive with a goal in mind. Some want to be more effective speakers on camera or on stage. Some want a makeover to look more professional, confident, and modern. Others want to feel different and refreshed, yet some want help crafting their public image and digital presence. In my opinion, all of this can be summarized as leadership development. The more an authentic image of you is put forward, the more powerful your story, your presence and your potential will be.

I care about this because it makes it easier for people to live their purpose and to reach more people with their work and wisdom. I also love witnessing the relief and joy that can come from a satisfied or joyful self-expression. For some, it's a little boost. For others, it's like being liberated from something that's been weighing them down and holding them back.

One of your most significant assets is your expression. Nurture yourself while finding ways to expand. Sometimes that means doing something that scares you. Maybe it's speaking up for a cause or telling someone how you feel about them. Perhaps it's signing up for a new adventure that accelerates the expansion. I've accepted an invitation and I'm about to leave on a motorcycle trip across Scotland with my friends Amy, Angie and Whitney. This is totally new for me. The first thought I had after confirming that I would join? If I do this, I'm going to feel like I can do anything!

True Authentic Expression Is Brave

Having style, charm, grace, and humor seems universally helpful and the perfect complement to intelligence. At the heart of it all is our voice and our story. Our own Kim Coles recently said, "Embrace, celebrate and curate your story in a way that unlocks the same for others."

We'll probably never know the extent to which we'll affect and inspire others. It can grow from a passing compliment you don't remember giving, an old embarrassing YouTube video you don't remember making, or something you wrote in a book chapter that will travel worldwide .

I was recently told, "You say things other people won't say." That was a powerful moment for me. Using my voice feels more important than ever, and I try not to hold back when it can make a difference. True authentic expression is brave.

You're standing up to receive speculation, criticism, celebration, affection and more. I believe it's not worth holding back self-expression. Declare yourself and stand for yourself. Dress the way you want to, go for the goal you're told is unrealistic, and tell people you appreciate and love them every chance you get. Be who you want to be *now*, regardless of who you've been. If it feels true to you and your purpose, say the things others won't say and do the things others won't do. Use your voice. Use your presence. Use your energy. Use your love.

You know who you are and you know what to do. Be intentionally authentic and proudly imperfect!

✡ ✡ ✡

Zayna Rose

I've been an Image Strategist & Consultant for 20 years. I'm a TEDx Speaker, podcaster, digital marketing nerd and confidante to my clients.

I believe everyone has the right to love the way they look and feel. I use a blend of creativity, image strategy and communication science to help you with your presence, branding or personal style makeover. I'm focused on making this fun and easy!

I want you to be happy when you look in the mirror, happy when you open your closet and happy when you jump on camera. You might find me dressed up in a serious business meeting and other times you'll find me chatting with a client over gelato while wearing ripped jeans and sneakers.

I'm committed to results, I'm relaxed and open with a global sensibility. I advise top industry leaders as well as those simply looking to find more confidence and joy in their personal lives.

I've been featured on the TEDx Shorts Podcast, CTV, BBC, OWN, CBC, The Globe & Mail and more. If you'd like to hear about working with me or about having me speak to your group, please do visit me at zaynarose.com or message me on Instagram @zaynarose.

The Womb of Harlem, The Birth of Wisdom

By Louise Miles-O'Shields

"I am humbly Sacred, and beyond all time measurements, you are Sacred Too."

I am Louise O'Shields, a Phenomenal Master Intuitive Life Coach. I am a Master at my craft of guiding others to their soul's desires mainly because of the mighty people who conceived & raised me within the "Womb of Harlem" New York.

In this fantastic journey to capture a full scope of how I learned about Wisdom, I have to give the credit and complete **Gratitude** to The Wise Ones of my home and my Community.

I was born in Harlem and raised in two separate communities simultaneously in the 60s and the 70s. The joy of living between two communities meant that I was always living in a wealth of emotional abundance and love.

Yet my life experience on 113th Street and St. Nicholas Ave was the vortex of **Wisdom** for me. My natural family had resided in the Art Deco Styled

Tenement apartment building since the early 40s. Attached to the building was a storefront space that my two aunts converted into a community center. Everyone in the neighborhood called this space "The Center" and that it was the Center of unlimited fun and wise counsel.

The Center is where children from 110th Street to 116th Street came to play; youth & young adults came for summer jobs; the elders sat inside and outside with watchful eyes being the vanguards over us all. The Center is one of the central locations where politicians and activists came to take care of the business for Harlem.

Here is where I will share with you some of my heartfelt experiences of how I was taught the art of Wisdom by those who dared to dream us all-powerful.

Without question, for as long as I can remember, every day of my life was an **Epic** exploration of Wisdom and knowledge created by **"The Wise Ones."**

"The Wise Ones" of Harlem, who lead the way for me, are a unique group of diverse guides who have experienced life on life's terms directing us all towards our most significant capacity for absolute success. The Wise Ones consist of; all the elders in my natural family, the neighborhood Aunties, Uncles, Big Brothers & Sisters. They are deeply rooted spiritual elders of many backgrounds and beliefs. They are coaches, lawyers, recovery sponsors, artists, substance users, activists, doctors, boosters, sports legends, entertainers, and nurses. They are grassroots politicians, educators, Nana's, self-created business owners, and community organizers; they are the ones who usher you into a lifetime of Wisdom. "I

am Forever Grateful for those who agreed to serve as "Wise Ones" with love.

The Awareness of Wisdom

My Aunts, who created our local community center, were vigorous community activists who took me, my cousins, and our friends to community meetings since we were eight or nine years old. They always had a task for us to do, like passing out the long yellow legal writing pads with writing pens to all community members before the beginning of each meeting.

When we completed our task, we would go to the last row of chairs and sit down quietly without ever being told to do so. We were well behaved because we knew that the meetings would be motivated by intellectual conversations, documented facts, heartfelt debates, and creative solutions. So we wanted to witness and hear it all! We also wanted to be the first online for the Curry chicken, rice and peas, and the Jamaican bun cake!

Suppose there was a problem in the Community on Monday. In that case, you could almost know with certainty there would be an active solution before the end of the week because the elders of the Community had no tolerance for community misappropriations or any manner of lack.

Swift community action is what Wisdom looked like to us! Wisdom looked like **planned self-actualization in action**! Our community leaders never begged for any services. Our community guides only demand access to resources that benefit community members who are neglected by the dereliction of social equality.

Our community advocates were Master Manifestors who often taught us that every living being is a mystical and sacred scientific Miracle that deserves dignity and self-respect. They often led us to practice the skills of Visualizing in Action. The Wises Ones guided us to see what we desired from our soul's eyes, then move forward to implement what we wanted in our power.

During this period during the early 70s, The Wise Ones are relentless about creating holistic community services. They nail it by acquiring unlimited resources to allow us to walk forward into creative greatness.

The Wise Ones contended that we, the descendants of formerly enslaved people, should always consider ourselves worthy, just like all humans should. Yet, because of the harsh life that our Ancestors endured, we should never forget that we are powerful because of those who dared to live free and create more.

I discovered that one's **Self-Worth** is a behavior that you practice by granting yourself the authority to soar forward even if you have to fly above expectation to feel the power of your rich source. **"I am grateful for knowing the power of Sacred Self- Love."**

The Practice of Wisdom

In preparing to share my experiences of how I obtained knowledge of Wisdom, I have realized that all of my foundational experiences concerning the use of Wisdom did not occur because I am an adult with a lifetime of experiences. My Wisdom came from The Wise Ones in Harlem.

I observed early in life that Wisdom for me is a combination of synchronized (harmonized) learning experiences that continue to teach me how to expand my capacity to discover and practice the skills of navigating through life euphorically. I further understand that as an adult, I have to consciously embrace and practice the life lessons of The Wise Ones daily so that I can become a gifted Wise One too!

The Wise Ones say that everyone is innately born with the ability to experience infinite Wisdom through wonderment and curiosity.

As my peers and I are coming into our pre-adolescence, The Wise Ones are upgrading the life lessons to match the life experiences we may encounter when independent of their close and wise supervision.

One of the primary life practices that we are encouraged to practice earnestly is the **Wise Actions of Discernment.**

The Actions of **"Discernment"** was often described to us as the ability to make wise decisions in complex situations without hesitation! You had to learn how to make decisions that served you well and kept you safe. Now that my peers and I were preparing to be independent of direct adult supervision within the Community, it became imperative that every physical move we made was well thought out and purpose-driven.

My cousins, peers, and I were mindsets ready for this illustrious moment when we could move through the streets of Harlem on our terms. But, in **"The Womb of**

Harlem," your freedom as an adolescent is determined by how well you listen and how well you stick to the community structure and protective rules. If you could not listen or pay attention to what was going on around you at all times, you would only get to watch everyone else move around freely from your front window until you learned how to follow the golden rules of **"Awareness."**

The rules for our pre-adulthood lifestyle were set in stone by The Wise Ones to ensure that we would flourish in Wisdom and evolve into our sacred creative flow.

"I am grateful for the Wisdom of Discernment and the Favor of Actualizing Illustrious Self-Love."

The Freedom of Wisdom

The time finally arrived when my cousin, my peers, and I were free to explore all of New York City to practice the art of life and the skills of Wisdom. We traveled everywhere together. The United Nations was one of my favorite places to go with my friends. We would run from room to room, listening on the headphones to representatives of different countries speak in their native language with translations being made by American Interpreters sharing concerns and possible solutions to some of the world's life dilemmas. However, my most enjoyable moment in this great adventure was to admire the beautiful stained glass windows inside the United Nations that often symbolize the notions of international peace and human rights order.

Going to adventurous places in New York City is what we did as teenagers; we surrounded ourselves with lots of fun combined with the Wisdom of impactful events that could change the world. We obtained this way of being because of how The Wise Ones exposed us to the laws of the Universe and the human rights agenda for sustainable equity throughout the world.

After our travel adventures in the city, there was nothing like catching the subway train to return to our native Harlem. It was priceless to emerge from the A train to the heartbeat of 125th Street. You could hear the music blazing from Mr. Bobby's record store playing the Staple Singer's song "Let's Do It Again" or any of your favorite songs.

The Marquee on the Apollo Theater is glowing with the announcements for the next show. The steak house aromas of flame-broiled steaks and giant buttered garlic bread are next to the Apollo, inviting you to dine with savory flavors that make you twist, dance, and explode with happiness!

Then as you walk a few feet away from the Apollo Theatre, you see true magic and artistry appear before your very eyes. Mr. Franco Gaskins, internationally known as The Picasso of Harlem (Franco The Great), is painting significant and vibrant murals of African American images on the metal storefront gates on 125th Street. Bus tours with people from all over the world come to Harlem on Sundays to see Mr. Franco paint and purchase his printed artworks.

I am in complete awe of Mr. Franco's ability to make all of 125th Street look and feel beautiful with his visions of greatness for our Community. We would ask him a thousand questions about his paintings, and his eyes would light up with glee because we were curious.

Mr. Franco explained to us that he painted the metal security gates on the storefronts with positive images of our people so that we would have pride in ourselves and Harlem. He told us that we all had unique gifts and talents that would take us far in life if we would promise never to give up on ourselves. Mr. Franco is genuinely a **"Wise One"** who painted our future powerful.

"I am Grateful to explore profound Wisdom with others who love to enrich the world."

The Knowing of Wisdom

My Mom has polished me well in my home life, for she is a Master Manifestor herself. She has provided me with infinite Wisdom, love, warmth, and a lifetime of affirming wise adventures, yet she encouraged me to explore my view of the world and bring her back the new knowledge.

Once a week, my cousin and I faithfully go to our favorite Harlem bookstore called **"The Tree of Life."** This book store is like standing in the tombs of Egypt itself. The walls are all covered with pictures of revolutionary vanguards for the liberation of black people worldwide. The wise men and the young men of the Community are in the reading areas having philosophical conversations about Marcus Garvey, Malcolm X, and the new knowledge pouring out in great quantity from the youth.

You are always greeted into the bookstore by the manager of the day with great salutations like **"Welcome to The Tree of Life, my beautiful Black Nubian Princess."** Then, of course, we would giggle and smile as we would respectfully respond, **"Thank you, my brother."** After the greetings are honored and completed, it feels like your soul leads you to the books that your destiny is seeking for you!

Most books feature the intellectual achievements of black people from all over the world since the beginning of time. Here, we learn more about how to expand your higher consciousness in The Tree of Life.

My cousin is entirely captivated by all things Egyptian and wise, and she is ever-expansive about all things African history. She will pick out books and large posters showing the stories about the great Egyptian dynasties and come back to the neighborhood to hold her African studies class, and we are only 12 and 13 years old.

On our walks back home from the bookstore with all of our literary evidence, knowledge, and proof of our combined cultural Wisdom, my cousin and I constantly analyzed everything in our surroundings. We often humbly give thanks to the "Heroin" addicts who would rise from their drug-induced nod to "speak life" into the power of our pre-determined success. Even the pharmaceutical dealers would hide their business exchanges from us to encourage us to stay in school and follow the path of The Wise Ones.

Harlem was just a 24-hour ocean of Wisdom. Everywhere you went, someone was encouraging you to win! **"I am grateful for those who practice the collective Art of Manifesting in Wonderment."**

Elevating In Wisdom

The time of my youth was long, enchanting, consistent, and steady. My peers and I are quickly approaching adulthood, not noticing that the wise ones are putting on the final touches of great Wisdom upon us to ensure that we are ready for the world in front of us.

In the community center on 113th Street, The Wise Ones have registered us of age to work summer and winter jobs in the Community. The wise ones ensure that the seniors have plenty of food and affordable housing. They are preparing the older community siblings for higher education and progressive employment. We, the seasoned teenagers, are teaching the younger ones behind us about the Wisdom of The Wise Ones.

It's now the summer season; the play street is open, alive, and vibrant with relentless laughter and endless fun. The sprinkler cap is screwed onto the fire hydrant, shooting rainbow-colored water from the sun's reflection. The boom box blasts Marvin Gaye's song "What's Going On" while The Wise Ones are sitting outside in their lawn chairs, keeping watchful eyes on us to make sure all are well according to our social norms.

In my mind, I planned to remain in Harlem to run the community center that I had grown up in my entire life. However, The Wise Ones had other plans for my life. So, I applied to colleges just like the community siblings before me. My high school teacher, a wise one in her own right, encouraged me to pick out an HBCU (Historically Black College & Universities) that I might like. So, I decided to select Tuskegee Institute, and Tuskegee Institute chose me.

Of course, after college, I returned to Harlem to work where else but on 125th Street in the Human Service field of foster care and adoption. I had to come back home to give my expertise back to The Womb of Harlem. So I have spent thirty-five years of my professional career practicing and serving humanity through the foundational skills taught to me through The Wise Ones.

It has been a pure honor to represent and lift forward generations of wise counselors. I bow in sheer gratitude for the lifetime of wise guidance granted to us all. I have learned in my great explorations that Wisdom is a lifelong adventure of practicing the majesty of living.

"I am grateful for the journey of Wisdom."

The Celebration of It All

As a Life Coach, I discovered that we are all spectacular Miracles navigating through the seasons of life. Our lives have unprecedented value, and each one of us deserves to live a life full of bliss and audacious existence. Wisdom helps you to relax in the unpredictable shifts in energy.

Wisdom is a life form of thoughts that often brings you ease, clarity, and new instructions to celebrate it all!

In my lifetime, I have heard people say that there is nothing new to be learned under the sun, but The Wise Ones say this is not true. The Wise Ones said, "There is always something new to learn under the sun, and it radiates from the new knowledge formulated by each of you."

Remember that no matter what you are growing through, you are supposed to be here celebrating your miracle! You are here to create, discover, learn and win!

I want to take this opportunity to give special thanks to my amazing parents for their profound courage and Wisdom in willing me to The Wise Ones in the Womb of Harlem. I am forever grateful for the many prayers that have granted me safe passage into my power of becoming a Wise One Too!

"I am always sacred, and above all things that matter, you are always sacred too!"
- Ask Mama Louise

Louise O'Shields

Louise O'Shields, known as "Mama Louise," is an Emotional Wealth Master Intuitive Life Coach. She is a graduate of Tuskegee University with a degree in Psychology and offers over 35 years of Life Coaching services to those who desire personal development and sacred capacity/inner growth.

She is an avid ever-evolving gardener, passionate about observing how all living things grow. She was born and raised in Harlem, New York, and now resides in North Carolina on a vision-board-manifested farmland with her amazing husband and instinctually gifted furry companions.

She loves to connect with ancestral guidance to support soulful victories and innate passions. Mama Louise loves the extraordinary adventures of antique collections, searching high and low for boudoir excellence.

Her ultimate goal is to ignite the hearts of humanity to see each other as one! Come and join Mama Louise on all current social media platforms under "Ask Mama Louise" and you can always book your Transformational Life Sessions on her website www.askmamalouisetoday.com

TRIUMPH in the Eye of the Storm

By Debra R. Baker

Fired! It was a sunny late summer afternoon. I turned to the back of the performance review document. There was a recommendation that I be terminated from employment for failing to perform. What?! How could this be? Three of us sat together in the small conference room, separated by a square wooden table. In the room, beside the table and chairs, were Katrina, my supervisor, and Martin, who was new to supervising Katrina. He had only arrived at our department thirty days before. I had been in this large 25,000-employee corporation and 200-person division about twenty-four months longer than either Katrina or Martin and I worked as a member of the company training team. I was asked to redesign an emergent leadership program and co-led their upper 700-person management program. Clear data of the emergent leadership program showed that 85% of my adult students, post program, went on to receive various promotions. 93% of participants said the program was "excellent."

These same adult students remarked that the program was "life changing." To accomplish this, I was teaching four days a week and designing one day a week. Sometimes, the day began at 5am and ended at 8pm, leaving me exhausted, but I would share with Katrina, my White supervisor, that I loved my job. Not once did she share any concerns about my performance. There was not even a look of dissatisfaction. Once, Katrina co-facilitated two four-day courses with me. Even then, I never heard, either verbally or in writing, any concerns. Likewise, I was never given a performance improvement plan, but then again, apparently these two did not understand performance management. Now, seated in this chair, I was completely aghast at the recommendation. Are they really talking about me? Are they firing me? This can't be! Katrina and Martin read the evaluation line by line. I felt as though I was having an out-of-body experience. I wanted them to give me something concrete - it wasn't there. This just couldn't be happening to me!

Breathing is a resource! During this meeting, I became anxious, and I was shaking inside. I was feeling traumatized, and I was thinking that my husband and I had a ton of financial responsibility, and I could not afford to be out of work at the moment.

While Katrina read line by line, I positioned my phone underneath the table and with a trembling hand I sent the following text to my husband, Kevin. "They are trying to fire me." He responded, "I'm on my way!" – that's my man!

Katrina and Martin cited the reason for the termination being that I didn't create an evaluation process for the emergent leader's program and that I had not completed the instruction manual. As they continued to nervously ramble on, something came over me and I took a deep breath in. I slowly raised my head and looked into Katrina's eyes. She sat in her white capris and yellow top shifting uncomfortably in the wooden seat. I watched the power dynamics at play. I saw Katrina frowning and leaning in, accusing me. I continued to focus on my breathing. I was nervous but staying grounded with each breath. I reminded myself that I am a creative, beautiful, African American woman, who had, at my desk, two years of completed program evaluations. The ones they said weren't complete. They never asked me if I had them. They assumed they weren't done. I also had a partial manual with the rest of it in pages to be placed in the manual – this Katrina knew. I made a conscious choice not to defend myself. I wasn't going to plead with them. As African Americans, we're acted upon and then asked to defend ourselves. The other inequity here is my White counterparts were given six months to design, research, text, and write all their programs, manuals, and evaluations. I, on the other hand, was given 30-days, with no resources, and I still succeeded. Oh, and it was strongly implied by leadership that I "should" help my White counterpart with her program because there was a racial training component included and, of course, they wanted a person of color to be involved. If I had not helped, I was told it "could" reflect negatively on my review. I remembered all of this with each breath I took. Katrina was now a bit more amplified trying to get me to become defensive. As she talked, I reminded myself I come from a strong family background of working-class people who instilled in us a strong work ethic. We always excel and do more than required. I reminded myself that I've led this work with integrity. I was clear about myself. So, I chose not to defend myself. The power dynamic continued – her voice was the only one invited. When Katrina finally stopped talking, I responded with dignity and an even tone, "Clearly, you have made up your mind. Please let me know what date you want me gone. I'm not going to continue this conversation."

The meeting was designed to satisfy Katrina and Martin, so I was expected to stay, while White Katrina continued and tried to get me to admit to receiving an email from her about the manual. I received no such email from her, and I asked if she could provide it. She ignored my request and went on reading line by line. Being a spiritual woman, by now I could feel the Spirit in each inhale – I wasn't alone. Katrina and Martin continued to stagger through words and accuse me based on the two issues outlined. For me, the meeting was over. This meeting was the last one Katrina and I would have because she had accepted another job and was out the door the next day. It was clear there was an agenda at play. The meeting ended and I still had no leave date.

Focused on the eye of the storm - PURPOSE. Clearly, I had been swept into some corporate agenda. My magnificent husband dropped everything to get to me. Upon arrival, he threatened to come in, "do I need to come in there?"- that's my man!! I asked him to remain in the car and let me come out. As he drove us toward the park-n-ride where my car sat, I re-counted the events for him. We were both stunned. There was a clear disconnect in our minds. We were in such shock, he drove right past the park-n-ride, as we absentmindedly forgot my car for the evening. While at our neighborhood market, Kevin pushed our small cart ahead of me down the frozen aisle of the store. I walked, dazed, behind him. Suddenly, he stopped in front of me, spun around and said these words, "You don't owe anyone an explanation about anything. Your reputation precedes you. I knew about you before I met you." He had my attention. A little shaken, I asked "What do we do?" He asked, "What do you want to do?" Well, his words and love were the gifts I needed to emerge from some of the shock.

Martin blundered around for over two weeks before giving me a leave date. The excruciating emotional pain would come and go, but I made certain to appear clear and calm on a daily basis. Finally, Martin called to see me. He said it was his job to believe Katrina and he didn't have time to do an independent investigation. I listened and then calmly repeated, "I would like to know my exit date." The brief meeting ended.

And then, one day I was on my way to teach my cohort and I heard in my spirit, "Remember, you are not here for the leadership of this department. You are here for the cohort who show up weekly to receive what you have to impart to them." That clear voice washed over me. I knew I had a purpose statement on my desk, written earlier in the year. I began to read it daily. I decided that if I was leaving, I was going to give this class everything I had. They became my focus, and my purpose statement became a compass in the eye of this storm. The longer the department took to share a departure date, the more it confirmed the issue wasn't me.

So, I did the following:

1. I got clear on who I am – gifted, educated, and resourced. I reminded myself of this daily!
2. I told myself the truth about the situation. I did the best I could do with the time and resources I was granted. I couldn't have done any better.
3. I leaned into my friends – male and female. I had them check on me regularly. I was in racial trauma. I didn't allow shame to bury me.
4. I remained intentional and focused on PURPOSE. I was there to influence and speak into the lives of the current cohort. Being focused on my purpose also helped to ease some of the emotional pain.
5. I documented the experience and I inquired about legal resources. The department didn't pay attention to the fact that I have a lengthy legal career as a social worker in my background and could access members of the legal community any time.
6. I devised an exit plan and worked on my purpose at the same time.
7. I made sure to care for myself by having a cry as needed to release anger. I then continued to resource myself with rest, prayer, good food, water, and by attending a couple of circles including a racial trauma healing circle.

Watch from the balcony. With a plan in place, I began watching department leadership from a distance.

I noticed everything like I was on a balcony looking down. There appeared to be other questionable things going on in the department. Leadership was also making more mistakes with me, and I was documenting them. Something was clearly amiss.

Department leadership finally came with a settlement agreement, including a leave date that was six months later! They wanted me to graduate the current class, package the program, and leave silently. In return, they would let me keep my paycheck and benefits.

For my human resource professionals, I know your hair is standing up on the back of your neck. Among other things, you might be thinking "When someone is separated from employment it happens almost immediately. Not six months later." ---Yes, I know!

About a month or so later, while walking, I was mentally reviewing for class, considering my departure, and thinking about the next meeting with my lawyer. I heard these words gently in my spirit, "Be still." Well, I've had enough experience with such a leading to know that Spirit was up to something. So, I held that note in my heart. I began to feel less urgency for making an exit. However, I kept documenting and watching from the balcony. While I knew I was following the voice of God and I had not gone through a situation like this before, some pain was still present, but a great deal less.

The departure. As the months went on, I made the decision to share my leave date with a handful of people whom I had come to enjoy in the department, a few of them African American. The sad thing is, we (African Americans) worked in the same department together and only knew each other by face and name. It seemed we appreciated each other from a distance. One day, I stepped into what appeared to be a casual conversation and in a gentle professional tone, I explained that I was leaving. They seemed stunned. With gentle dignity, I went on to tell them that I was being fired and shared my exit month. They became visibly outraged! Little did I know, these now precious co-workers had witnessed and admired my work from afar.

As time progressed, I was heading to class one day and was told to see our office manager and the director's executive assistant, both African American. During a break, I went to find them. On my way, I slowly turned my head and looked to my right. While looking through the glass front double doors, I saw the back of what I knew to be Martin's head and a bag on his shoulder - he was leaving the office. I didn't think anything of it until I found the executive assistant and the office manager. I slowly walked into the same room where initially I had been fired. I was told Martin was no longer employed in our department. Martin was let go! It was further explained, Martin had made serious mistakes and my termination was one of the most egregious.

This was not my demise, I was shocked. I finished class and found a quiet area to calm myself and express my gratitude in prayer.

New leadership was put into place. Now, I must decide, would I stay in the company or go? It took new leadership months to undo much of the harm previously done. When they got to me, it took a while for them to be sure there wasn't something credible in the action taken against me. Once they found no merit to the termination, new leadership (which were predominately White) apologized. The allegations were reversed and there was no mark on my employment record. Furthermore, get this, no one could explain why this happened.

I was still traumatized! The trauma set into me like smoke captured in the lungs. I wasn't sure I could stay. I did know I had to find a way to heal. The deputy director scheduled time to speak with me. With a soft voice, she wondered what they could do to make amends. I didn't file legal action; money would not be on the table without that documentation in place. I heard a whisper in my spirit, ". . . it's up to you. You can forgive and remain, or you can forgive and leave. It's up to you!" I knew this whisper and I was curious and wanted to see what God would do. So, I told the deputy director I would get back with her. For three months, I actively pursued my healing. The deputy director waited patiently.

In the end, I chose to remain. The department agreed to pay for educational opportunities for me, which later proved to elevate my career in ways I couldn't imagine! Shortly thereafter, I received surprising news that I had been selected to receive a national award for my work. I was then promoted to be the manager of the training team. "You mean the team I was fired from?" I asked the deputy director with a slight bit of sarcasm. I turned down the role twice before finally accepting. While in this position, I could clearly see the discrimination in my earlier situation and the significant racial issues woven throughout. Nonetheless, I performed well and left the training position to be promoted to another team.

Thereafter, I was one of a handful of people chosen for special assignments related to COVID. I excelled in this work and returned to my new team. Following the murder of Mr. George Floyd, I was sought out to facilitate discussions on race for White community members, both inside and outside the organization. You know I had to dig deep and pray to be sure I was healed enough to do this work, given what I had endured earlier. The new education prepared me for this work. After careful consideration, I accepted the opportunity and, to my surprise, the workshops were attended nationally. Since the time of being fired, I have been catapulted further into my purpose. I was promoted within the same organization three times and my total income has increased exponentially.

This situation became my promotion and not my demise.

The WISDOM G.I.F.T.S.
What to do in the eye of a storm to
then experience **TRIUMPH.**

1. **Breathe.** When you find yourself in a challenging situation, breathe to resource yourself. This keeps trauma from being trapped in the body.
2. **Be truthful with yourself!** Tell yourself the truth about who you are and your skills. Don't accept responsibility if it is not yours to take. Be honest with yourself. If you've not

performed the job as expected or if you've acted poorly in a situation, ask for an extension and then do the job! Or find an opportunity to correct the situation. Be in integrity.

3. **Have a spiritual practice.** Don't wait until you're in trouble to develop a practice. Your spiritual practice will resource you and guide your steps. We must spend time in the practice to recognize the guidance when it comes. For me, the practice includes speaking with Spirit in the privacy of my heart.
4. **Have a tribe.** Develop friendships and take time to nurture them. Don't expect a spouse or partnership to be everything. These situations can be tough on our loved ones, too. They shouldn't be your only support.
5. **Have a purpose or mission statement.** Look at this statement weekly. This statement should guide life decisions, including marriage and employment decisions. My purpose statement focused my attention.
6. **Respite.** Find rest from the pain. Find fun things to do and give your emotions and your heart a rest. And, exercise!
7. **Walk away!** You always have options! Walk away if you desire. Get advice and be sure you're not missing a gift that could be on the other side of the situation if you remain.
8. **Heal.** Don't get stuck! Often, people wrap themselves in the trauma for years, impairing personal growth. When we are stuck in hurt

feelings, we can miss out on the gifts and opportunities ahead.

Beloved, may love burst you wide open and propel you into the arms of your purpose. May you feel the TRIUMPH as you find your purpose.

✡ ✡ ✡

Debra R. Baker

"Debra Baker is one of the most authentic, vitally intelligent, and compassionate leaders in the land."
~Dr. Michael Eric Dyson, Vanderbilt University and Author~

Debra is a published author, speaker, and a well-respected thought leader. She is a national award recipient of Training Magazine's Emerging Leaders Training award for developing adult leaders. She has a Master of Theology and studied business at Columbia University. Debra is an associate professor at Seattle

University where she co-teaches with her husband and is also known in government spaces as an Organizational Development Practitioner.

Debra's jam is cultivating and calling forward the person who is emerging as a global change maker, social influencer, and community healer. She develops exciting and zesty development experiences where participants become liberated and embody the heart, soul, ministry, and artistry of leadership. They go on to shift social atmospheres and make significant impacts in the world in vibrant, brilliant, gracious, and generous ways.

Debra lives in Tacoma, Washington, and is married to Kevin Baker. Together they have two sons, a daughter and a whole host of family and friends. She enjoys cooking, traveling, learning about different cultures, and good conversation.

For more information about Debra's upcoming leadership center and other offerings www.DebraBspeaks.com

Finding Greatness Through Gratitude

By Lindy Lewis

"GRATEFUL"

One day she realized that she was…
FABULOUS because of her flaws;
AMAZING because of her adversities;
WISER because of her wounds;
STRONGER because of her scars;
EXTRAORDINARY because of her errors;
PERFECTED because of her pain;
INCREDIBLE because of her imperfections;
HEROIC because of her hurts and hardships;
COURAGEOUS because of her crises and chaos;
TENACIOUS because of her tragedies;
BOLDER because of her breakups and breakdowns;
TOUGHER than her trials and tribulations;
GREATER than her grief;
FIERCER than her fears and failures;
MIGHTIER than her mistakes and missteps;
BRAVER than her battles;
She is GRATEFUL!!!
She is ME!!!

**The Challenge

Lights out! When the world shut down and we went into lockdown, I felt my own light go out. The first couple of weeks of the pandemic were the hardest. The lockdown restrictions, the precautions, the social distancing, having to wear masks, sanitizing hands, wearing gloves, quarantining and only going out for essential services and activities like groceries, medical appointments, getting prescriptions filled at the pharmacy and work, if you were classified as an essential worker. This was all too much to deal with.

As a curriculum and online course specialist for over 20+ years, I was able to work from home. I realized how blessed I was to still have my job. But I still felt financially vulnerable, even though I was building my business on the side. In the back of my mind, I knew I had to create additional streams of income for my own peace of mind, as I saw many people have their hours reduced, and their pay cut. Some saw their jobs and incomes disappear completely while others had to close their businesses after having had them for decades.

Everything happened so fast. Overnight the world went from offline to online. In-person events and activities became virtual. We were no longer able to do the everyday things we had been accustomed to doing. Even as an introvert, it was a lot to adjust to. I felt robbed of my freedom.

I had recovered from Covid only a few weeks before the pandemic was declared. I was still in a very fragile place mentally, emotionally, spiritually and physically.

For ten weeks I fought for my life. There were days where I questioned if I'd ever recover. I'd never been so sick in my life. What scared me even more was the thought of going to my grave with my gifts still inside me. These are the gifts that God specifically chose for me to share with the world: gifts of exhortation (writing and speaking), faith, craftsmanship, discernment and giving. There was still so much I wanted to do. My story couldn't end here.

I got a text from my best friend "CJ," Claudia John. I was still recovering from Covid and she wanted to know how I was doing. She asked me if I had heard about Kobe Bryant. I had no idea what she was talking about. She told me that he had died, along with eight others in a terrible helicopter crash. The news shook me up. I was devastated. I had followed Kobe's career for years. I had graduated nursing school the year he was drafted.

When I looked back over Kobe's career, and what he accomplished both on and off the basketball court, it was nothing short of phenomenal. At the age of 41 he had achieved and accomplished so much... five NBA championships, two Olympic gold medals, eighteen All-Star acknowledgements, and four All-Star Game MVP awards, an Oscar Academy Award for Best Animated Short for 'Dear Basketball,' New York Times Best-selling Author and Publisher of young-adult fiction and sports fantasy novels, charitable and philanthropic activities, i.e., NBA Cares initiatives, reading initiatives, After-School All-Stars, Boys and Girls Clubs, Make-A-Wish, combating youth homelessness, scholarships, and donations to worthy causes were just a few of his many acts of greatness (service).

I remembered Lewis Howes had interviewed him on his School of Greatness Podcast, and he asked him about his definition of greatness. Kobe said,

> *"I think the definition of greatness is to inspire the people next to you. Yeah, I think that's what greatness is or should be. It's not something that lives and dies with one person. It's how can you inspire a person to then in turn inspire another person that inspires another person and that's how you create something I think lasts forever. And I think that's our challenge as people is to figure out how our story can impact others and motivate them in a way to create their own greatness."*

I had never thought about greatness that way before. Despite being in the midst of a global pandemic, feeling anything but inspired or motivated, Kobe's definition stuck with me. I was still heartbroken and grappling with the immense loss of his passing, though grateful for having gotten over Covid. My grief was then met with rage over the racially-motivated, senseless murder of George Floyd by police that May. I was struggling. I was overwhelmed with emotions, plus I was missing the way things used to be before the pandemic. I was missing being able to go out when I wanted, visiting my family, hanging out with my friends, the day-to-day contact with people, interacting and engaging in face-to-face conversations, celebrating birthdays, holidays, family dinners and get-togethers, socializing, going to restaurants, shaking and holding hands, hugging, kissing, shopping, traveling, seeing people's whole face and their cheeks rise when they smile, going to events, and the movies. What made lockdown extremely hard for me was that I was so used to enjoying physical touch and quality time with others and now I couldn't. Then living alone only intensified these feelings of loss and deprivation. I felt shut in and isolated, cut off from the people in my world.

Most days, it was difficult to get out of bed in the mornings, to focus on work, build my online business and be productive. Mentally, the lockdown had taken a toll on me. My mind was all over the place. I found myself stalking the news, binging on every breaking news update, feeding into the media frenzy and constantly refreshing the daily case numbers. There were many days where I found myself plagued by dark thoughts, suffocated by the fear and uncertainty. I wasn't ok.

That's when something in Kobe's definition of greatness came back to me. He said, *"our challenge as people is to figure out how our story can impact others and motivate them in a way to create their own greatness."* How could I expect to *"motivate someone to create their own greatness"* if I was struggling to create my own? I started to think about what I wanted my story to be when all of the restrictions were lifted and the pandemic was over. I asked myself, *"Who did I want to be on the other side of this pandemic?"*

**The Choice

Then a few days after they'd declared the pandemic, I'd gotten an email from Dr. Tracy Timberlake, my very first coach. She said, *"NOW is the time! The opportunity that is in front of you is unprecedented - and it's time you meet that opportunity with YOUR greatness!"*

At that moment, I knew that I didn't want to be the same person I was when I went into the lockdown. That was not how I wanted to remember 2020. I didn't want to look back at that time in our history with regret. How I came out of the pandemic was on me.

I had to make some changes.

The *first thing* I did was I stopped stalking the news and checking the daily case stats. The less I focused on things that were outside of my control, the better it was for my mental health. I shifted my focus to what I could control, like my environment, how I structured my day, my daily routine, my words, how I responded to my circumstances.

The *second thing* was I knew that who I wanted to be required a different version of myself, a new identity. I wanted to be someone who stood for greatness, who lived their greatness everyday, who inspired greatness in others and who served with their God-given gifts. I wanted to be a human for greatness. Jesus was the ultimate human for greatness. Serving others was his greatness. I wanted to love, serve and impact like Jesus did. This was who I wanted to be on the other side of the pandemic.

The *third thing* was, I asked myself, *"what was one simple thing I could do everyday that would help me stay positive, grounded in the present moment, would drown out the negative soundtrack in my head and silence the mixtape of my mind?"*

It was gratitude. I realized that what was missing from my life was GRATITUDE. I was so preoccupied with the pandemic that I didn't stop to appreciate what I already had, like early morning phone calls from my sister Lisa, cards in the mail from friends, wellness check-ins from my mom and dad, time to read and write, work from home, virtual meetings, a flexible work schedule, build my business, enjoy home-cooked meals, and a reliable internet connection. There was so much I had to be grateful for.

I made a commitment from that day forward to make gratitude a part of my day, every day. Each day I would focus on what I called the 5 G's: ***God, gratitude, grace, gifts and goals.***

God: I'd spend time in His presence in prayer, meditating on His word and who He said I was in Him, reading my Bible, giving thanks, praising Him. This helped ground my day, and gave me a sense of peace and calm.

Gratitude: I'd write down what I was grateful for, then I'd set them as daily alerts on my phone as reminders throughout the day. My apartment became the "Gratitude Zone." This helped me to focus my mind on higher things, like empathy, compassion, generosity, love, kindness, humility, gentleness, and patience.

Grace: I'd hold space for myself and others and would treat myself and others with empathy, compassion, and generosity. This helped me to acknowledge and be more mindful of what we were all experiencing, and to be kinder, gentler and more loving.

Gifts: I'd look for ways to share my gifts with others, such as an encouraging text, a card, an uplifting phone call, dropping off groceries, or lending a helping hand. This helped me to feel like I was making a difference in the lives of others.

Goals: I'd make a list of what I needed to accomplish for the day. This helped me to focus, keep on track and be more productive.

These were just a few of the many gratitude practices I did daily. Before long, the more I practiced gratitude, the lighter I felt, the happier I was, the more joy I experienced and the more my light started to shine again. My mind was quieter. I felt calm and at peace. Gratitude was my rainbow after the storm. It changed everything. It became my superpower, my secret weapon against the tough emotions I wrestled with in lockdown. "Grateful" became my power word. Anytime I felt the negative thoughts come bubbling up, I would say out loud, *"I am so grateful that..."* and I would name 5 things that I was grateful for in that moment, to nip the negativity.

**The Consequence

"The most important thing is to try and inspire people so that they can be great in whatever they want to do."
–Kobe Bryant

Gratitude was contagious. It wasn't enough for me to express and experience gratitude. I had to pay it forward in some meaningful way outside of myself, beyond the walls of my apartment. I had to put my gratitude into action.

As God would have orchestrated it, I got a text from Korrie Silver, a dear friend and fellow entrepreneur. I've known Korrie for over a decade. We go way back. I used to walk her dog, Isaac, affectionately known as Zak or Mr. Silver.

A friend of hers, Janice Findlay, emailed her with a request for support for Milika Tomlin, a young single mom in my area. Korrie reached out to me and asked if I knew anyone who could help. *What if this was my God-given assignment?* I couldn't say no. In my heart I had to help in any way I could. I felt I was being called to serve. This was when I met Milika, her 4-year-old son, Elijah, and her 5-week-old twin girls, Malayah and Aleena.

When Milika called, without hesitation I would be there. It didn't matter the hour of the day. If she needed diapers, formula, baby wipes, clothes, groceries, anything, I was happy to help. I wanted to do whatever I could to support her and let her know that I was there for her. It was my way of putting my gratitude into action and being of service. I had found a purpose outside of myself. It was the greatest feeling to know that I was making a difference. What I learned was that the secret to true greatness is serving.

What started out as a request for support turned strangers into friends, and friends into family. I am so grateful. God knew exactly what was needed when he placed us in each other's lives. Had it not been for Janice reaching out to Korrie, then Korrie connecting with me, I would not have met Milika and the kids. That is the power of gratitude.

"You can do some phenomenal things individually, but they'll never reach their full potential unless you do them collectively."
–Kobe Bryant

Before 2020, I honestly felt like I was having a breakdown. I was on the brink of burn-out, feeling overwhelmed with life, overworked and dealing with Covid. Then on March 11, 2020, the whole world was blindsided. It was not how any of us planned to start that new year.

Looking back, 2020 was my purposeful pause. There were no more 3 a.m. alarms, long days, 5-hour commutes, being stuck in rush-hour traffic or constant hustling and grinding. My life slowed down.

Living in lockdown allowed me time and space to pause; be present in my life; breathe; feel all of my feelings; ride the mental and emotional highs and lows; examine myself; take inventory of my life; reflect on who I wanted to be when the pandemic was over and all the restrictions were lifted; remember who I was born to be and who Christ said I was; and rediscover my greatness through the practice of gratitude.

It was a catalyst for my personal growth and metamorphosis. I learned things about myself that I could only have learned in a lockdown. In hindsight, it was exactly what I needed – time to rest, restore, reflect, remember, reconnect and rediscover.

Had it not been for rediscovering my identity in Christ, being a human for greatness, cultivating a daily gratitude practice, creating four additional passive income streams using Web 3.0 technology while still maintaining my 9-to-5 and building a legacy brand; I'm not sure how I would have survived the lockdown. Gratitude saved my life. It was what allowed me to unlock my own greatness and be the greatness for Milika and the kids. It was what kept me afloat spiritually, mentally, emotionally and physically, when I could have so easily fallen apart. But God, in His grace, love and mercy got me through.

Now two years later we are still dealing with the aftermath and impacts of the pandemic. We are nowhere near normal. I don't think we ever will be. The world has changed. We all have changed. We are no longer who we once were. Our priorities are different. What matters to us is different. The life we used to know is no longer, and will never be again. And we cannot change that or go back.

But what we can do, is we can co-create the world we want to live in for ourselves, our families and our communities... now and for future generations.... a world where we love, serve and impact those around us...where we take nothing for granted...where we inspire others to their greatness...where we change the world with our collective greatness...where we are humans for greatness.

Never has there been a greater time to love, serve, and impact others and the world around us than now, because the world needs our collective greatness now more than ever. Right now, we have the greatest opportunity in our history to be the greatness we want to see in the world.

Les Brown always says, "There is greatness in you." I believe that *"we are all born from greatness, with greatness, for greatness."* You are not here by accident or mistake. You are here to share your gifts and greatness with the world. When you focus on being grateful every day for what you already have, even on the hard days, you make room for your greatness to show up and amaze you. You make room for the flow of more and greater into your life. Think of it like this, gratitude is the match that sparks the flame of greatness within, that allows you to be the greatness for others and make an impact in the world.

Let us take time during the course of our day to be grateful, to unlock our greatness with gratitude, chase our greatness, be the greatness and share our greatness with the world together, because together we are greater. Together we can spread more love, serve at a higher level and make more impact in the world around us. It is no secret that we achieve more collectively than we ever can individually. We are not meant to do life alone. Our greatest legacy that we can leave the world with is our collective greatness. Together, we can be humans for greatness. Will you join me on the journey?

Thank you to all the Health Care and front-line workers around the world who continue to risk their lives to keep us safe. You are all truly humans for greatness.

✲ ✲ ✲

Lindy Lewis

Lindy Lewis is a Human for Greatness, who is here to love, serve, and impact others. As someone who found herself struggling during lockdown, she shares how she rediscovered her greatness during the pandemic of 2020. As a nurse of over two decades, an educator, course curator and an award-nominated curriculum writer of 20+ years, Lindy has a heart for people and education. She is on a mission to inspire others and believes that we are all born from greatness, with greatness for greatness to be of service to others. This is why she has launched

Humans for Greatness™, a socially conscious apparel line to be a powerful reminder of our greatness.

As author, thought leader, and speaker, Lindy wants to create ripples of change in the world. Through sharing her own wisdom and life lessons, she's here to show others what's possible when they unlock their greatness with gratitude.

Not to mention, Lindy is also a Web 3.0 educator and blockchain enthusiast, who is excited to show others how to leverage this new technology to fund their dream life. She loves all things planners, pens, journals and notebooks. She is also a die-hard Y&R soap fan. Get your #HumansforGreatness™ Planner right now! https://bit.ly/HumansForGreatnessPlanner

Fighting With Cement: An Unorthodox Transformation

By Priscilla Damas

All I can say is, if your face gets into a fight with the cement, the cement is going to win.

In a way, this is how my personal transformational journey began, however, to make it work, my business also needed changes.

I was ill during the summer of 2019. Though the illness was not life-threatening, it went downhill before I got better, lasting longer than anticipated. My doctor confirmed that the bronchitis developed into pneumonia, twice, during a short period of time. I was alone most of the time and refused to go to the hospital. At one point, I was contagious. Friends checked on me, dropping off soup, leaving it on my porch. During that summer, I thought about the wonderful experiences I have been blessed with. I have a strong family unit, beginning with my parents. Both parents gave my siblings and I a foundation in the church with creativity, discipline, and a strong work ethic. My siblings and I were seldom allowed to just sit. There was always something to do in the apartment complex, at least folding clothes while we watched television. That strong family support extends to my husband and two adult children. Reading and researching then was the backdrop of my convalescence, as I dozed in and out of sleep. Most importantly, during the time I had to be still, I pondered my life. I considered my last several decades and visited and revisited the question of purpose. I have been a trainer of conflict resolution and topics relative to conflict for many years. I have had a blessed life that has taken me to national and international situations that still fill me with awe. I have also been involved with the community and have paid it forward.

But still, this was a time of reflection. I asked myself if I had been doing what I am here to do. Was I fulfilling my true purpose? I also thought about where I was in life, asking if I had gotten all that I wanted out of life? The realization that I was 67 surprised me. Not that I had not kept up with age, but it was the sudden realization that there was much more time behind me than in front of me, that I did not know when age would catch up with me. At what point would one of life's variables of age catch up? I could lose sight, hearing, or not be able to walk across the Great Wall of China, one of my life goals. It has always been more important for me to experience life and its adventures than to acquire things. My mom told me at one point that I treasure the items that I had gotten through travel so much, too much. She was correct. My artifacts represent my memories and the people, the cultures, that have crossed my path, that welcomed me. Yes, these are the things I treasure. However, I had slowed down my travel to a snail's pace. I was not in school and was putting myself in few, if any, learning situations. But I was busy all the time. I wondered if I was busy doing a lot of nothing, not really being productive, not traveling, learning anything new or even reading much, as I had once enjoyed tremendously. At that moment, I knew I needed to make changes in my life.

This thinking resulted in major decisions. I made three goals:

- Readjust my life so that I would have more time to focus on leisure activities, travel, and things I enjoy doing - large and small.
- Change my business model. Give myself the permission to make necessary changes to allow time and space for pursuing other challenges and dreams. It would also leave more time for self-care and enjoying life. I needed time management.
- And third, and the most important, make my health a priority. I knew I needed a change in habits for a healthier life.

To put myself on the right path, I had to jack myself up. I know me. I could not pitter patter. I had to do something drastic, make serious moves to jerk myself into place. I had to be intentional to find the time for myself and to give a jumpstart to each of the three goals. As I re-evaluated my time and focus, I had to adjust the number of hours spent on business and related activities, including chambers, boards, and committee meetings. These were engulfing my time.

That summer of 2019, I made the decision to learn how to relax, de-stress and meditate. The program, "Mind, Body, Medicine," was offered to community leaders in Broward County because of the Marjory Stoneman Douglas tragedy at that high school. It teaches community leaders how to assist those that have been involved with a traumatic situation and how to use their mind and body as natural resources to help them through stresses and tragedies. Once accepted, I went on to become certified. The program was 9:00-5:00 daily for two weeks. It offered optional extensions three mornings a week for participants that wanted meditation and relaxation activities. These were usually in a closed room for quiet or around the pool. The locations were both selected to provide the right atmosphere for learning and practice. I bought the book, *Just Breathe,* by Mallika Chopra, on meditation, mindfulness, and movement. I also purchased, *The President's Devotional,* by Joshua Dubois, which provides a year of meditations. The daily mediation has a Bible scripture and an explanation as to how it relates to today, and a prayer. These meditations were sent to President Obama daily and later compiled by his White House Director of Faith-Based Partnerships, Mr. Joshua Dubois. To implement this learning into my own life, I had to find the time. I changed my working hours for my business, Wingspan Seminars, to 10:00-5:00. This gave me a solid block of time prior to work. I began to meditate, read my morning devotional and exercise during this time.

I often recall and repeat parts of Van Jones' interview with Oprah Winfrey. He asked her what she does differently that most people do not do. Without hesitation, she answered, "meditate."

The business transition was and continues to be a huge undertaking. I have been a trainer and involved with peace and social injustice initiatives for forty years. The community service began at the YWCA in Indiana, then continued when I moved to South Florida. Training for the Anti-Defamation League, Wingspan Seminars and becoming a full-time trainer for Miami-Dade Public Schools, made my transition very difficult.

Being invited to be a part of multiple national and international teams proffered acclaim and reinforcement of value, fortitude and purpose. However, those reflections during the summer made me realize I was neglecting Wingspan Seminars, self-care, and had gotten off track, busy being busy. My grandfather used to say, "Time waits for no man." Time was whispering in my ear, now is the time to make changes before it is too late for you to experience new things. You have yet to include learning and trying new ventures, traveling, and writing. Wingspan became a theme. I learned, through the hiring of coaches and my business attorney, not to throw out what I had done for years, but to, instead, pivot and build on that expertise. I was advised to build a strong foundation and learned the importance of clarifying my niche. The business transition encompassed these three goals:

1. Completing *"99 Conflicts to Avoid,"* a book I had begun six years previously
2. Hosting an international seminar
3. Creating an online seminar

By early fall of 2019, I had planned a business trip to Belize and South Africa to explore and begin establishing relationships for a future seminar. With my business attorney's assistance, I found a home for my international summit. Several trips resulted in The W.O.W. (Wings on Women) International Summit in Belize, March 2020. Its theme was Domestic Violence which, I learned, was a government focus there.

As I returned to Florida, Covid 19 had hit the U.S. and Florida had begun to shut down. Limiting movement of residents worked well for me as I was able to use the summit's success as a mental springboard that created a 'can-do' force. I thought that if I could pull off a successful international summit in such a short time, which I had deemed as the most difficult goal, the additional two goals were a piece of cake. Well, they were not. However, they were both more in my control and doable since now I had the time and a major endeavor under my belt.

As I took online courses to learn how to create an online seminar, I completed "*99 Conflicts to Avoid.*" Second goal, done!

During the summer of 2020, Americans' daily lives were affected by the pandemic and racism hit a global nerve with the death of George Floyd. Its impact on me personally, along with my business, was formidable. To address the conflicts caused by Covid-19, Wingspan Seminars released a series entitled *Tips, Resolutions and Resources* on social media platforms. I also created three eBooks, *Conflicts Caused by Covid 19,* for self-care, couples, and homes with children. They were free and remain available to the public. Initially, I had planned to create an online seminar about conflict resolution basics. However, I realized there was a dire need to help parents address the topic of race and racism with their children. I entitled the online seminar, *Race, Racism and Your Children.* This is when I took my own advice for couples and purchased a bike. I was so excited when my husband and I brought it home, I immediately began riding it around my neighborhood. A car approached me, and I felt another behind me. I did what most people who have no idea what they are doing do, I panicked. When I grabbed the brakes too tight, the bike flipped me off and I landed face down on the cement.

I knocked each of the business goals 'out the park.' "*99 Conflicts...*" has a workbook and journal. It is also listed on Amazon with the Vice-Mayor of the city where I reside, Miramar, Florida, sponsoring the book signing. Creating an online seminar has resulted in Wingspan Academy. This goal, along with the health focus, has taken much longer than I anticipated. However, the result is having an online academy with a team and multiple instructors and classes. That collaboration and potential for growth is invaluable. The international summit surprised me by taking less time than I had imagined. Once I learned of a need in Belize, which was domestic violence awareness, it was a perfect entry point for collaboration. It was all about developing relationships thereafter. I met the director and staff of the Women's Department, Belize. This gave me a strong base of support. The marketing assistant I hired was able to include an appearance on a popular television show in Belize, *Open Your Eyes Morning Show,* the day prior to the summit. This led to reporters attending the summit. A delegation, led by an elected official from Florida, attended and spoke at the summit. Now, as Covid concerns lessen in the United States and Belize, I will decide if Wingspan Seminars will host an annual summit.

Giving myself more time to enjoy life and gain improved health was more difficult than pivoting for business. This required a lifestyle change. Though I initially enrolled and became certified in the "Mind, Body, Medicine Program," it has never been easy to change old habits. Kicking off my day with meditation and exercise worked at first. I was intentional. Things had been moving along regarding business. I had even begun to breathe, relax in place and meditate. I had traveled to Belize multiple times leading up to the summit and had traveled to South Africa, which had been on my list for years. Taking time for myself every morning, then going to a park to exercise three or four times a week worked for a while. I do not know what took me off target, perhaps falling off the bike. After being too easily deterred from the personal goal, I once again had to jack myself up.

This time jacking myself up meant investing in myself. I needed a personal trainer with nutrition as a focus that did not require going to a gym. I found that in Tony Major. He had just released a book, "*Sit to Get Fit,*" for seniors who were hesitant about going to the gym with Covid lurking. Many of his clients are over fifty. To cap it off, one of my girlfriends had lost one hundred pounds with Tony's guidance. People were saying Covid 15 because so many had gained fifteen pounds sitting at home dodging the pandemic. By this time, I was approaching two hundred pounds at 5'1", a weight I had never reached in my life. It scared me. I was huffing and puffing as I climbed the stairs in my home, and I knew I could not blame it on Covid. It had been creeping upwards for years. Tony did not ask about my weight and never said the word "diet." Instead, he began by telling me to use a journal and draw three circles. Afterward, he told me to write the words time, quantity, and choices. He said it all boiled down to understanding how these three words affect your health. When you eat, how much you eat and the choices you make are what make the difference. He also said that if I did 70% of what he told me to do, I would lose weight and have a healthier life. It was interesting that we began with three-pound weights and Tony never asked me to sit down. Periodically, Tony added words for me to look up, such as patience and forgiveness. He also sent me videos, especially on intermittent fasting and meditation. I began to take Tony everywhere with me by phone. We used cans, bricks, and bottled water when I did not have weights. I did not share with anyone what I was doing until I had lost twenty pounds. This was a big enough benchmark for me and any listener to know I was serious. I posted pictures of Tony and me in Grenada, New York, and with my 91-year-old mother in Indiana.

As I lose, the dermatologist is working on my face to get it back in order. While in Dr. Moore's chair, I realized how much I have been working on myself and in multiple areas. Over two years, by the time this book is released, I predict, I will have lost fifty pounds, be eating correctly, and be bicycling with my husband. I decided then that my 70th birthday would be a perfect goal point. My skin, weight, nutrition, business model, book, time for fun, meditation, and travel all equals total transformation by seventy!

To reach my goals and transform I had to open myself up to learning. I wanted different outcomes. This meant I had to do things differently. I did not want to hire people to create an online seminar, new website, finish my book or to do all the branding and marketing. Instead, I wanted to learn, at least the basics, myself. I signed up for programs that included consultants or coaches. These were time-consuming endeavors that were costly. It has taken over two years; however, it has been an investment in myself, and worth it.

None of this was easy. Note - I began during a period of illness that forced me to be still, then the pandemic again kicked that force of stillness in place. It made my body rest, then slow down. During these periods, I massaged, maneuvered, and implemented goals. This process went from my head to writing and researching, then putting action behind my thoughts. It continues to be a journey, but I am getting there. By my 70th birthday, November 23, 2022, I will be there.

"When you get right down to it, **intentional** living is about living your best story."
John C. Maxwell

"If you're going to grow, you have to be **intentional**."
Curt Kampmeier

* * *

Priscilla Damas

Priscilla Damas is a conflict resolution trainer, educator, and author with over forty years of experience. Her latest book is *99 Conflicts to Avoid and 100 Ways to Resolve Them*. She was selected by the Anti-Defamation League as a Consultant and sent to racially tense situations throughout Florida. As conflict heightened in schools across the country, she became a Safe Schools Specialist, responsible for conflict prevention and intervention, crisis response and staff and community training. Her lifelong interest in diversity led her to an internship with the Martin Luther King

Center for Nonviolence. It began at the Conflict Center for Resolution in Kenya, Africa, and was completed at The King Nonviolence Center in Cuba. Ms. Damas was invited to train ex-militants in the Nigerian Amnesty Program in Nigeria, Africa, in Kingian Transformational Nonviolence. She has received numerous awards, including Mayor Gimenez and the Miami-Dade Commissioners proclaiming April 4th Priscilla Damas Blake Day. When Priscilla is not writing or training, you may find her with women, encouraging them to enjoy life and have 'silly fun'. Ms. Damas is Founder of Wingspan Seminars, whose mission focuses on improving organizational relationships and conflict dynamics. You may find her online at www.wingspanseminars.net

Sow What's Worthy!

By Toye Cook

Whatever a man sows, he (or she) will also reap.
Galatians 6:7

What are you sowing into your life? When he disrespected me in the restaurant's parking lot, I asked myself that question. But before I tell you about that night, let me give you more information about myself. Stay with me, beautiful readers, and see why this information is relevant. Throughout my story, you will learn how GRATITUDE penetrates. I am blessed to share the wisdom that I learned along the way—I am blessed to share it with you.

My parents taught, guided, and led me into adulthood when I was a child. So, my reaping what I sowed had nothing to do with my upbringing. The fact that Mama was mid-way through her forties and Daddy was in his fifties when we were born, proved their readiness to have kids. My parents raised us with plenty of insight and sound wisdom and, even though my father was masculine and dressed like a cowboy and owned a shotgun, he lovingly read bedtime stories to us at night. Daddy was an entrepreneur. I have two siblings (my brother was an adult and lived independently), and the rest of us went to church together as a family on Sundays. Therefore, I knew about the Lord; however, it would be a while before I understood His power in my life.

Now that I am a parent, I realize the challenge it must have been for my parents to raise us. Once, my father walked up to me in our local park's recreation room while I was "slow" dancing with a boy and told me to come with him. Ha! They did whatever it took to help us become respectable young ladies. My father did not discuss his reasons for interfering with that dance, but I knew from his silence that my behavior was not in line with their expectations. They wanted to keep us safe, but I'll admit that I tried to get as far away from their rules as possible. Honestly, I wish they would have shared more with me about their failures when they were younger, because it made them seem too perfect for me to ask questions and share my deepest thoughts. Of course, I have no way of knowing if that would have stopped me from veering off their moral path and learning some things on my own—because I was stubborn and enjoyed discovering things.

I am eternally GRATEFUL that I grew up knowing I was loved and feeling that love was instrumental to me loving myself. I wish I could have told Mama about my school crushes and have spoken with her about sex, without judgment. But, I understand that my childhood was during the time of the "silent generation," and open discussions from parents were rare.

I was not promiscuous; however, I'll admit that I did share intimate expressions in the confines of my relationships. Even though my parents taught me differently, I looked at it as a natural way of loving my partner.

In my late twenties, I married my one-and-only husband, and we had a son whom we adored. My husband had a job, and when the money ran low, he started making money illegally. Eventually, he was arrested and received more than 20 years in prison. Our relationship did not survive, and we divorced.

After my divorce, I became determined to date someone qualified to become my son's stepfather—I knew that I did not need a father for Lucien (not his real name). Still, I had benefited from having two parents, and I wanted him to have that as well (for his sake). I knew that there would be times that he would need to know something as a man-child that I would be incapable of teaching, simply because I am a woman.

I met Raymond (not his real name) after eating at his restaurant near my job. The food was delicious, and I started eating lunch there almost every day. I admired that he was making a living as an entrepreneur, which reminded me of Daddy. I was excited to hear the goals that he had set for himself. In my eyes, he was a prime candidate and marriage material.

We dated for a few months, and our communication was lively. We had a lot in common; we laughed and enjoyed playing racquetball and exercising together. I envisioned a great future with him, and he proposed marriage. We moved closer to both of our jobs, got an apartment, moved in together, and everything was lovely...until it wasn't.

After a couple of years, his insecurities got the best of him, and instead of growing closer, we grew further apart. My vocabulary had become much more colorful, and we started lacking in the bliss department and having more arguments. Doing that in front of my son was a definite no-no. So, we decided not to get married. I ended the relationship, and Lucien and I moved in with my sister.

After our break-up, Raymond and I remained in contact by phone only, never in person (simple catch-ups once or twice a year). We weren't good together in a relationship; however, we had remained friends. It had been 20 years since our relationship had ended, and I hadn't seen him. So, when he invited me out to dinner, I accepted.

The Night of the Incident

I lived with GRATITUDE for many reasons; Lucien was well adjusted, and I was healthy and enjoying a great career as a supervisor of the nurses. It was nice to see Raymond (again, not his real name); we greeted each other with a friendly hug. The restaurant was cozy, and I was mindful not to order wine because it was late, and I didn't want to fall asleep while driving home. Raymond didn't drink alcohol at all, ever.

The two of us shared friendly banter about the past 20 years, my son, his sons, how he had sold the restaurant and started working in what he considered a more stable field—as a security guard. I spoke about my promotions in my nursing career.

When we finished eating, he moved over to my side of the booth and planted

a kiss on my lips. I should have questioned his reason then—but, in my head, I rationalized the unique nature of our relationship in the past, and I allowed it. It had been 20 years since our relationship had ended, so in my mind, it was innocent. The restaurant was closing, and Raymond asked me to join him in his truck for more conversation. Again, we hadn't seen each other in 20 years, so I agreed because he was someone I trusted, and I am a bit of a night owl. I'm not usually a naive person, but that night... I was. Once we were in his truck, he started the engine and drove to the opposite side of the parking lot. I was assuming that he did that to create more privacy, and that was when I understood he wanted more than conversation.

When we arrived at a different spot in the parking lot, we did not talk before he reclined and pulled his pants down, exposing his genitals. Now mind you, I had not done or said anything before this action to lead him to the conclusion that this was what I wanted, and we had not been intimate with each other in over 20 years. Insulted at his gesture, I hopped out of the truck and slammed the door. I left him with his pants down around his ankles, stomped-walked to my car, and drove home. "Wow!" I thought, "I have been inducted into the 'me, too' movement."

Oddly, immediately I started to feel a sense of responsibility for HIS actions. "Did I mislead Raymond, or were his advances in some way my fault?" I asked myself, had I unknowingly done something to encourage his behavior? But, as soon as those thoughts popped into my mind, I dismissed them because I knew that I had not. Women! —Sometimes, our wacky hormones can take our thoughts in a weird direction.

According to Webster, a false sense of responsibility or misplaced guilt is when one feels responsible for the actions of another person—usually connected to a traumatic event. So, that explains my willingness to think that I was accountable for Raymond's sexual advance.

If I had not learned to love myself, I would have felt that I deserved his actions. Instead, I knew he disrespected me because my parents ensured that I had a great understanding and love for myself. If anyone ever violates you, my beautiful readers, I pray that you will love yourself. No one has the right to disrespect your feelings—because you matter.

Six months later

I was still thinking about that night. With the encouragement of my friend—I called him to ask why he had done that. He asked, "Was I supposed to ask you, if we have done it so many times in the past?" I said, "Yes, Raymond, we had sex in the past, but that was 20 years ago! Come on!"

He said he wanted to have sex with me, and that, coupled with the fact that we had done it in the past, was the reason he felt he was permitted to expect that it was okay. I asked him if he thought his actions were selfish, and he agreed they were. I reminded him that respect was an act of giving consideration and my feelings were important. So, he had disrespected me. Entitlement is a belief that one is deserving of or entitled to certain privileges, and it is a narcissistic personality trait. When you are looking for a suitable mate, pay attention as to whether your potential mate possesses any of these "red flags":

Do they have an exaggerated sense of self-importance?

Do they have a persistent need for admiration?

Are they snobbish?

Do they lack empathy for others?

Do they have a condescending attitude?

It was not okay for Raymond to disregard my feelings while pursuing HIS desires.

I ended this experience by educating him and reminding him that it didn't matter whether the two of us had a relationship in the past or not. I told him that he needed to consider MY choice today. I told him it was wrong to assume I wanted him simply because he wanted me. I reminded him that he had sons and would not want to leave them uninformed on this topic and that it could keep them out of severe legal trouble when they became old enough to date.

In my case, I chose to educate him—but some people might need to involve the police. Everyone has their own unique experiences, and I advocate for anyone, woman or man, to handle their case in whatever manner they deem necessary.

In conclusion, based on his responses, I decided that his actions were selfish but not intended to harm me, and he was simply clueless. I'm GRATEFUL that my friend encouraged me to ask him about his activities because I needed closure, and asking him empowered me and gave me clarity. Following that night, our communication dwindled even more than it had when our relationship ended. It was a great learning experience for Raymond and me.

My WISDOM G.I.F.T.S. - GRATITUDE

Regarding the "Indecent Exposure" incident - I am GRATEFUL to God for allowing negative experiences to happen because we grow and learn from them. When Raymond disregarded my feelings and exposed himself, I was GRATEFUL that I was only harmed emotionally and not raped or hurt by violence. I feel that Raymond must have damaged me emotionally because the incident continued to haunt me six months later.

As the Bible cautions, "I had reaped what I had sowed because, even though I did not deserve what happened that night in the truck with Raymond, I had not respected the power of sex over my lifetime. I feel that I sowed the seed of disrespect from Raymond when I trivialized the act. And because God created me and knew everything about whom He had made, He knew that I would share this experience with you, and we hope that you will use it however you most need it, and pay it forward.

I understand that my parents were strict because they loved and protected me. Thinking back on my experiences, I believe that it is good to discipline and also good to share life experiences with children. Allow children to speak openly. Use discernment to decide if open communication is appropriate for your circumstances. Some conversations might be embarrassing, but it will benefit their development into adulthood if you can endure a talk or two. We live in days when parents can be more transparent than in my parents' days. My parents did not talk to me about sex, but they did equip me with essential knowledge in other areas of my life. I am eternally GRATEFUL that they took me to church and taught me the importance of having a good education, leading to a fabulous career. I knew right from wrong, and I loved myself and expected men to treat me with the same respect that my father had shown me.

Sex is an act that requires responsibility, which is why it is spoken about so many times in the Bible. It can have positive and negative outcomes. The positives and negatives will depend on the circumstances. Remember that rape is an unlawful sexual activity against the victim's will. So, my final advice is to please make sure that you have received consent (every time) from the other person before you engage in sexual activity of any kind.

Regarding "Parenting all by yourself" - Giving honor to God first because I was only the vessel, but

Lucien's outcomes were because God's love flowed through me. I prayed and continued to pray without ceasing, which means that I pray when I'm awake, when I eat, when I get in my car to drive, etc. My son Lucien (again, not his real name) is 26 years old now, and I am eternally GRATEFUL and proud to report that he is a responsible adult—well-mannered and thriving. I spoke this outcome into existence when he was a child. (There is power in our tongues, beautiful readers.) He has a wife, one toddler girl, and another girl on the way. Because of God, I didn't need a man. He provided me with a village of people to help me raise him. I did not know how to be a parent, so I led with love. My ex-husband shared his fatherly advice on the phone (Oh, and I am GRATEFUL that he came home early from his time away, and he and Lucien have rebuilt their relationship). My husband reminded me to hug Lucien because boys needed that. I am GRATEFUL for many people; however, one person stands out in my village, the loving man my ex-husband chose as our son's godfather. I knew Lucien was safe when I left him with his godfather. Utilize the people around you like my parents did for me. I tried everything—think outside of the box.

Yes, we had a rollercoaster of experiences, but the total outcome was positive because I did not allow any negativity to penetrate. I kept inspired by positive literature and television shows. I fed my soul with positivity. Pulling Lucien away from his peers in school and teaching him at home was one of the best decisions I made. I did not have experience being a teacher, but you do what you have to do. I spent time talking to Lucien, sharing myself totally with him. If he watched television, I watched it with him, and we had conversations about what we saw. I spoke, and he listened, and vice versa. Because of that, he was not lonely. God's love flowed through my mother, and she made a similar decision when she sent me to a high school outside of my neighborhood. Give children a good foundation of values, and when they leave you, to paraphrase the Bible, they will not depart from those values. I had two beautiful parents, and that was not enough. I learned that the respect I deserved needed to come from inside, and I am eternally GRATEFUL that my parents taught me to love myself as God's love flowed through them. If you are a parent, there will be challenges, but if you lead with love...You've got this!! I am GRATEFUL that He chose me to comfort you with my story.

"I am grateful."- Gratitude is a prerequisite to happiness.

I am grateful for the ups and downs.
Everything has contributed to who I am.
Today, I express gratitude for it all.
~ author unknown

* * *

Toye Cook

Toye Cook, aka "Nurse Toye," is the CEO/Founder of Compassion Masters International, which provides advocacy and support for nurses and women in general. After working for 40 years, she recently retired but still stays connected to the purpose and profession she truly loves.

You will see Toye on social media supporting, inspiring, and motivating nurses and women to take great care of themselves so that they can take even better care of the patients and people they love. When she is relaxing, you will find her doing puzzles or picture finds. She loves to laugh and enjoys socializing.

Nurse Toye has lived with her family in the beautiful city of Chino Hills, California, for 30 years.

To learn more about Toye please visit www.compassionmastersintl.com or stay connected with her on Facebook and YouTube or email at: Compassionmastersintl@gmail.com

Be Intentional...Choose Peace On Purpose!

By Sharon Allen

How many times has a situation come about and you've almost lost it?! You and a friend may have been discussing something and the next thing you know you end up in a disagreement. You both are raising your voices, trying to out-talk one another just to get your point across. The situation has now become heated and before you say something that you may regret, you agree to disagree. At that moment, you chose to keep your peace on purpose!

However, your friend does not feel the same as you. He/she wants to finish the conversation. They must get their point across before they will let the matter go. Your friend is not maintaining their peace at all. The situation at hand took his/her peace away. Other circumstances that can take "peace" from someone are very broad in range. These circumstances may include, but are not limited to, a divorce, loss of a loved one, loss of a home or job, or maybe the loss of a friendship or relationship! The lack or loss of peace may also be due to a life-changing health issue. By the way, I have experienced

ALL of those situations previously mentioned, plus some! Yes, I am divorced. Yes, I have lost several loved ones. Yes, I have lost my home. Yes, I have lost a job. I have even lost several relationships. I have also had a life-changing health issue! As for the plus some, I'll just say there were more than I could count. All of these circumstances definitely caused me to stretch and shift from the person I was back then and blossom into the person I am today.

Here is a common scenario. You are starting out your day as usual, driving in traffic and someone cuts you off! It really ticked you off, causing you to use a few "poor choice" words and a hand gesture or two. In the midst of this situation, it may have made you feel out of control or a little heated, to say the least. I am quite sure I am not the only one who has experienced this. Yet, somehow you managed to pull yourself together and move on with your day. You chose to keep your peace on purpose.

I want to elaborate for a moment on that "feeling" you may have had during that moment of negativity, that sense of being uneasy, anxious, worried, or even agitated. At that moment you have lost your PEACE! Nothing and no one should ever be able to steal YOUR PEACE.

That was a lesson I had to learn the hard way and, unfortunately, more than once. Let me share with you some of those moments that helped me learn these lessons. I'll begin by saying I was not always so mellow. I would get angry fairly quickly. Growing up in a household where yelling or raising your voice was a normal way to get your point across, I had no problem letting whoever made me angry know that I did not appreciate them causing me to lose my temper! That was my dad in me. I also had my mom in me, as well. She was always the voice of reason. She had a way of calming people down with just the tone of her voice. My mom knew what to say and when to say it. I often admired her for not letting a situation allow her to change her temperament. I so wanted to learn how to maintain my temperament as well. This is where I first discovered about choosing peace deliberately and wanted to utilize it in my everyday life.

I was about six or seven years old and my mom had put my hair into two curly ponytails that day for school. During those days, we went outside during recess. It was a beautiful day, so warm and the sun was shining really bright that day. Taking in the warmth of the sun, I was in my own little world playing hopscotch when, out of nowhere, one of the boys in my class ran past me and pulled my hair. I could not believe he did that! I got so mad! Instantly, I wanted to punch his lights out! However, God must have been on his side that day. I chose not to give him a knuckle sandwich, instead I stayed cool. I willfully chose peace. Besides, I think I had more fun watching him squirm while trying to figure out what I was going to do since I didn't punch him.

Another time that helped me with learning to choose peace was when I was in the fourth grade. It was during a volleyball tournament between the fourth, fifth and sixth graders at my elementary school. My fourth grade class, and our opponents, the sixth grade class, were the only two classes left standing. We had won against all the other classes, so now we had to play against each other. The team that won the most out of four games would win the tournament. Now, after one of the teams won a game, the teams would switch sides on the volleyball court. As we went to switch places on the court, I noticed those sixth graders looked huge compared to us fourth graders! Needless to say, because I was small (but not the smallest in my class), I didn't seem to be a big threat to the other team. So, as luck would have it, I became a target to be picked on. One of the sixth grade girls (one of the biggest on the team) decided she wanted to bump into me as we switched sides on the volleyball court. She almost knocked me down - pure intimidation on her part. However, I grew up with two brothers so I was used to the rough housing. I could have paid her back by shoving her back when we had to switch sides again. Instead, I chose to keep calm. I gave her that look of "try it again if you want, but I'm not responsible for what happens next!" As difficult as it was, I chose peace yet again.

Although I experienced many more incidents, I'll fast forward several years. I am a senior in high school. This time I went to visit my cousin in Virginia for the summer break. I always enjoyed visiting her because I always had loads of fun with her and there was always something going on. It may have been the fun of us sneaking strawberries off the vines or picking apples from the trees. It may have been the excitement of the carnival being in town! Whatever it was, I had a feeling that this time was not going to be the same for me. I did not know how true that statement was at the time it entered my mind. My cousin was well known and well liked throughout her school and her town. It was the type of town where everyone knew everyone. This particular day, my cousin, a few of her friends, and I decided to go to the carnival. It started out just like all the other fun times with a lot of joking and laughing. Then the atmosphere changed really quickly. A girl that my cousin had argued with several months previously decided she was going to show off for one of the guys that was hanging out with us. I later found out she had a crush on this guy. Yes, you guessed it! She decided to start another argument with my cousin and I. Now, she began to get loud, trying to cause a scene. Now, I would like to say I kept my cool the entire time. However, that would be a lie. Every part of my being wanted to pounce on her and snatch the weave off her head! I made a move toward her, but the guy she was causing the scene for, grabbed my shoulder before anything happened, motioning to me not to do anything that would cause my vacation in Virginia to be shortened. Instead, I began to do what my mom used to do. I stayed calm and began to talk in a calm voice. Before I knew it everyone had calmed down. We had reached a point where everyone was no longer yelling, but talking! Once again (with help this time), I chose peace. Now mind you, I'm not saying choosing peace is going to be easy all the time. However, I am saying choosing peace on purpose allows you to stay in a more joyful place. Choosing peace intentionally will take practice, but it becomes easier over time. I have also noticed that it takes less time to regain my peace in situations now than it did years ago.

The more I choose peace purposefully, the faster I can get back to enjoying my day. So if I can help you not to go down the same path as I did in the beginning of this life experience, then this message was meant to be shared. Having peace means different things for different people. Peace for me is being able to find that place where I can collect my thoughts and emotions enough to not react or respond in a way that takes me out of character or leads me in a negative direction. When some people are pushed to their limit, they may shout. Others may throw things, and someone else may storm out the room, throwing up their arms, fussing and stomping. These are just to name a few. You may respond similarly to what I have described. Or you may be a person who gives people the "silent" treatment. How does that work for you?

I can recall an incident with someone whom every time they chose to call me on the telephone they would try to start an argument with me. Now I could've simply just not answered the phone. However, I was not in the same space back then that I am at this point of my life. Again, I know I am not alone in this. Now, I would sometimes go back and forth with this person and other times I would give little or no response or energy to the situation. In doing this, I noticed a great difference in me. I noticed if I chose to go back and forth with this person, my day was spent replaying the phone call over and over in my head, reflecting on "I should have said this instead of that" moments. However, if I gave the circumstance little or no energy… I had a great day, well, at least a pretty good day anyway. I kept my peace and stayed calm throughout the day, which, in my mind, beats feeling uneasy or agitated any day.

So, from that day on, I began to become more conscious of myself being less agitated and staying in my definition of tranquility. I have learned different things to do to give me peace. Daily affirmations and meditation, writing poems, reading, listening to music, making my own soaps, candles, and bath salts are big on my list. The list goes on and on. Basically, what I am saying is, find something that works for you. It may be painting or drawing. Whatever it is, as long as it is legal and does not cause harm to anyone or anything, go for it. Some people may cook, bake, sew or knit. There are thousands of things to do. You just need to find a few that take you back to your peaceful self. Be intentional with your choices. Make sure they guide you toward a peace that includes self-love, and love toward others.

The feeling you get when loving on yourself or loving on someone else is amazing! It is one of the best feelings I have ever experienced. The whole experience will shift your mindset. It will put you in a space or place that allows you to view everything differently. You no longer look for the negative in situations. You seek out the positive in everything you do or say. Yes, you will begin to choose words that uplift and bring joy to you and others. In turn, being and staying consistent with this type of mindset will allow you to not only experience peace intentionally, but to extend peace to someone else as well.

I am sure you have heard the saying "peace-of-mind means everything!" Well, that saying changed my mindset. It was what allowed me to take a good look at my life and make a few changes. It granted me the ability to incorporate things and activities that brought love, joy, and peace into my space. I often use some of the items I mentioned earlier or just take a walk in the park, as a means to release stress and obtain peace. I am at a point in my life where, as I said before, "peace-of-mind means everything!" I choose to be happy and stay joyful, which, in turn, ushers peace into my life. I no longer "sweat the small stuff!" I make a conscious effort to maintain calmness throughout the day. Hence, I obtained one of my nicknames, 'Mellow Yellow.' I laugh every time I hear someone call me that.

I can not imagine that the not-so-positive reactions mentioned above could bring any peace or tranquility to anyone involved. So now I am asking you to reflect back on a matter that may have happened in the past, or more recently, that interfered with your peace. I'll give you a moment to think of an incident that took your joy and peace away. Acknowledge if your joy or peace was taken for a good length of time or for only a short length of time. Think about how your body began to feel. Did you tense up? Did you clench your teeth? Did it have some other effect on your body, such as a headache? Stress (lack of peace) affects everyone slightly differently. However, in that moment of time, we are usually aware of what is happening to us. I am not sure about you but, I DON'T LIKE IT! So, I try to avoid those feelings when I can. Now let's be realistic, you can't run from or ignore these feelings. Yet you can find better ways to view them. All of these circumstances definitely caused me to stretch and shift from the person I was back then and become the person I am today. I refused to stay stuck in the cycle of disappointment and being upset. Yes, we are back to the mindset. It now becomes a matter of whether you handle the experience in the same way… getting upset, shouting, stomping, etc…or do you decide to do as the GPS says "reroute." What could you have done differently before your peace was interrupted? What are some things that bring you peace or tranquility that you can incorporate into your routine? You can decide to look at the situation and say to yourself "I will not allow this to steal my joy!" At that very moment YOU CHOSE PEACE ON PURPOSE! Yay, you did it!

You see, that was not as hard as you thought it would be. It was just a matter of changing the way you view the circumstance that allowed you to experience peace. Feeling at peace helps us in many ways, including how we handle stress. We only have one life to live. Living it with energy that promotes peace and tranquility is very important. So stay calm and do things that bring positive energy rather than diminish it. I thank the Lord everyday for reminding me how important it is to stay calm, willfully.

It does not take a magic trick to enjoy or participate in this experience. It is simply the decision to INTENTIONALLY CHOOSE PEACE.

* * *

Sharon Allen

Sharon Allen is a Certified Breakthrough Coach, a best selling co-author of *"Her Story Our Story: Different Faces, Same Trauma"* and is a Certified Registered Central Sterile Technician. Sharon also has a background in Physical Therapy and Diagnostic Ultrasound, as well as being a licensed nail technician. Above all else, added to the list of many hats she wears, Sharon is the mom of three wonderful young adults.

Fueled by a great passion and her own life experiences, she founded *7 Peaces, LLC*. This is a place where women who have experienced life's challenges (i.e., trauma from divorce, loss of a loved one, loss of a job or home, and/or life-changing health issues) can come to find Peace. She is inspired to help women who are "stuck" in their life challenges to "breakthrough" those challenges and begin to live a life with purpose again.

You can connect with Sharon here via email Sharons7peaces@gmail.com

Forgiveness: Open Mind Leads to Open Heart

By Monica Crowell

When I turned fifty, it was so pivotal because my mom, who was my best friend, had passed five years prior and wouldn't be there to celebrate with me. I was dealing with perimenopause, issues with my job, and a failing marriage. My children were growing up and thriving, yet I felt stagnant. The 'happily ever after' didn't exist for me. My thoughts became different, and the person that I knew myself to be, didn't seem to exist anymore. There was a communication bridge in our marriage and a brick wall to where we couldn't seem to meet in the middle. I was tired of arguing about the smallest things. My sanctuary for peace at home was currently non-existent. Also, there was a lack of trust between us that we couldn't move past. After ten years of marriage, I was convinced that he had started cheating, because I had started getting bladder infections whenever we had sex. He would deny it when I asked, but I didn't believe him because he seemed to be closed off and uncommunicative. At that time, I couldn't tell if he was lying or not. After almost twenty years of marriage, I asked for a divorce; I needed to find peace of mind for myself because we had hit a place where it just didn't look like it could be fixed. His reply to the divorce was, I was blocking his blessing.

I had to look inside myself to realize that if God can forgive me every time that I ask, then who am I to hold on to unforgiveness. When you forgive someone, you shouldn't continue to speak about what they did to you. Forgiveness is about letting go completely and moving forward. The Bible says, *"And when you stand praying, if you hold anything against anyone, forgive them, so that your Father in heaven may forgive you your sins,"* Mark 11:25. I was raised with this verse, but I didn't discover a deeper understanding until I became an adult. Forgiveness is not easy for anyone, but I needed to release all the negative feelings that I felt for my ex so that I could move on with my life. The ramification of not forgiving is not worth it for me because I'm the one suffering and having feelings, when the other person is moving on with their own life. I had thoughts about reconciling with my ex over the last couple of years, but we needed to fix our communication and trust issues to make it work a second time around. When my ex-husband asked for another chance, for the third time since our divorce, I had to at least consider the possibility that this was the right time, even though we had been divorced for 11 years.

Let me start at the beginning with how I met my future husband, E. We grew up in a small town where there were no strangers; everyone knew everyone, especially my grandparents. His grandmother went to the same church as my grandmother. E was in my kindergarten class as well as the first, second, and fourth-grade classes (yes, we go that far back). We did go together for one day in the fourth grade. The next day, he broke up with me with no explanation. I never found out the reason until I was grown. He was told by another boy that I liked the other boy and not E. I would have told him that he was lied to if he had asked me. We had moved away, so I didn't see E again until I was in college and he was in the Marine Corps. While I was visiting my grandfather one summer, I connected with my childhood friend, Nita. She wanted to go to the park where we used to hang out when we were younger. As we walked back from the park, a car stopped near us. Nita had no problem approaching the car. Someone called her by name, so I hung back, since I didn't know who they were. After a few minutes, Nita called me over to the car. Initially, I was hesitant. She convinced me to walk to the car.

I didn't know anyone in the car until a familiar face leaned out the back window. It was E. I could still recognize him. He was mature, tall, brown skinned, broad shoulders, and looked as handsome as ever. We chatted for a few minutes and exchanged information. We kept in touch for a while through letters and phone calls, then the communication stopped. There was a reason for the "crickets." E had gotten married, and even though we were just friends, he decided not to tell me. I found out when I called his house and his sister told me that he had taken his wife to the store. Imagine my surprise, only because I didn't hear this from him.

In the meantime, I moved on with my life after graduation. I enjoyed the single life and living on my own. My mother wanted to see me married, and she prayed for God to send me someone. I told her that it couldn't happen unless I accepted it and believed it. At that time, I was nearing my thirties, and all I wanted was to make a career, buy a house, and adopt a few kids. Then I had this dream in 1988. I remember everything about the dream, which was so vivid and seemed real. When I tried to recall the baby's father, I couldn't see his face, but I knew that it was someone I was familiar with from my past. The first person that popped into my head was E, but I knew at that time he was still married, and it couldn't be him. My mom didn't believe my dream would come true, but I knew! Let's say that it was instinct. I would hear from him now and then. As I said, we were friends and nothing more, at that time. I didn't see him any other way. Anyway, we had lost contact.

A year later, after the dream, my mom told me that she had spoken to his grandmother a few weeks prior and had given his grandmother my number, without my knowledge. She always thought that we should have been together. Several months went by before he called. At this time, I wasn't dating anyone due to a stalking scare; I had decided that I would chill for a bit. I was going through some drama at my job, as well. When he called, the first thing I asked him was if he was still married; I always asked him that when we spoke. He still was. I wanted to make sure that I was always respectful of his marriage anytime I spoke with him. Our conversations always stayed on what was going on in the world, very basic. We never talked about his marriage, not once. After that call, I didn't hear from him for almost a year.

He told me that he broke off communication because he was going through a divorce and needed to deal with the ramifications of the fallout. When he finally contacted me, his divorce was final. The first thing he told me was that he didn't want to get married again, ever, and I was fine with that because I wasn't sold on getting married anyway.

Months passed; we would talk on the phone quite frequently, sometimes for over three hours, which allowed us to get to know each other as adults. Around six months later, he came to visit during the holidays, and we spent time with each other. We only went on one official date. He surprised me on Christmas day by popping the question. I didn't see this coming, even though he had told me he was in love with me. I was in love with him, so I said "yes." He said that he wanted to take care of me for the rest of my life.

Six months after we were married, I was pregnant with my firstborn. I thought initially that this was going to be like the dream I'd had a few years prior and I would be having a girl. During my seventh month, I had another dream in which it was revealed that I was having a boy, and we had chosen only one name. When I became pregnant the second time, 2 ½ years later, I knew at that moment I was having a girl. The dream that I had six years previously had come to fruition. Everything in that dream was exactly how the labor and delivery went. Trust the vision that God gives you.

We had our ups and downs the first ten years. Around that time, I realized that I had changed and not for the best. There were some good times, but I had to ask myself, did the good outweigh the bad? I had lost the essence of who I knew myself to be. I had fallen into a deep depression that was expressed by my shopping addiction, which was out of control. My self-image was low, partly due to the pregnancy weight gain that I could not lose. We had just bought a house, and at that point, I realized that I didn't want to be married, and I thought that it was not a good thing to have these thoughts. I prayed for clarity. I still loved my husband, but the trust between us was not there. My best friend didn't seem to exist. I thought that we could still make it work without trust, but a marriage without trust is impossible to grow.

When turning fifty, I took a good look at my life and started to reflect on how to move forward. I just didn't see staying married. I wanted to work on my marriage, but we kept having the same conversation over and over, with no lasting changes. It wasn't that I wanted him to change, I just wanted the man that I knew, to materialize. E was more attentive, communicative, and romantic before we married, and once we said "I do," a wall went up. I found out six months into our marriage that he enjoyed watching pornography. I realized, years later, that this was an addiction, which affected our intimacy and other aspects of our marriage, over time. I did seek counseling and prayer before I asked for the divorce. We decided to have an amicable divorce, not just for us, but also for our children. The hardest part was telling our children. No matter how old they are, it's never easy to accept, because children want their parents to stay together. My son did not react, but my daughter took it very hard. It took years for her to forgive me for breaking up our home. I promised that we would continue to do family things together, and we kept that promise, even though there were times I questioned myself as to how long we could continue.

The first year of separation, my husband decided to visit his family for Thanksgiving and take our kids with him. That was my first Thanksgiving without my kids. My best friend and her husband had Thanksgiving dinner with me, but it just wasn't the same. After that, I didn't want to spend another Thanksgiving without my kids. So, we continued to have Thanksgiving together as a family. Our divorce was final the following year, but I didn't move out for another year. In the meantime, my son left for the Air Force.

Moving from a house to an apartment while downsizing was an adjustment the first year. Reality hit when I realized I would be paying rent again, which was something I had never imagined I would be doing again. Financially, it wasn't a good time, but I didn't care. During the adjustment time, I started going to concerts again to at least give myself some much-needed self-love. I was fortunate to win tickets from a radio station or find some free concerts. This was my way of dealing with the downside of being single again. I wasn't interested in dating, since times are different with social media.

I worked as a caregiver in clients' homes. There were times that I would have couples as clients. For the married ones, I would ask them how they met their spouse. To my surprise, they all said that it was love at first sight, and they just knew that they had met the love of their life. Until this time, I did not believe in love at first sight.

The fact that they weathered the storms and made their marriages work gave me clarity. While taking care of my clients, I developed compassion, which I had lacked during our marriage. I developed more compassion to help and serve others, but, unlike my mother, I do have a limit when it comes to others trying to take advantage of my good heart.

When our children were grown, I felt that we needed to see less of each other so that we could move on. We were still having Thanksgiving as a family. One year, I told E that this would be the last Thanksgiving together, and he needed to figure out what he was going to do the following year. My daughter had a different idea to keep that family time going. She had just moved to another state for her job and decided that she wanted to have Thanksgiving at her place, and she was inviting her dad. You guessed it; I went because my dad and my sister were coming. I had a feeling that this was going to be my dad's last Thanksgiving, and, unfortunately, I was right.

We were better at being friends at this time than we were at being married. I had to have nasal surgery due to being clogged most of the time. An ENT doctor had recommended surgery over a year ago, but I wasn't ready to hear that. E told me that he would pay for it. I reluctantly agreed to have the surgery in January of 2021, with the promise that my daughter would come to stay. When that time came, she couldn't come because she had to pack to move into her new home. She recommended that her dad should be my caretaker. I was very hesitant at first, but I relented. He came and stayed with me. He prayed for me before I went back to surgery. I was touched (this was not something he would have done in the past). It was the pivotal moment that my heart started to melt again for him. He was attentive and caring as he took care of me, and made sure that I took the medication and rested. The healing process was long and extremely painful, and I'm still healing, after more than a year.

E was going to come back to Virginia to get his taxes done, so I suggested that he come on my birthday weekend. He did. We talked, laughed, and he took me out to dinner. It was nice to not argue. I felt that I had my friend back at this point. I told him that I wanted to get rid of my storage unit, and he offered to help. During that weekend, we talked about seeing each other undercover until we figured things out. I had a conference that I was going to attend, so he came down for us to spend some time together. Our time together was different than it was in the past, as it should be, considering we are older and wiser. We are taking our time, and we don't want to capture what we had; we want something better as we move forward. Our familiarity has now become our "brand new."

During the time that we spent apart, I had to grow and find the person that I loved and liked again. He needed to grow without me, as well. We have finally come full circle in forgiving each other and forgiving ourselves. It was hard, initially, to forgive E for the hurt that I dealt with over the years. I thought that I knew the man that I had married, but there was a part of him that I did not know.

We had always been friends, but when we divorced we had to rebuild that friendship and the trust. We began to build a different bridge for us to cross together, and as one. The love between us may have waned, but it never died. Our love just evolved. We were both open to a different type of relationship, and the possibilities are endless. The support that I get from my E speaks volumes. He's my inspiration for my jewelry line and keeps me going.

Covid has taught me that life is too short to hold on to the negative thoughts and the drama that comes our way. I'm choosing to resist the drama and embrace life. My mom once told me that you can't change a grown person; you must decide what you're willing to tolerate. Never say never because God may have you circle back to where you came from. God knows the master plan for your life.

Pray for God to show you His vision and be willing to receive it. I now have peace and hope for the future. I look forward to my journey the second time around.

FORGIVENESS is one of the WISDOM G.I.F.T.S.
I am so grateful for it.

* * *

Monica Crowell

Monica Crowell is an author and entrepreneur who currently resides in Virginia Beach, Virginia. The Southwestern Ohio native attended The Ohio State University and Bryant and Stratton College where she received a Bachelor of Science degree in Psychology and an Associates of Science degree in Information Technology respectively. Her love of reading and her creativity was cultivated when she began hanging out at the library with her mother when she was young. In her spare time, she creates beautiful jewelry for those looking for something unique and lightweight. When she isn't spending time with her two children, family and friends, you can find her at a good old-school concert.

You can reach her via email at hmmrqsb@gmail.com

A Rose Is Still A Rose

By Sharon DuMas

A plus-sized woman's journey to
self-love and self-esteem

It is no secret that people love roses, whether they are buds or in bloom. That is my analogy of being a small stature (bud) or a plus-sized woman (in bloom). Allow me to share my journey to self-esteem and self-love.

I was an insecure, dark-skinned teenager before sayings like "Black is beautiful" became popular in the '60s. I was fairly quiet, considered overweight, and the one thing I truly lacked was confidence. Like so many young people at critical points in their lives today, I was trying to find my way without a compass. My real growth didn't begin until I learned my worth. Knowing my worth led to understanding my potential.

My lack of confidence affected more than just the way I saw myself physically. I was shy, so I didn't go after a lot of the same opportunities young people my age were pursuing, coming out of high school. When the senior prom rolled around, I was available – probably more available than I wanted to be! I didn't have a boyfriend, so I hoped I'd be asked to the dance by one of my senior classmates and that we'd have a great time. Well, I did get a prom invitation, but it was *nothing* like I had in mind. A boy did ask if he could take me, but he said he wanted to be paid! I remember telling my mother about it and she wasn't about to let me sacrifice my pride, even if I wanted to.

I didn't get any more invitations, so I went to the prom by myself. My mom insisted. No, I didn't have a good time. I was a full-figured girl, so I didn't get much attention, and I was too much of a "wall flower" to shine on my own. But I got an important lesson at the start of my self-esteem journey, just by showing up. My mother had said, "Let no one stop you from doing something you want to do." It was a lot like the lesson my counselor, Mr. Littlefield, taught me without even meaning to, when I told him I was going to own a business. He said "Sharon, you will never own a business and you should only aspire to be a secretary, because if you can't manage your weight, you will never be able to manage people." My lesson– **no one can set limits for someone else's life.**

I was truly what you'd call a late-bloomer, and I believe those two experiences, coming out of high school, deeply impacted my self-confidence so much so that I didn't even start driving a car until I was 23 years old. Well, if high school had been my initial visit to the doctor's office, and poor self-esteem was the diagnosis, I would have to find the right prescription sooner than later. After all, I wanted to enjoy my life and make my dreams come true just as much as everyone else around me. I wanted happiness and fulfillment. A lot of people don't realize it, but self-esteem issues can get in the way of almost anything we allow them to, from personal growth to professional goals. Every minute, hour or day that you talk yourself out of believing you can succeed, is a minute, hour or day you can never get back. My low self-esteem led me into bad relationships with men. I recall being in a relationship and my male friend, at the time, told me that: "I would never make it without him and it was apparent I had low self-esteem and didn't love myself; that I was incapable of being his woman because men like women who are confident." That statement was meant to hurt me but it actually motivated me. After crying for 48 hours straight and re-playing the two scenarios in my head from high school, I decided it was time for a change. I set out to prove to myself that I was worthy of loving myself and being loved and respected by others. I decided to put into action the lessons my mother had taught me.

My first step was to look in the mirror and figure out how to like the person staring back at me, so I became a Mary Kay Beauty Consultant to learn how to wear and apply makeup. My work with Mary Kay led me to discover a gift that took me places I had never imagined I'd go. While selling the cosmetics, I saw an ad in the newspaper that described an opening for a beauty director or makeup artist. I was always trying to come up with creative ways to attract new customers, so I thought the position could be a good opportunity. Even though it was a volunteer position, it felt like one that would work out well for me because it called for someone who knew how to do makeup and modeling.

I didn't have any experience in the modeling area, but makeup had become a specialty. I got in touch with the person who was listed in the ad. Her name is Amina Fakir and we are still good friends today, forty years later. Well, after talking with Amina, who was in charge of the Miss Black America Pageant, I did a makeup demonstration on one of the models and she was impressed.

"I would love to have you," Amina said, recruiting me as a regular part of the pageant's backstage team. So there I was, serving as support while Amina trained and prepared the young ladies to participate. Little did I know, this would be just the tip of the iceberg of my experiences to come, as far as modeling and beauty showcases. Defining one of the things I was good at doing, opened the first door. I felt good about making an important contribution to the program and it was a great experience. Not only did I enjoy it, doing something that was recognized as valuable helped boost the self-confidence and value I felt within myself. It can work the same way with you.

I learned that recognizing outer beauty can be a result of building inner beauty. Have you ever known a person who had great looks, but who never seemed happy? Maybe he or she had a gloomy personality, or just wasn't pleasant to be around. The thing about having a poor self-image is that it doesn't let us see the good things other people see when they look at us. We can have the most wonderful hair and the smoothest skin; we can paint amazing portraits, write poetry or sing well, but low self-esteem is what blinds us from seeing the good in ourselves. Sometimes we not only fail to see it, but we also bury it completely after listening to the wrong inner voice, that says, "You don't have what it takes."

I remember hearing that voice when I watched the Miss Black America Pageant from backstage. I had done my job by helping to make all the contestants look their best – but I realized they had the spotlight, not me. I stood there starry-eyed, basically in tears because I knew I wanted to be one of those models. But, just like it had been in high school, I knew I wouldn't be accepted because I was a plus-sized woman. I really hadn't ever thought about becoming a model. That felt a lot like what the high school counselor, Mr. Littlefield, told me when I said I wanted to own a company, it's something I wasn't supposed to do.

After the Miss Black America Pageant, my self-esteem soared, and I had the confidence and the plan to start my organization, Full & Fabulous. My purpose was to provide a vehicle for plus-sized women and girls to cope with the peer pressures of being overweight. This was done through personal and professional development to motivate and enhance them in the areas of self-esteem, health and beauty. My first event was the Miss Full & Fabulous Inner Beauty Pageant, because I wanted to shine a spotlight on women like me, but I wanted to stress that inner beauty was more important than outer beauty. The highest-paid motivational speaker at the time was "Zig" Ziglar and he said, "The best way to learn it is to teach it." So, as I taught others how to present themselves with confidence, I learned it for myself.

Being exposed to beauty and fashion led me to new places and new experiences. It also helped that I was really starting to come out of my shell as my self-esteem bloomed within me. Like the soft petals on a flower, I was beginning to see myself develop into the rose I had always wanted to show the world, but hadn't yet become.

I recall my first photo shoot with Chester Price, who was an excellent photographer, who took pictures of celebrities who came to Detroit for different shows. Through Chester, I had a chance to style the makeup for different celebrities, male and female. Then one day, he said something I never expected to hear: "Sharon, let's take some photos of you."

What? I was surprised and a little nervous, but I followed Chester's lead. He gave me instructions for how to pose and kept snapping shots until he felt satisfied with what he had. A week later he had developed the photos and I came to his darkroom. He handed me one of the images. I took a close look.

"Who is that?" I asked.

Chester started laughing at me. His photo lab was at his house and his family was around. They chuckled, too. What was so funny? Of course, the laughter was because I didn't even recognize myself in the shot Chester handed me! I had been dressing modestly, creating this person who looked old-fashioned. I truly didn't know I had created, using the formulas from working with the women in my program, a vibrant, attractive woman under those layers, until I saw her looking back at me from that picture.

When I think back all those years to how I started my organization, Full & Fabulous, it brings me joy that I became known as Full & Fabulous. I've done a lot of things that I never imagined myself doing when my self-esteem didn't allow it, including taking the training to own a car dealership! (I wonder what Mr. Littlefield would think about that.) But creating Full & Fabulous, with all the learning I did to recruit participants, promote and operate the programs, is the biggest proof that I never had any real limits. My forty years have included national TV interviews, magazine and newspaper stories, fundraisers with celebrity guests and other achievements – most of all, helping other women and girls realize they had as much potential inside them as I had in me. Of course, it was a huge challenge to build the vision into something I've become so proud of today.

As a girl growing up on Detroit's east side, I would have thought anyone telling me I'd start an organization for plus-sized women and girls to promote health, beauty and self-esteem was smoking something illegal. Not only would I have disagreed, but I might also have laughed! If they told me that one day my organization would do a fashion show for the Prime Minister of the Bahamas, Hubert Ingraham, have our name listed on the website and become a sanctioned event of the Super Bowl, the biggest sports celebration in the country and seen around the world, I might have rolled my eyes. That I would appear on a national TV talk show; receive the key to the City of Detroit from the Mayor; and receive a proclamation from the Governor of Michigan for the work I do with plus-sized women and girls? No way! Sorry – wrong Sharon.

It turns out, all these years later, that I would have been the one who was mistaken. My future, after discovering self-esteem, included all those achievements and more. I've met presidents and millionaires. I created and led a team to have a street in Detroit named after the Motown legend and icon, Stevie Wonder (Stevie Wonder Avenue). I've dined with divas and mingled with models. On a few occasions, I even found myself on the runway or in the spotlight. I've received awards and been celebrated for the work I've dedicated myself to performing for the past forty years. I don't share all of this to brag. I share it to explain the importance of what I want you to become knowledgeable about: how to learn and maintain healthy self-esteem.

Building confidence has become a career for me. Influencing lives is a calling and a ministry. What's interesting is, I didn't start with any special training or advantages. As a matter of fact, I was one of those folks who might be described as overcoming the odds. From being raised by a single parent to coping with a life-changing injury, I've walked a road without yellow bricks. I have faith in God and I've made some good friends, but confidence has been my closest companion. By sharing the steps on my journey, I hope that self-confidence and a positive self-image becomes yours, too.

Just like the fact that roses are beautiful, whether a bud or in full bloom, your position doesn't limit your power. With the right focus and determination to live your potential, you can bloom in greater ways than you ever thought possible. It's time to start watering your rose.

I have two questions for you:

ARE YOU READY FOR THE JOURNEY?
WHAT ARE YOU GOOD AT?

If your answer is "nothing," you're losing the battle for healthy self-esteem to one of its biggest enemies: self-doubt. Every one of us has some kind of gift, talent or skill, even if we haven't discovered it. Since self-esteem is fed by self-confidence, we all need to have a source within us to make us feel good about something we can offer the world.

Finding it can be a journey all on its own, but it's one of the most important keys to overcoming self-doubt. Everything is a process, so discovering what you do well, what people find interesting about you, or even whatever small thing you might have that makes you feel proud, will help move you to the next level of building your confidence and comfort in your own skin. No matter how big or small, as long as it's a talent or asset that doesn't involve letting others use or exploit you, count it as something that makes you valuable.

Depending on how long you've suffered from low self-esteem, it might take a while for you to identify your gifts and assets. It might even take a while for you to develop them, but don't be discouraged – it doesn't mean you don't have them; it only means you haven't fully explored them. Start the search by thinking about what you enjoy, because the things we like doing often reveal the places where our skills can be found.

I like to say, "Today is the best day of the rest of our lives." In other words, as soon as you learn your value, don't waste any time making the most of what you learned.

Here are a few ways to Water Your Rose:

> **Affirmation:** Write a positive adjective about yourself, starting with every letter in your first name. For example: Sexy, Happy, Attractive, Responsible, Outstanding, Nice. Now repeat it (with your own letters and name) as follows, at least 100 times daily (in increments of 20).
>
> – ***I am the sexy, happy, attractive, responsible, outstanding, nice Sharon and today is the best day of the rest of my life.***

Remember that what you say about yourself is more important than what anyone else says about you.

Take a few minutes each day to reflect on your worth. Think about things you like and feel proud of, the things you have to offer the world, whether big or small. Write a list of these things, post them where you can see them and, reflect on them daily as reminders of what's so special about you.

Inner Beauty breeds confidence. Smile more! Be kind to yourself and others. It's not just a feel-good saying: Beauty truly does come from within. And yes, there are those with natural traits that make them more physically attractive – but not even the most amazing looks or the hottest figure can hold a candle to the appeal of someone who truly feels good about themself. Being comfortable in our own skin means accepting ourselves and knowing our value.

Write a list of five things you do well (or want to explore doing because you enjoy or find them interesting). Don't get frustrated if you have trouble coming up with five things you do well right away; ask a friend or someone close to you to add their thoughts. You might even include things like "showing kindness to others" or "taking care of my health," because these types of skills can be developed into talents, too.

Make a list of things you've wanted to do but haven't had the confidence to try yet. Beside every item on your list, come up with one or two small things that will move you toward these goals. For example: You might not feel ready to start a business, but you can grab a book about how to become an entrepreneur or challenge yourself to find a mentor who is a business owner. Now get moving!

(Watering your Rose) – Keep a journal of the things that motivate and inspire you and be consistent saying your affirmations. Even if those positive adjectives don't describe you now, they will and that's why journaling your progress is important.

You've heard my journey, now enjoy
your **journey to SELF-LOVE.**

✲ ✲ ✲

Sharon DuMas

Sharon DuMas, CEO/Full & Fabulous Inc., author, speaker, and philanthropist. "Full and Fabulous is a state of mind, not a dress size." Positively impacting the lives of plus-sized young ladies has been a lifelong journey. Sharon's unique formula has delivered spectacular results. Founded in 1982, the Full & Fabulous program has had ZERO teen pregnancies in its 40-year history.

Growing up as a plus-size girl was extremely stressful. Body shaming by loved ones was a frequent source of pain. Searching for advocates and finding few, she decided to be the heroine that she was looking for. Acceptance of insults was replaced by affirmations.

Cleansing her mind was her first step towards mental hygiene. Enhancing body image is essential. Sharon looked in the mirror and gave herself permission to be pretty.

Self-esteem and confidence pushed Sharon to share her formula with the Detroit community. She's been featured on television, been tagged a W.K. Kellogg Foundation Expert-In-Residence, was awarded Michigan's Hometown Health Hero of the Year, given a Key to the City of Detroit, and partnered with the NFL for Super Bowl XL community outreach.

To book Sharon for a conference or organization meeting:

LinkedIn: Sharon DuMas
Website: www.sharondumas.com
Email: sharon@sharondumas.com

Lightning Strikes Twice

By Aretha Y. Ballen

Triumph through trust in God,
and SELF-LOVE

Growing up, I was that young girl who preferred to hide in the shadows. I was, and maybe still am, that shy introverted young lady who never felt like she measured up. This was mostly due to my father's expectations. I don't think he believed in me at all, and boy it was hard for me to be me, each and every day. My mother, on the other hand, was always there for me, and she made me feel like there was nothing that I could not accomplish and nothing that I could not do! Little did I know that lightning would strike and change everything.

I didn't hear the words, "I Love you!" and to be honest, I don't know if I ever have heard them from my parents. It was just something my parents never said. But I always felt the love, especially from my mother. My parents were not that "lovey-dovey" couple in public. The examples of love I saw and received from my parents and other family members did not compare to my expectations and what I was looking for in a relationship.

Every year, my mom, sister and I would take our yearly trip to Washington DC around Labor Day. We would visit with family and friends, go shopping, site seeing and attend church on Sunday. If you have ever been to DC, you know that there are tons of federal government buildings everywhere and we just so happened to end up in front of the Department of the Interior (DOI). I looked at the building and wondered, what did this organization do? It impressed me.

After graduating from college, about two years later, I relocated to the DC area and I began applying for federal government positions. After about six months, I finally got a job offer, and would you guess where! The DOI! I was like WOW!!! I remembered the building and my first day on the job was Monday, August 12th.

I was so grateful to a family friend, who helped me get my foot in the door. I met my sorority sister and friend Lacey at church, who also worked at DOI, and we became fast friends. But one particular day, I remember standing at Lacey's desk and we were just talking and then I turned to my left...and there he was! I was like who is THIS!!?? I felt like I was Struck by Lightning!!

He was tall, lean, and handsome, wearing a crisp white shirt, black tie, black slacks and the biggest smile I had ever seen. He proceeded to walk over to me, extended his hand and said, "Hello, I'm Lennox." I literally felt the room shake! Did I say, "struck by lightning!!!??" You could have SOLD me for a nickel, because I was SOLD on him! Now, I had dated before, but this was different. The love Lennox and I shared was magical. I found out later that on the day we met, he had told his best friend and roommate,

"I met the woman I'm going to marry." The ironic thing is, my first day at DOI, August 12th, was his birthday, and he would often tell me that I was his birthday gift. We had the most amazing times ever!! Dinners, movies, concerts, trips to the beach, trips to New York City, amusement parks!! We did it all!! We had so much fun and there was just so much Love and my heart was happy. I knew this was what I was looking for!! I finally found it.

Lennox was kind and caring, but he was also tough as nails and he did not play. He was the kind of man who gave respect but demanded it in return, regardless of who you were or your title. You either loved him or hated him, but he was it! He was what I was looking for (in a man, in a husband). How did his Love Language show up? He would speak words of love, he would buy me the most beautiful gifts for my birthdays and holidays. Valentine's Day was always my favorite holiday to celebrate with him. He would always buy me these beautiful long-stem red roses and, even though we didn't have a ton of money, price was never the object for him. He wanted me to feel LOVED. And oh, how I did! He was my protector, and he showed me how much he loved me each and every day.

We were planning our future and I knew that the sky was the limit, and I began to settle in and to follow the lead of my future husband. Then, around 1993, he began to have some health issues. It started with some tingling in his feet and hands, and later, with his breathing. After a number of tests, he was diagnosed with Scleroderma. Scleroderma is a disease that affects the skin, internal organs and connective tissue. There is no cure and it is fatal in many cases. This disease attacked his lungs, heart, kidneys, eyes, and skin. I remember the day he was diagnosed; I called and he wouldn't answer the phone. I went to his apartment and he wouldn't answer the door and I knocked repeatedly. He wouldn't come to the door. Because he lived in a basement apartment, I was able to peek into his bedroom window. That's when I saw him, just lying on his bed. I can't remember how long it took for him to finally talk to me about his diagnosis, but he was devastated and sank into a deep state of depression. This disease not only took a toll on his body, but also on his appearance, and he always took pride in his appearance!! He was a FINE ASS KAPPA ALPHA PSI Fraternity, Inc., man, and this was more than he could possibly endure!!

He tried everything he could to end things with me, but nothing worked!! I was not leaving his side, NEVER! We wanted to be married and to have three kids, and I was still believing in God. He would go to the doctor, almost weekly, but he continued to get progressively worse and he would not take any of the medication that was prescribed to him for the disease. He got up and went to work every day in spite of the pain and the change in his physical appearance. I could see the struggle each day, but he pressed on. I was just so thankful that we were able to carpool to work every day, so now I could watch over and protect him. His health continued to deteriorate and it truly broke my heart to see him suffer the way that he did. There was a point where I literally cried every single night, but I continued to pray to God, not for my strength, but for Lennox's.

As time went on, he realized I wasn't going anywhere and then he said, "It's time to get married" and boy was I ready!! I didn't care what people thought or what people said. His physical appearance didn't matter, nothing mattered but us! So, on September 2, 1995, we tied the knot. It was a glorious day. I fondly remember my friends and family arriving from out of town and just having a great time. My sisters were my maid and matron of honor and my best girlfriend, Tam, was one of my bridesmaids. Tam came up a little early and we had a BALL!! Tam's only job, other than being a part of my wedding party, was to make sure I picked up my birth control pills from CVS the Friday before the wedding. Well, let's just say my daughter, Lauren, arrived nine months later and I honestly believed that was by God's design.

Having our daughter was the JOY of our lives. He loved being a husband and a dad and I loved being a wife and a mom! Every night he would hug and kiss her and spoil her rotten.

Once Lauren was born, he knew then that he wanted to live. She was his motivation. He wanted to do everything he could to live a long life, so he started taking his medication. The reason he was so hesitant about starting the medication when first diagnosed, was because one of the side effects was that we couldn't have any more children. So the dream of having three kids would be gone.

Lennox worked and attended school full time. He was determined to be a provider, but three months shy of Lauren's second birthday, God called Lennox home. March 9th, that's the day my world changed forever.

I was so used to having him lead, and now that he was gone, I had to figure out how I was going to parent and take care of the house alone. I wasn't even focused on my career. I was happy being a wife. I didn't have any huge career goals. He and my family were my career goals. I wanted to be a happily married wife with him leading, because I could hide behind him. It took me a while, but eventually I learned how to maneuver and move in the world without him. Every day I talked to God. I wasn't upset or angry, just heartbroken and disappointed. But I knew that I wouldn't want Lennox to be disappointed in me, because I believed that he and I were brought together for a reason, not only to bring our daughter into the world, but to share a life filled with love and true happiness. She's here and she's blessed and highly favored. And she's destined for greatness and I hope that she will read this and realize that she was brought here for a purpose.

I had to figure out how to move in the world without my life partner. No one thought I could do it. My mom, who was always there for me, was still trying to protect me. She told me one day, "Okay, well, I know it's time for you guys to come and move back home." But I just couldn't do that. I couldn't do it because I knew deep down inside, that's not what I wanted for me or my daughter.

So, after I decided that I wasn't moving back to my hometown, I had to figure it out. And thank God, I had some great people to help me along the way. Shout out to my village of friends and family!! They held us up and they were/are the Biggest Blessing Ever! I had tremendous help; I must admit, my help came from some places that I never thought that it would! Some people really stepped up to the plate. They were there no matter what. My sister, Sheila, in particular, was my "ride or die." She was there for me, even though she lived in the town that we grew up in. I remember when I needed time to deconflict and I needed some time alone, she would tell me that she would take care of Lauren for as long as I needed time. She would meet me on the interstate to get my daughter, her niece, whom she loved dearly. We would always meet in the middle between our homes. But two years after Lennox passed, she passed away tragically and I no longer had that support from her. But fortunately, there was also my Godmother, my girlfriend, Lisa, and Lauren's Godfather, Greg, who are all just the greatest. They were there when I needed them to be.

But, at the end of the day, I was still heartbroken. I still wanted what I wanted. I still missed my husband, and I just could not understand why God had allowed for this to happen. We were good people. We were honest people. All we wanted was to be happy and to continue to live and to thrive. Why snatch all of that away? Why put me on center stage? How can I lead? But, I had no choice. I realized that I could no longer hide in the shadows!!

After a while, I got to a point where I was lonely. I was young and attractive. I still wanted what I wanted. But that part of the road is where things got a little cloudy and I tried to create my own path instead of allowing God to create it for me. I decided that there were certain things I wanted and instead of me giving it to God, I said that I was going to create my own path. And you have to be careful when you decide to create your own path. You also have to take the responsibilities that come along with it. That's what happened. This is when I learned that you can't convince God to create something that you are not ready for. The one great thing that happened out of this learning period, is I had my beautiful, handsome son, Joshua. My son is the greatest blessing ever to come from that learning experience. So I set my sights on being alone…just working, taking care of my children. And that was it!

And I tell you, when I got out of my own way, followed God, told him the desires of my heart and became obedient to him, my world changed. I started to practice self-love. I focused on my life, being a mom to my children and taking care of us. And even though I decided that relationships and love were off the table, God had the last word!

A short time later, my good friend Chuck's birthday was coming up and he didn't want to celebrate his special day. But I said no, he has always been there for me so I was going to give him a party to celebrate. I told him, "Okay, it is your birthday and we are going to find a way to celebrate you!!" So, we planned his party. However, two weeks before the party, I had surgery and I was in so much pain. I was taking painkillers, but I was determined to attend and celebrate my friend. The day of the party, I got there early to help set up.

Well, I'm there early…setting up food, drinks, etc., and in walks this guy. He was so handsome and he had the most beautiful caramel silky skin, but he wasn't making any eye contact with me. I had seen him before and later I realized I had actually met him years ago. So I walked up to him and I said, "Hello, my name is Aretha." And he stated, "I know who you are." I'm like, okay, and then I remembered, Harold. He actually knew Lennox and he was his fraternity brother and we had met before. I was like, "Oh wow! Nice to see you again."

I then walked away. By this time my back was killing me. The painkillers weren't working, so I went into the living room and laid out on the floor to try to ease the pain in my back. Then Harold walked in and sat down on the floor next to me. That was so nice of him. I'm lying face up and he's just talking to me and we had a really, really good conversation. I must admit, after so long of not having fun, I had a really, really good time. I went home thinking to myself, "Wow, that was a really good conversation that we had and he is the nicest guy."

About a week later, my girlfriends and Chuck and his friends and I attended a Congressional Black Caucus event in the city. After meeting up, we all headed into the party, and Harold proceeded to head to the corner to camp out, but yet he was never too far away from me. I walked over to him and said, "Why aren't you dancing?" he replied "I don't dance!" Well, a short time later, he pulled me onto the dance floor and we had the best time ever! Little did I know that this would be the beginning of a beautiful relationship and marriage. After that night, Harold and I were inseparable. We did everything together from movies, dinners, concerts, trips to Jamaica in Vegas, we did it all! Granted, I had matured as a woman, so I was looking for a lot more than a pretty face and a nice smile! I was a mom now, and my kids were my top priority. It took quite some time for me to introduce him to my children and to have him involved in that part of my life. I tell you, he would show up at Lauren's cheer competitions, camera in hand, and at all of Joshua's sporting events, rooting louder than most of the parents! This made my heart smile!! When I began to feel that the love that he had for my children was genuine, that's when lightning struck! So for me, lightning struck twice, and I fell head over heels in love!! I still remember his beautiful proposal on that moonlit beach!! His love made me believe in love again!

So today, I am a happily married mom of three, yes, three! I had my handsome baby boy, Trey, at the ripe old age of 44 and he is definitely HEAVEN SENT. My children are…Heaven Sent!

Life has taken me on a true journey, but I realized, even after finding it, that life and true happiness are not about having the perfect husband, three kids or the house on the hill. Happiness, I mean true happiness, comes from the relationship that you have with the Creator! It was in my relationship that I developed with God that I was able to triumph over every obstacle that was placed in my way. When I began to focus on Him and trust Him, every crooked path that I had, was made straight. He has made me the woman that I am today.

So, if you want to find true happiness, I recommend that you do the following:

(1) Trust God, (2) Know that you are Worthy, and (3) Get Out of Your Own Way by practicing Self-Love!

Once you truly do these things, be prepared for Lightning to Strike!

* * *

Aretha Y. Ballen

Aretha Y. Ballen is a South Carolina native who currently resides in the Washington Metropolitan Area. She is a supervisor with the Federal Government and has over 30 years of experience in the Budget arena. During the Bill Clinton and Barack Obama Administrations, she was chosen to represent her agency during the National HBCU Week, which is a part of the White House HBCU Initiative. She graduated from the prestigious Claflin College (now Claflin University) with a Bachelors of Arts degree. While at Claflin, she became a member of the Illustrious Alpha Kappa Alpha

Sorority, Inc. She is currently an active member of the Zeta Chi Omega chapter in Northern Virginia. She is also an active member of the historic Alfred Street Baptist Church in Alexandria, Virginia, who made history by donating $1 Million to the Smithsonian's National Museum of African American History and Culture.

She is happily married and the mother of three, as well as the owner of My Sacred Temple, LLC, which caters to the healing of the Mind, Body and Spirit. She enjoys watching sports, movies and spending time with her family.

She has a passion for empowering and supporting those who are on their journey to healing, after suffering from the loss of a loved one. She simply wants to help heal those whose hearts are broken!

If you need support in finding your path to happiness, check out her course *Rediscovering Joy*.

She can also be contacted at MySacredTempleLLC@gmail.com for one-on-one coaching and additional support.

Be sure to follow her Facebook and Instagram @ArethaYBallen.

From Invisible to Inspirational

My Triumphant Journey to Women's Empowerment

Dr. Teresa Jeter

Many years ago, I stood on a stage alongside five others in a singing group during an annual event, waiting for recognition for our faithful contributions and services. One by one, I watched and listened as each one received plaques and vacated the stage. The leader made an apology and ensured that my plaque was coming soon. I was surprised and embarrassed when I was left standing alone without a plaque, as if I was not a member of the group. Imagine the pain behind my smile as I wondered, again, how could you possibly not see me as I glanced at my flesh to confirm I was visible.

More recently, I became the Chief Operations Officer of a wonderful women-owned organization that provides great services in the community and around the country. One day, one of the directors, whom I had hired, was making a PowerPoint presentation about our organization to a potential client. The client and our team were present in the conference room. The director talked about the organization, and he identified key individuals that would be involved in some capacity with this potential project. Photos of each key individual were in the presentation - everyone's photo except mine. Except for the Chief Executive Officer, I was the highest executive in the room. I was sitting next to the director in the meeting. He apologized profusely for his oversight. He was embarrassed and others were embarrassed for him. Again, an all-too-familiar occurrence in my life. I was invisible.

I will share a little about my family because it will provide a backdrop about my feelings regarding my birth order. You will find that some of my personality characteristics are as a result of being a middle child, and you also will become aware of the insecurities and painful moments that have put me on a triumphant path to women's empowerment.

I grew up in a family that included my mom, dad, and two siblings. I was the middle child. My sister was 13 months older than me, and my brother was 16 months younger. We traveled together. We sang together in the gospel field. We played together. We were such a blessed family that others in the community gravitated towards our home because they felt the love and they saw the respect people gave to us. Were we a perfect family? No. Were we a wealthy family? No. We were and are a close-knit and loving family.

My childhood was not one of drama. It was one filled with adventure and fun. I was successful at everything I tried out for in school. I was a cheerleader, a head majorette, and a pageant winner, twice. I participated in many school organizations, and I led a major high school musical production. Everything I thought I could do, I did. From the outside, I had it all together. However, what people, including my family, did not know was my childhood was often one of self-struggle. Why? Unbeknownst to me at that time, I was a middle child experiencing some of the middle-childhood traits. Let me explain.

I am not a therapist or psychologist. However, those who write and conduct research on the middle child will tell you that a middle child will have unique feelings and exhibit certain behavior because of the order in which they were born. "Middle child syndrome is a set of feelings and a relationship style that's common in middle children," says clinical psychologist, Aimee Daramus, PsyD. "It's not a psychological disorder or even anything that 'officially' exists, but it's a pattern that people have noticed for decades." Based on my findings, I will highlight a few of the middle child's characteristics that best describe me.

According to several experts who conduct research on middle children, one characteristic of the middle child is the feeling of being overlooked, left out, or not seen. Much is written about why the middle child experiences these feelings. I strongly identify with this trait, which is why to this day, the invisible treatment can impact me more than anything. However, as an adult, whether on purpose or not, if I am overlooked or not seen, I acknowledge my thoughts, take control of my feelings, and move on. This approach has empowered me to manage these occurrences, as well as my feelings.

Dr. Daramus identifies other characteristics of the middle child as having a serious and ambitious drive. I am serious, ambitious, competitive, and an overachiever which all have served me well as an adult. I've never been afraid to take risks, which has led me to experience many new and exciting things and to pursue opportunities that I wasn't equipped to take on. As an adult, I live a fulfilled and meaningful life.

I will identify four of my middle-child syndrome characteristics and discuss how they have propelled me to be empowered. I share them here in hopes that you will have some takeaways that will inspire you to move beyond whatever insecurities or struggles you are facing, toward having an empowered life.

My Casper Moments

Casper was an invisible cartoon character whose full name was "Casper, the friendly ghost." He was called friendly because he was unlike other cartoon ghosts who had the reputation of being mischievous and scary. I can sometimes be in a meeting or attend an event and not be acknowledged when everyone else is acknowledged. Fortunately, on occasion, someone says, "You forgot to mention Teresa." During those times I am not trying to be seen, heard, or seek attention. I am in the same space as everyone else. I was invited to be in the room or at the event or be part of a group when those situations happened. This does not happen every day of my life, but it occurs more times than I care to remember. During these moments, I mutter the words, "Am I Casper or what?"

Whether by accident or on purpose, being treated as though you are invisible is hurtful, embarrassing, and wounding, no matter when or where it occurs in your life. I call them my *Casper* moments.

How do I use my Casper moments to empower myself and others?

First, I recognize and acknowledge that my Casper moments are painful, due in part to my middle-child syndrome. Next, I give myself the power to control how I feel about those moments. I do this by understanding why my Casper moments create the level of pain I feel. Knowing the reason for the pain helps me to level my emotions. Last, I know that Casper moments will always be lurking around. They will happen sooner or later. Therefore, I choose not to dwell on my Casper moments because I know there will be others. As such, I don't embrace them. It is at those moments that my pain subsides and I'm empowered to move on.

My Casper moments have given me insight into being sensitive to the fact that I am not the only person who experiences painful moments. Therefore, whenever I am given the opportunity to lead others, whether through supervision or by serving as the president of a board or speaking to a group of women, I am mindfully intentional about creating opportunities for those who are not usually called upon to participate, or for those who do not speak up because they are timid or feel inadequate. I am aware that these persons exist in every segment of life. Therefore, I make it a point to know who those persons are and to involve them in a way that allows them to be visible, heard, and empowered.

The Need to Overachieve

Another middle-child trait is being an overachiever. That is me. I could never be involved in just one or two things at a time. My plate has always been full and, somehow I have been able to carry them off. In high school, I was in several activities each year and none of them involved sports. Throughout my adulthood, this has not changed. If I mention what I am currently involved in, you would say, she has lost her mind!! It is because I am an overachiever, which is a middle-child trait that continues to this day.

Being an overachiever isn't necessarily a bad thing. As a matter of fact, it has been very useful for me in a number of ways. It has caused me to be very organized. I learned early on that if I was going to continue being an overachiever and juggle many things at one time, I had better learn how to be organized or experience a chaotic and hectic life. I feel that organized people are empowered people. Therefore, I make many to-do lists and I use a lot of post-it notes. They are my go-to tools for helping me manage my projects as well as my life. My desk and dining room table are full of to-do lists and post-it notes. I have lists for everything, whether personal or business-related. While piled-up post-it notes can seem unorganized, they are key to making my life less chaotic. (Just know when to throw them away once the project is finished!) Figure out what tools you need to help manage your life, your dreams, and your aspirations. Post-it notes and to-do lists are my best friends because they help me stay on top of things and they empower me to manage my life.

As an overachiever, I also learned quickly how to ask for help, be flexible, rearrange my schedule, and not be disheveled if I had to drop a ball because I knew all of the balls could not stay in the air at the same time. I learned how to juggle everything as a single mom commuting 130 miles six days a week for two years while finishing my undergraduate degree. I also worked part-time. That was grueling. During that time, I temporarily moved back home with my parents so they could help me with my child, when necessary. That was humbling. However, I recognized that I could not make every appointment, attend all the parent-teacher meetings, or make it to every class, without assistance or without being flexible. When I am in my overachiever mode, which is usually most of the time, I am not ashamed to holler HELP.

There is nothing wrong with being an overachiever. I learned early on that I do not have to do everything by myself. I am okay with that. So, if you are an overachiever with a full plate, which is usually a woman's experience, ask for help and pivot when necessary.

Independent Creative

Being a middle child meant figuring out how to stand out. Remember, middle-child syndrome is feeling ignored. Therefore, for me, standing out afforded me the opportunity to be unique by being independent and creative. I learned how to stand out by being different from my siblings. Instead of playing in the high school band like my brother and sister, I became the head majorette. Instead of just being a person in a high school musical production, I produced the musical production. While one sibling graduated with an undergraduate degree and the other sibling attended college without graduating, I finished college with advanced degrees. I moved the farthest from home. I learned how to snow ski. I created women's empowerment conferences on cruises. I raised a lot of money to produce several successful concerts. What is my point? While I was motivated by my need to stand out from my siblings, I became an independently creative person, who was empowered to undertake new challenges that were unfamiliar. Some of the challenges were risky in that I did not know how everything would turn out. However, that did not stop me.

Being independent and taking risks should not stop you. Take what is unique about your experiences and use them to empower yourself and others.

Shameless Negotiator

As a middle child, I learned how to be a negotiator, a shameless negotiator!! I crafted this skill in the fifth grade. My teacher was a coin collector. One day in class he mentioned that he was looking for a nickel that had a specific date when it was minted. If a student located the nickel, he would give the student a quarter. Needless to say, we were all excited to locate the nickel and get a quarter in return.

Several days went by and no one had located this nickel. I had a nickel. It was not the nickel that my teacher was looking for. That did not stop me from trying to figure out a way to get my teacher to take my nickel and give me the twenty cents. At this point, my middle-child negotiation skills kicked in. On the way to school one day, I took my nickel, spit on it, polished and shined it up to the point where it became clean and shiny. I figured that all of this effort would be my child-like way of negotiating. I waited until recess to approach my teacher with my nickel. I handed my nickel to my teacher and said, "Here is the nickel you were looking for!" He looked at the nickel and then stared at me for what seemed like an eternity. He said nothing and reached into his pocket and gave me a quarter. I can only imagine what he was thinking. It did not matter to me what he was thinking. When I think about that day and what transpired, I laugh aloud. To be frank, I do not know what I would have said or done if my teacher would have challenged me on my shameless negotiating stunt. What I did not know at the time was that I used a top negotiation skill which was not being afraid to ask for what I wanted. Wow!! Who knew?! While I didn't verbally say to the teacher what I wanted, handing him the nickel was my way of saying I want the quarter. That day I felt empowered.

Don't be afraid of asking for that raise or promotion, starting that business, or adopting a child as a single person. Ask for what you want because you just might get it!!!

As my journey continues, I have been very blessed to become a CEO, a COO, an Entrepreneur, Non-profit Founder, Consultant, Professor, Motivational Speaker, Mommie, Auntie, and Oil Painter. And the list could go on. Oh, did I mention my dissertation has been reviewed in 700+ institutions in more than 100 countries? I read these accomplishments and I say, "Who is this person who has achieved so much?" However, while I reflect on my achievements, my journey on this path means more to me because it has taken me from being invisible to being someone who inspires others, especially women, to figure out what empowers them.

My journey is not just about the middle-child syndrome, my feelings and experiences are worth noting because they are the basis for much of my insecurities, as well as my successes. They also provide insight into the choices I have made. They have created the pivotal moments of my life and they have led me to this moment in time that is very fulfilling, which is helping women understand how they can use past hurts, pain, wounds, and insecurities to be empowered.

I have covered my middle-child syndrome feelings and behaviors, my Casper moments, the need to overachieve, my independent creativity, and my shameless negotiation skills. While these are my experiences as a middle child, you have experiences that are unique to you.

It could be very easy for you to turn your insecurities into excuses for running, hiding, and never experiencing life to its fullest. The usual outcome is a devaluation of one's existence. Ask yourself this question: *How can I take the unique experiences of my life and turn them into positive, impactful opportunities to empower myself and inspire others?*

The main takeaway from me telling my story is that you can embrace your experiences as pain and stay stuck, or you can use your experiences to be inspired to do great things. What starts out as pain, hurt, and embarrassment can become the thing that empowers you. Just in case you didn't know, here are a few famous middle children: Diana Ross, Warren Buffet, Madonna, John F. Kennedy, Jr., Walt Disney, David Letterman, Jennifer Lopez, and Bill Gates. I think I am in good company. Now all I need is their wealth!!

Feel the TRIUMPH of being empowered and inspiring others!! Use your WISDOM G.I.F.T.S.

* * *

Dr. Teresa Jeter

Dr. Teresa Jeter is the founder of Midwest Women's Empowerment Summit, a nonprofit organization that inspires and encourages women to live empowered lives by Stirring Up The Gifts Within ©. As Chief Operations Officer for a Black-owned women's business, she received a Master's in Urban and Regional Planning from Ball State University and a doctorate degree in Public Policy and Administration from Walden University. One of her most fulfilling experiences was building houses for first-time homebuyers and handing a single mom the keys to her first home. A sought-after speaker, Dr. Jeter has been the recipient of many honors, including a governor's appointment to the Indiana Commission for Women and recognition as a Distinguished Hoosier for Public Service and Contributions to her Community. She is the mother of one daughter, Talia Jeter. When Dr. Jeter is not working or speaking, she is facilitating exciting women's empowerment cruises to Europe and other interesting places around the world. Check out Dr. Jeter's women's empowerment events at www.Midwestwes.org.

Unbecoming The Strong One

Intentionally emerging into the well-rounded one!

By Dr. Tekeilla Darden

A great philosopher once said, "when life gets you down, do you wanna know what you've gotta do? Just keep swimming, just keep swimming, just keep swimming."

Okay, you got me. That philosopher was Dory from the movie, *Finding Nemo,* but long before Dory reminded me to just keep swimming, it was pretty much how I lived my life. This coping phenomenon is found in many of the "strong ones." Yes, I am "*the*" strong friend, the one from the trend where folks tell you to check in on because, GASP, we, too, can be struggling. However, I get why many do not or did not check in on those strong friends. I know, as well as those well-meaning loved ones know, that everyone has their own challenges.

The "strong ones" are often perceived as being more equipped to handle their struggles independently. The strong one is often defined as a person who is capable of always holding it together. The term "it" is usually expanded to include many forms of strength. Truthfully, from many of my loved ones, my strength and my ability to bounce back were just expected. Another hard truth for those "strong ones" is the inability to answer the question 'when is it okay to not be strong?' This is especially true if I ever had to apply that question to my own life. I have never given much of any indication that I could not or would not be "okay." This began from my experiences in childhood. First, I was independently traveling by plane by the age of five, every summer, to visit family. These were often long summer trips where I was subject to meeting many new people. Secondly, I was the only Black child in many of my classes; therefore, I was often a "spokesperson" for other Black people, whether I wanted to be or not. Lastly, my first name is pronounced like the famous alcoholic beverage, Tequila; subsequently, I had to endure unending teasing and questions about my name. I could not articulate that I was anxious, afraid, annoyed, and hurt in many of these situations, so my "strong one" mentality was birthed, to counter the amount of anxiety I had daily.

Being the strong one is a job I have perfected in the spirit of vulnerability. It just made, and still makes, sense for me in many of the roles I have in life. In most of my relationships, I am the advice giver, the solution solver, and the open and caring listening ear. In my career as a clinical psychologist, I make a living helping others navigate the most complicated intersections of their lives. In this profession, I do much of the same thing as I do in my personal life, only with applied research and science to aid my practice. In my everyday life, my level of independence suggests, that most times, I can work things out on my own because I rarely have crises where I require assistance from others. I would rather help solve a problem than to admit I have one. To come off as anything else but strong would undermine what I know as my whole existence. This may be the reason why checking on your strong friend sometimes leaves loved ones in a state of confusion. The "strong ones" have built-in sure-fire responses to even the most well-meaning attempts at trying to understand us. A simple "how are you doing?" can often be met with, "I'm good; how about you?" and then a quick change of subject, where we add something like, "How are you keeping up with that thing that was thinging?" Deflection at its finest.

So, when do I start getting real and vulnerable, you ask? Remember, I am good at deflection. It comes naturally. However, I had a turning point (admittedly, that's still turning). Not too long ago, there came a time when I had to challenge what being the strong one meant. It came during a period in my life when many of my defining labels that I happily wear today were emerging. In my early thirties, I was still enjoying my honeymoon stage with my husband. It was also one of the most intensive stages in my Ph.D. program. I was relying on my husband's income (I've always had my own "Lord have mercy" funds before), and being pregnant with our first child, a son. I was at the point in my Ph.D. program that if I missed any point of this significant year, I'd have to start it all over again to receive credit. I knew I was taking a risk when I found out I was pregnant with our first child. I would only have a maximum of six weeks, the standard acceptable American way of believing that's all you'll need to adjust to parenthood, to get back to the program without any penalty. Nonetheless, I was prepared and more than confident I would have my baby and come back to my program with little to no fault because I've always been good at keeping things going, you know, just keep swimming.

I had my days, weeks, and months planned out for how work, school, and life would look, with some reasonable flexibility for what a newborn baby may bring. However, I could not and did not have any inkling about how to plan for what was about to be my new reality. Ten days before my due date, I went to the hospital with the expectation that I would bring home my baby boy, but when I got there, I was told he didn't have a heartbeat. I had to go through labor and delivery knowing that my son was not alive. The first few thoughts were that maybe he will be okay, and we won't know this until I deliver. Denial, often the first process of grief, was strong with me. After delivery, I had all the emotions usually associated with that type of pain, including confusion, overwhelming sadness, heartbreak, disbelief, guilt, and anger. There was no obvious reason my OB-GYN could tell me why this happened, nor anything else any other doctors could tell me, as the reason for my stillbirth. I was drowning.

Shortly after my stillbirth, I did the thing I always do to minimize and invalidate my own pain. I told myself there are women who could never get pregnant and why should I think I was special or exempt. Horrible, I know. I would never do this to someone who would tell me this is their story; I would have more compassion and empathy to share and give to others. I am just not practiced enough in offering the same grace to myself. After my birthing experience, I internally beat myself up. I went back and forth between 'this is something I have every right to be upset by' to 'I have been so blessed in other areas in my life where others have not.' I often tell myself there are people in the world who have had it harder than me in order to not feel sorry for myself. I tried to make excuses for answers I never had. Here's one of those excuses; maybe I just wasn't destined to be a mom. I forced myself to be better for those around me. My husband was experiencing his own grief process, and I wanted to be mindful that he needed me as much as I needed him. I knew my mom, wrecked in her own grief, would not be able to be okay unless I appeared to be, so I seemed to be better.

I took the six weeks I was allotted from work and part of my clinical program and went right back to work. I did not take any time off from my course work because it served as one of my greatest distractions. Many knew what had happened; I tried to run my own PR campaign about my birthing experience before going back in, so I wouldn't be faced with the expectations of showing off or talking about my son. However, I couldn't reach them all, and those questions were inevitably asked. In addition to the surmounting support, I was met with statements such as "wow, you're so strong," "I couldn't do this right now if I were you," and "how can you focus on helping others after going through something like that?" I had one professor pull me aside and tell me how inspired they were by my strength. I took these questions and statements in but did not bother to answer or give them much thought because, well, you know, just keep swimming.

I am a person who stands on my faith and spirituality, albeit quietly. However, feelings soon began to emerge that I had never really considered as a part of my story before. Being the strong one meant that I often did not want to burden others with the ruminating thoughts of my experience, even if someone were to directly ask how I was. While my anxiety was something I always had issues with, I never knew it, or put a name to it. It was, for the first time, evident to me after my stillbirth experience that I suffered with anxiety. In addition, challenges with fear and self-blame plagued me. I worried about what the unknown reason for my stillbirth meant for me. What did I not see? Could there be something wrong with me, too? Because there were no clear answers to those questions, they evolved into fear of becoming pregnant again and having to go all the way to the end of it with the same outcome. When I just couldn't resolve the unknown, I blamed myself. I just needed a reason, any reason, to settle my analytical mind. Sadly, I was my easiest target.

Not soon after my intensive year in my program ended, I now had to endure clinical training, where I would do more independent counseling and psychological assessment with patients. I love working with women's issues, and soon, before I knew it, I had many women with infertility, child loss, and pregnancy concerns. Many of my mentors and supervisors, who knew my story, would gently ask if I were okay, especially if I had a case very similar to my own (and I had several). However, I am good at compartmentalizing, so I rarely compare what anyone else went through to my own experience. I have never disclosed my own history of stillbirth to my patients. I often get from them how much I have helped them through their struggles and challenges, so I have never felt moved to, because I have accomplished their goals without the need. I also walk a fine line between what is helpful for them to know for their own healing journey and what is not. Vulnerability is not my strong suit. Even when it is just me, myself, and I, who I need to be vulnerable with.

I had my rainbow baby, the child born after a stillbirth (the angel baby), nearly a year and a half later. However, during my pregnancy with my daughter, I was wracked with so much anxiety. No one knew how much of my worry consumed me because my façade said I was okay. I even hid many of these feelings from my OB-GYN during checkups. During my stillbirth, I noticed the tears she so desperately tried to hide, so, in the spirit of being the fixer and the helper, I didn't want her to worry about me worrying.

There's a dichotomy that exists within me because I have unwavering faith in the belief that happiness is always in reach, and a fear of what may be that will make the heart ache. I have a great amount of gratitude and an equal amount of self-doubt. My story of being the "strong one" is not about wanting to deny my strength. It's quite the opposite. I am extremely grateful as I feel blessed with this gift, which has afforded me the life and coping abilities I have today. Similarly, where I may have only been able to highlight my strength, I am now intentional about highlighting the times I am not okay, even when I don't have an answer as to why. Many times, people believe there is always an answer, but the truth is, that is not always true. Like with my stillbirth, there was no answer, and still, none for me. I had to make a choice to either keep searching for an answer that may never come, or accept that no answer would change my reality. Some events, situations, and areas of life just do not have an answer, so rather than working on finding the answer, time may be better served finding acceptance or forgiveness. This is not your momma's definition of forgiveness where the other person, place, or thing is actively involved in the process in order for you to forgive. This is forgiveness of yourself, self-doubt, hurt, anger or confusion, lack of control, or the shattering of what you've always known something to be and the acceptance of what the reality is. Even in my anger after coming home to an empty nursery, I knew it wasn't appropriate to take out any anger on anyone/anything, so I had another choice, to forgive. I needed to forgive that my birthing experience was a real and painful moment in my life, but I will be able to move forward. Just keep swimming.

It is difficult for me to think others will read this and automatically see me as anything other than strong. When I think of all the ways in which I have adapted to and accepted this "strong one" personality, I feel sad for that version of me. I believe, for those who have the true strength of vulnerability, they can be often perceived as authentic, genuine, and, you know, great bestie material. I have always struggled with others' perceptions of me, including being an authentic and genuine person. This is where my "strong one" attitude has challenged me. My ability to analyze and calculate things and situations to get to a destination that is usually positive, is often initially received as if I am holding back. I am often thought of as having an air of conceitedness that presents a 'no new friends' vibe. That's just not me, though. I love new and old friends, am an open (in-person) person, and am very friendly. It just takes me a minute to adjust subconsciously. Like when I was a child, in order to counteract any anxious feelings, it's like I need others to see my strength first.

I now define myself as having strength, but I'm no longer claiming the mentality of being the "strong one." At least, not in the way I have done before, because it was harmful to me in the times I really needed help from others. I am still, to this day, trying to undo a lot of the precedents I have set up in relationships, where I am solely the advice giver. Sadly, it has been uncomfortable for those who have that expectation of me. I have set an unrealistic bar of responsibility and obligation that has been hard for me to turn off and hard for others to accept of me. Anytime I'd see a quote that said 'check in on your strong friends' I'd say that's me and wait around for those to check in on me. That never came in the way I thought it should. However, this attitude paints the picture that no one was there, and this is not true. The truth is, I still have anxiety around pregnancy and childbirth and have set out to find someone like me who can understand mutuality in the depths of sharing these types of feelings. I had a miscarriage after the birth of my rainbow child, and, as I write this, am in the second trimester of my fourth pregnancy. So, you can imagine that many of my fears remain.

Do I still think it is important to just keep swimming? Yes. However, when I get tired, I stop, rest and practice self-care. If I am swimming too fast, I slow down and reflect and when I seemingly don't know where I am going, I circle back for a deeper understanding.

The gift I offer through my story is INTENTION.

**"I am intentional in unbecoming the 'strong one' and emerging into the well-rounded one.
A well-rounded person is intentional
about acknowledging all the areas and
personal moments of weaknesses
without denying all the strengths one possesses."**

That's it. That's my quote. Oh yes, and "just keep swimming, only with applied breaks and reflections when you need it."

* * *

Dr. Tekeilla Darden

Dr. Tekeilla Darden is a licensed clinical psychologist with a passion for helping others to heal through storytelling. Being a lifelong lover of bringing stories to life, she realized how storytelling can be a tool to help others open up in therapeutic settings. She received her PhD in Clinical psychology from Walden University and currently has her own thriving private practice, focusing on psychological assessments and therapy. Inspired by her professional practice, Dr. Darden created a luxury mindfulness-based tea line after she saw the benefits of utilizing tea in some of her therapy sessions to help others become mentally wealthy through the practice of self-love.

In addition to her professional practice and tea line, Dr. Darden is a business owner and a published author in multiple genres which include written works in academia and fiction. Dr. Darden offers therapeutic writing retreats to assist other writers to mentally prepare, navigate, and complete their written work. She is a wife and mother, loves a good girl's trip, and currently resides in the Dallas, TX, metroplex. To learn more about Dr. Darden and checkout her products and services, please visit her at www.drtekeilla.com.

I Left The Church And Found God

By Rev. Patricia Dershem

Ok, I was born into Christian Science. It worked well for me as a kid growing up. I learned a lot about the Bible. I also learned that we create a bunch of pain and dis-ease by our own minds. I saw nearly-instant healing first-hand when I had an accident on my bicycle and ripped my leg open. My mother quickly scooped me up, covered my leg in a towel and began "knowing the truth" (praying). Her faith was so strong that within 3 hours my leg was totally healed, no scars, nothing to see that would indicate there had been an injury, except some very bloody towels. That helped me to understand, as a kid, that healing was not only possible, but had actually happened.

Well, all was well until I turned 18 and was asked to join the church. As I was filling out the application, there was a part where I had to promise not to read any literature about other religions, philosophies or streams of thought. I was offended. I was about truth. Why were they afraid for someone to read other literature? I was out, forget it, not interested. It hurt my mother, but I was now more curious than ever to read other religious material.

I am so very grateful to have the personal memory of a hands-on experience of healing as taught by Jesus, channeled through my mother. I also learned how our actions are based on our thinking, and thus, the results we experience in our lives are directly connected to the thoughts we entertain.

I found myself visiting other churches with various friends of mine. I went with a friend to a Buddhist gathering. I began to chant and meditate. Oh, how I loved chanting. I would do it out in a garden or anywhere in nature and feel myself get totally into rhythm with nature. It was so calming yet energizing. In meditating, I felt like I was getting messages from God. Just simple little messages of love. In one meditation I had I was seeing a tea cup. It was black and white and had the pattern of yin/yang. I asked a Buddhist priest what that might mean and he said it indicated I would probably come together with a Black man and we would become a powerful couple.

When it came to getting deeper within the religion, I was not interested. Some of their rules, ideas and beliefs didn't feel right to me. But to this day, I still enjoy chanting and I am grateful to know the divine feeling of hugging a tree. I took with me the experience of the connectedness of ALL beings. That means people, flora and fauna.

My next adventure into the world of religion was the Mormon church. A gentleman I had fallen in love with was a Mormon, so I thought, let me check this out. I had been a hippie with forays into "sex, drugs and rock 'n roll" but now I was asked to be a group leader with the 12-year old girls, sooooo I put my bra back on and cleaned up my act so that I could be a good advisor to the young ladies. As I studied this religion, I found many of their rules, ideas and beliefs to rest well with me UNTIL I discovered how they discriminated against Black people AND that they considered homosexuality as aberrant behavior and something to be "healed". This did not feel right to me at all. Time to go!!!

I am grateful for the many experiences I had in the Mormon church. One of them is how to make a decision when stuck between two choices. Go in prayer and seek guidance, then simply make a choice, and if things then begin smoothly, you've made the right choice. If things begin by being chaotic, quickly reverse your choice or move on.

They also have a great business plan. They don't register as a non-profit, thus there's far less government control than most churches have. Also, the church charity program is set-up so that if you need help paying your rent or buying groceries, etc., they will bail you out AND you must "pay" for it. For example, you might be asked to help out stocking shelves in the grocery warehouse, or by reading to an elderly congregant, or any of many different neighborly acts. This way, it's not a hand-out, it's a fair exchange and a person retains their dignity. They have various activities throughout the week for the different age groups, such that no one has to feel alone or ignored. Young people have many choices of different church groups to hang out and participate in. This helps families greatly in raising children in this time of rampant social media addiction.

A few visits to a Catholic church and attending masses was enough for me. I wanted a direct connection to a higher power. Didn't want to have to go through an intermediary for my prayer to be heard, even though it's Jesus' mother.

My next "church" adventure was the Congregational Church. This was on a recommendation from my uncle, Carleton Booth. Uncle Carl was a very devout Christian and had been one of the founders of World Vision, so naturally I was interested in this recommendation. Well, the people were lovely and helpful but it just didn't go deep enough for me.

The next church I found was Unity Fellowship of Christ Church (supposedly non-denominational) - somewhat Pentecostal. Why were the clergy always asking God to stop by? If God is within, then what? If God is like the ocean and we are like scoops of water from that ocean, that means we have the same spiritual DNA. We are alike, basically, and very much a part of each other. This church was created for the purpose of letting Black LGBTQI+ (plus all the other alternative labels) people know that they were made in God's image and likeness and were loved equally by God. This really appealed to me. I was there for nearly twenty years and became a member of the clergy.

While going through their seminary program, I had the opportunity to study many different Christian ideologies, also man's inhumanity to man during the reformation, and saw all the blood that was spilled during the Holy Crusades, all in the name of Jesus.

This church had many great programs to assist the disenfranchised communities of Black, gay people, especially during the height of the AIDS pandemic. There was help in the form of hope, housing, food, health training, AIDS meds, self-empowerment programs, Bible study, and a community coming together to assist each other.

After a while, it seemed to me there was no spiritual growth happening within this church. And I am one who knows that truth becomes more available as we search and study, so apparently the leaders were resting on their laurels and didn't see a need to continue learning and evolving. I understand this church now has a different leader so maybe we will see evolution there.

In my research I discovered that many religions were created out of a need to bring like-thinking people together, get them to support a particular religious thought, and bring their money and talents into a controlled program. Often, these started out with good intentions, but after experiencing the power of what had been unknown, very charismatic egos took over and corruption began.

I started studying and researching on my own and discovered that there was so much to be found in various groups that were studying spirituality, i.e., Huna, Agape International, Abraham-Hicks and Kabbalah, to name just a few.

I drifted away from organized religion and started going to Agape. I was very interested since I had found out that Rev. Michael Bernard Beckwith had broken away from the Church of Religious Science and was teaching spirituality. From religion to spirituality was when I started discovering what I call "magic." It's actually what Jesus was teaching when he said "…you can do the things that I do." I had had a taste of that from my mother healing my leg when I was very young, now I wanted to know more.

Going to Agape I learned how to meditate. I love it. Rev. Michael taught meditation and manifesting and picked up where "The Secret" left off. At the same time I went to a Huna Level One Training. It is a beautiful Hawaiian spirituality program. One of the things you learn is how to connect with the elements and shift them. It's beautiful and amazing, all the things that Jesus teaches, while not being a Christian philosophy at all. Huna was created long before Jesus was on earth.

During this time I also tried Shambhala Buddhist Meditation. It was gentle and beautiful. I started really appreciating nature and the messages it has for us. The squirrels and birds and all critters are trying to communicate with us, if we'd just listen.

I continue to read spiritual books, such as Louise Hay's "You can Heal Your Life." I'm re-reading an amazing and eye-opening book by Philip Yancey, "The Jesus I Never Knew." The Biblical Apocrypha are absolutely fascinating reading. I am now taking Kabbalah classes. I totally love this way of thinking. You discover that your life is a movie and there are many different versions of that movie that can be produced. It all depends on your mindset. And you can change your mindset as you evolve. "Change your Mind, change your movie." One little thing I found amazing with Kabbalah, they teach that when you are praying, you must be certain about God hearing you, CERTAIN. Certainty is very important, not doubting, questioning, but certainty. Kabbalah has free Level One classes online. Try it, you might love it. Kabbalah.com. I also follow Abraham-Hicks. I experience many miracles and answers to prayer all the time.

One thing that really helped me get clear on how we create our circumstances through our own individual thoughts, words and actions, was taking the Landmark Forum, and the Advance Course. Check it out!! You'll be totally empowered when you do this work. "Manifest" seems to be a popular word currently. Once you're empowered, you'll be manifesting right and left. Enjoy!

Everything I read and see that feels right and true tells me the following:

> The Universe, God, Jesus, Holy Spirit, Superconscious, Creator, your own name, or whatever you call your higher power, is real. Everything is energy. Science proves that energy can be rearranged to be a different thing than what it once was. What I call "miracles" are simply shifts in energy.

I learned one of the keys to finding God is being grateful for everything that happens. Yes, everything! No matter how awful a happening might be, there is ALWAYS at least one blessing to come out of it. Then start researching and studying to find the goodness that is revealed. Out of chaos comes new ways of order. I saw something on social media that said "With Religion, you learn of others' experiences - With Spirituality, you have your own experiences." I experience many miracles and answers to prayer all the time. I am so grateful that I have found God, God everywhere and God within each of us.

Study, research, read, take classes of anything that speaks to you. I promise, you will find God. There is no place where God is not.

I am GRATEFUL that I left the Church and found God (everywhere).

✡ ✡ ✡

Rev. Patti Dershem

Rev. Patti is definitely a local girl. She was born in Glendale, California. When she graduated from Business College she went to work in a law office and absolutely loved working in law. Then her father convinced her that she should go to work where he worked, work for a year and save her money and then travel the world. Well, she went to work at Lockheed Aircraft Company and was there for 23 years. The last 13 years she was there she worked with the L-1011 airplane sales team as a Customer Relations Rep. When the L-1011 was phased out, Patti worked for two years as a Business Consultant to Lockheed.

Patti went into Banking briefly. She then went back to her first love, Law, and had a great time as a Legal Assistant for the next 10 years. Then, while helping a friend in need, discovered Unity Fellowship Church. She left the law firm and went to work at Minority AIDS Project, an outreach of the church. Patti felt "the calling" and joined the clergy class and two years later was ordained. She was fortunate to be able to spend three years as an administrative assistant to the late Archbishop Carl Bean.

Rev. Patti is currently pursuing her entrepreneurial interests. She is a Certified NLP Master Practitioner, has completed the entire Landmark Curriculum for Living, and thrives in her practice of manuscript proofreading/editing. Oh and yes, she loves performing weddings.

Ready to share your WISDOM? Download my free Idea Generator worksheet at www.saidwrite.com

Embracing Success As A Gift From God

By Saprina Allen

Do you ever look at someone who is "successful," in whatever situation you think of, and say to yourself, "That person is lucky! They've achieved something that the rest of us can only dream of!"

Think about Nobel prize winners, CEOs of major companies or even your friend down the street who seems to "have it all." You know the woman I mean. She has a great career, balances caring for her family, and makes it look easy and maybe she has the same body she had in high school. I know these people, and sometimes, I feel jealous.

But then I look back on my life and realize some have wondered the same thing about me. Well, certain of these ideas may not have applied, but I have been asked many times about my story.

I just bought a building in Chicago. How many people can say that? I have a great family I adore and, on the surface at least, I *seem* to have "it all." But there is always more to the story. And I'd like to share some of it with you. I say some because *all* would take volumes and no one has that kind of time.

I share this now because I want to share some of the tragedies in my life, some of the triumphs, and the lessons I have learned along the way. At the core of it all is the idea of forgiveness. This idea, and the surrounding thoughts, have helped define who I am.

As I share these stories, that question, "Who is Saprina?" has returned to me time and again. Mostly, I've enjoyed the memories. Other times, this question and the answers, or lack of one, has haunted me and left me a wreck. It can be hard to deal with all of these emotions, especially when your heart is overwhelmed.

That thought brings to mind a scripture I have had on my mind since I was a little girl. You see, as a child, I had some strong influences in my life, i.e., my fourth grade teacher, my grandmother, especially, and the Bible. I was taught the Psalms and Proverbs, memorizing some, and one always seemed to resonate with me. It's the 61st Psalm and I especially like this first part:

> *Hear my cry, O God; attend unto my prayer. From the end of the earth will I cry unto thee, when my heart is overwhelmed, lead me to the rock that is higher than I. For thou hast been my shelter and a strong tower from the enemy. I will abide in thy tabernacle forever. I will trust in the covert of thy wings.*

Coming to trust God, that He has been there with me, leading me and protecting me, has been a thing I have both trusted and struggled to identify all my life.

Nevertheless, at the end of the day, I do trust God, that His intentions are for my best life. So, I try to follow that trust, even if I don't understand what is happening at the moment.

I was both blessed and abused as a child. It's heartbreaking for me to think upon it now, but I also realize that these experiences of pain have been the catalyst in my life to start my Dirty Dress Foundation. We all have dark days in our past that we'd prefer to forget. Sometimes we can't forget them, but must still move on and accept ourselves for who we are and the experiences we have had.

Still, losing your father at five years old hurts. Being abused hurts. Being broken, as well as broke, hurts. I feel I have a deep understanding of these issues in people's lives, and I have compassion, understanding and empathy, because I have experienced these things, too.

At one point, I was such an emotional mess that I thought the pain would never go away. I asked God why I had to deal with such a terrible situation. In time, though, He healed me. I think it's still a work in progress, but I don't hurt as much anymore because of those traumatic experiences. In fact, after my father was murdered, I had to come to grips with forgiving the man that did it. That was hard. It was, perhaps, the most difficult thing I've done, yet it was liberating.

Maya Angelou once said that "Forgiveness is the greatest gift you can give yourself. It's not for the other person." I never realized how true and profound those words were, until after I forgave that man and then had to try again years later in a completely different situation.

After that tragedy, I relied on my grandmothers more than ever. You see, my father hadn't left a will or plans or anything for his children. Maybe he thought he was young and had time to do it all later. And he should have had that time, but I learned another thing from that whole experience: planning is critical in your life.

I've since made it my mission to plan to "make it" in the world. I have planned for my children and grandchildren's futures, with college and discipline and love. I've planned for my own future, realizing that I had to do it myself, but that God would be with me, supporting me. That way when I failed, and I did – sometimes pretty spectacularly!–He would still be there to shelter me in the cover of his wings, as it were.

God works through people, I've learned. A good pastor will help you understand the Good News better. A friend will listen to your stories of pain and commiserate with you. That same friend will motivate you to get up and try again, and again. People you work with, for and around, these people in my life have influenced me in big and small ways, sometimes for years, and sometimes, in the very moment I needed it. I thank them all for this.

So I want to tell you a story. I first met Mark when I was younger, working as a barmaid. He would constantly ask for my number, or to go out on a date and I would constantly decline. I didn't like him much. He seemed cocky and arrogant. Later, I learned he would travel some 40 miles out of his way, just so he could be rejected. And he was my best tipper!

Mark was in the military. He loved this country, he loved service (he later became a great minister to a great many people) and the idea of serving in the military was a natural fit.

He moved away and I moved on. I became driven during this time to provide for my own. Not only that, but I wanted success like I had seen from afar and remembered words from my grandmother resonating with me: "I don't want you to feel that this job is ok and something for you to do for the rest of your life. I don't want you to feel it is okay to leave a mess for other people to clean up." She was a cleaning lady and wanted more for me.

So I went about getting and making more. The funny thing about the rat race in the corporate world is that it gets you looking inward and focusing on what you want. Sometimes that introspection is a good thing, and sometimes it can be bad, but it is something that I needed to grapple with over time.

Some years after working as that barmaid, I saw Mark again, in a grocery store. He was wearing a uniform and said, "Hello, Saprina!" I was confused. It took a minute to remember who I was talking to. He asked me to dinner. I said no. He asked for my number. No, again. And I made an excuse and left.

A week or so later he called me. I am still not sure how he got my number, but there he was. I accepted a dinner date and we went out. It was probably the best dinner date I have ever been on!

During the last 15 years, I had taken upon myself the role of wife and mother and matriarch to the entire family. I considered myself the backbone of our group. It was exhausting always being the supporter, organizer and problem solver. At our dinner date, Mark took on that role. I let it all out and he listened and supported me. He had changed from the arrogant self-centered person I had known way back then to someone humble and considerate.

Within three months, I met his whole family and he asked me to marry him. His mother became one of my best friends. His siblings and aunties and uncles and everyone became my family, too. I finally got the family support I had been craving for so long, and I felt at home.

But all of us carry baggage. I talk about it in my Dirty Dress meetings. Men are no different, they carry it, too. In Mark's case, the baggage included military service and PTSD, which dramatically changed his mental health and life.

In a marriage, you both try to make things work. You love the other person and try to support them in what they need when they need it. This included making sure that therapy was attended, that the proper medications are gotten and then consumed, and more. I did everything I could do to make sure that this man, whom my children called "Papa Smurf" got the treatments I thought he needed.

But the demons still fought through: alcoholism, addictions, dreams. He spoke other languages in his sleep! Loud noises were devastating, causing a fight-or-flight reaction. So, no thunder bowling, no dropping dishes, no thunderstorms, ever. It was challenging.

At the same time, I was taking off in my career. I was working many, many hours and when I was busy, I was busy and couldn't be disturbed. This was my own baggage and it caused a lot of stress, pride and exhaustion.

So here I was "making it" and here he was trying to slow down and deal with the tragic things he had seen. One way he dealt with these demons was through a church ministry. It helped him have some sort of valuation in his life. I valued him for who he was, but people have different things that bring value to their lives. For many, it is the sense of "bringing home the bacon" and he wasn't, so that was hurtful to him.

One day, he called me at work and said he wasn't feeling well. I thought he was just being whiny and told him to lie down. I went back to work. A few minutes later I had the thought to call him back. I still think it was God nudging me. When he got on the line, I could tell something was definitely wrong. His voice sounded like he was drowning.

I called 911 and sent an ambulance to him, but I didn't stop working. I had things to do! Some time later I got a call from the hospital telling me to get down there right away or I may never see Mark alive again. I rushed down there, forgetting my phone at work, and joined him in the ER.

As he was struggling for his life, the nurses gave me his things and I used his phone to start calling his family about him. I noticed some things on his phone indicating he was having an extramarital affair, but this wasn't the time to confront him on that. Not yet.

The doctors put him into a coma and he woke up a couple of days later. After the doctors said he was finally going to be okay, I said we needed to talk. I asked him if there was anything he needed to tell me, and if he was happy in our marriage. He assured me he was fine.

I was angry. My mother in-law saw it and on a later visit, asked me what her son had done to me. I told her that *I* was fine. She saw through that. She saw my breaking heart and told me so. She also asked me to stay with her son till she died and then I had her blessing to leave him if I so choose. She had cancer and was wasting away at this time. A month later she was gone. A month after that I left Mark because of the hurt he caused with this affair.

I am being vulnerable here. The reason I am is to show you that behind everyone's façade is some trauma and baggage that you may never see, so be kind in your judgments. I also want you to know my story. I am an advocate for three things in my life: ministering to women, especially abused or distressed women, helping my industry to see there is a real person behind each mortgage they are working on, and veteran services. That building in Chicago I bought? It is to be a home for veterans.

After I left, I threw myself into work again. I moved across the country for a while and got to know people and places all over. But we would keep in touch. Why, you may ask? Because I knew him. I knew he still needed a type of support that his new wife couldn't understand. I knew he needed to be reminded that life was still worth living and that he needed to work through it. I still love him, even though I felt it was a better choice for me to leave.

About ten days before he died, the day before he had the aneurysm that would take his life, Mark sent me a text message that I still ponder. In it, he expressed his regret for not being there when I needed him to be. I feel I should have been more "there" in return.

> *"Good morning. I know you are probably sleeping or working, but I've been thinking and praying and listening to God and seeking answers to so many things, including my feelings and love for you. I'm so torn right now because I'm so desperately trying to let go and just move forward and get you out of my head, heart and soul. I love you so very much to the point of pain. I'm not asking for the same in return from you because I know you are not there anymore. You will always be my Queen and the love of my life. I'm slowly accepting that you have no room for me in your life. It doesn't make my feelings go away but it makes reality a little closer. I pray for you daily. I pray for the boys daily and your entire family. Please forgive me for not being there when you needed me. Because now I can't get close enough to you. I love you forever. I'm still in love with you. You'll always be Mrs. Allen –"*

Unfortunately, I usually responded, "Life's too short. Leave me alone." I did this time, too, and sometimes it haunts me.

I've been thinking about forgiveness lately. I worked hard to forgive the man that murdered my father and haven't regretted forgiving him. It brought me freedom and lightened my soul. Now I have been working on truly forgiving Mark for the things he did. In truth, I think I forgave him a while ago, but we never got back together because of pride. I didn't want to hear the gossip of what others were thinking about my decisions, so I stayed away.

I don't know whether that is the right or wrong decision, and it doesn't matter now. Still, I wonder. Mark is the love of my life. True, he hurt me, as only great loves can, but he also accepted me for who I am. He was my strength and support when I needed it. The news of his death came as a great shock to me and left me wondering if there was a lesson in all this that God was trying to teach me.

Mark tended to live physically better than I did. He ate right, exercised, and went to the doctor. I did the opposite, pretty much. So why did he die and I didn't? Rather, why did he die so young?

When we were married, my husband didn't come first. Work did. Work and more work. It was all about the MONEY for me. But I couldn't see it, or I didn't want to. Our home was divided. He wanted to be the best minister he could be and I wanted to be on top in "corporate America." I worked toward that goal at all costs. The cost was this family.

Now that I have achieved everything I wanted to achieve in my career, it's not enough. It's not enough because I don't have him here to share it with me. I don't have my prayer partner. He would pray for me every day before I walked out the door to go to work, and he would pray for me before I went to sleep at night. I miss that dearly.

As I contemplate forgiveness and love now, I wonder what could have been and I wonder about the lesson God is teaching me, if I will listen to it.

> *Hear my cry, O God; attend unto my prayer. From the end of the earth will I cry unto thee, when my heart is overwhelmed, lead me to the rock...*

In the end, I have another scripture that comes to mind and I think that this is what God wants me to be. Really, He wants all of us to be this way, but it seems especially poignant to me right now. In the KJV "love" is translated as charity, but not like the charity you have when you give to some poor beggar on the street. Rather, it has been said that Charity is the pure love of Christ.

When I read this, I am reminded that this is how Jesus is and how He wants us to be, so I am trying. The following is from the NIV. I Corinthians, 13:4-6

> *Love is patient, love is kind. It does not envy, it does not boast, it is not proud. It does not dishonor others, it is not self-seeking, it is not easily angered, it keeps no record of wrongs. Love does not delight in evil but rejoices with the truth. It always protects, always trusts, always hopes, always perseveres.*

In every stage of life, if you let him, God will lead you to "green pastures" (Psalm 23) and a better life. For now, this green pasture is healing what is broken in me. So I take a little better care of my body. I exercise a couple of times a week and I no longer drink soda pop. More than this, I focus on helping veterans.

That building is temporary housing for them near the VA hospital in Chicago. I am helping them repair their credit so they can get a VA loan for a permanent home. Finally, I am helping military families for whom mental illness is real. It is an illness that can be treated and we are working on best practices and guidance for that.

Perhaps this was the lesson all along, to reach out and serve others, using my own experiences in the process. This way I would come to understand who I am, and what my life is about. Jesus said anyone who wanted to save their life must lose it, so I am losing it in this work.

* * *

Saprina Allen

Saprina Allen is an active advocate in the communities she is part of. She works on and promotes causes as varied as home ownership, veteran's issues, corporate responsibility and women's issues affecting society.

Saprina is known for her work on home mortgages and advocating for the homeowner. "Every home has a heartbeat" is a mantra that she reminds the companies she consults with to engage their sense of accountability to the people they are working with, in turn. Her work in the mortgage note industry has garnered accolades and attention industry-wide, including "Top 100 People in Finance" and leadership awards from Note Summit, among others. Saprina gets more satisfaction through her outreach work, noting that she sits on the Alliance YMCA board. She is especially proud of her "How Dirty is Your Dress" series of conferences and through her work with helping the mental health of veterans.

A recent project has been collaborating with house flipping expert Vance Smith. Together, they create a better process for real estate investors to realize gains in their industry by flipping houses for a profit. They also help the home owners purchasing the real estate to have better experiences and be better financially grounded in their purchases.

Connect with Saprina at https://saprinaarletteallen.com/

With Intention Comes Triumph

By Tam Smith

Resilience is a necessary factor in order to realize true triumph. According to the Merriam-Webster definition, resilience is the "capability of a strained body to recover its size and shape after deformation is caused, especially by compressive stress" . . . the "ability to recover from or adjust easily to misfortune or change." Triumphant would be described as a conquest and being victorious. Allow me to share just a few stories of many life struggles I have personally been faced with, in order to help you grasp a better understanding of how both words function in tandem for me.

As I awoke from a very restful sleep, I could vividly hear my name being called in the distance. I was perfectly nestled in, with an overall sense of calm and pure relaxation, yet oddly, I could hear the rustling of what sounded like footsteps on the forest floor around me and an earthy scent. I quickly found myself laying on a bed of leaves, instead of a Serta. I attempted to raise my head but quickly lost consciousness, though not from fatigue, I'd discover later. When I came to (again), I was surrounded by legs, although, never seeing any faces, I immediately understood those legs belonged to rescue paramedics. There was one individual kneeling in front of me and I instinctively began rubbing their thigh in an attempt to connect to the reality of what was happening to me. I was instructed not to move at the same moment that it became obvious I couldn't.

The realization of what had occurred came rushing back to me in a flood of details. I had been driving down the highway when I encountered a red sporty vehicle whose driver was adamant about ruining my day. Mister red car was quite successful in running me off the road at seven-thirty in the morning during rush-hour traffic. Due to being an inexperienced driver (I was only 19), I veered off the road to my right attempting to avoid a wreck, but inadvertently overcorrected to the left, managing to flip my tiny SUV into the grassy median of the commuter-filled freeway. I have a lucid recollection of all sounds being muffled and seeing a beautiful patch of green grass in front of me. I was dangling upside down from the car ceiling by the defective seatbelt, while my belongings were tossed about as if in a tornado simulation. Shards of glass fragments and other bits of debris were thrown towards me at whirlwind speeds. As it was told by many witness accounts, my body was ejected from the vehicle, once hitting the lovely grass median, then carried by what I know as my guardian angel over 250 feet into a wooded area off the opposite side of the freeway, and gently placed in a perfect clearing of fallen leaves, delivering me from irreversible injuries. Let's fast forward to me being maneuvered through various emergency platforms, where

I would be partially conscious of experiencing extreme cold due to my clothing having been removed, to extreme hot sensations from being injected with dye to enable the ER team to scan for internal injuries. Seven days and two blood transfusions later, I was leaving the hospital with a nick on my nose, a gaping leg wound, and a metal rod in my femur, anchored by a pin in my hip and two pins in my knee. Unknowingly suffering from PTSD, the ride to my grandmother's home to be nursed back to health proved to be petrifying. I had become deathly afraid to be inside a vehicle again. I found myself reliving the experience each time, and simply seeing brake lights took my breath away. I slowly recovered, learning to walk again and finally getting back behind the driver's seat of life.

"How did I get here?" - both physically and emotionally - was the question racing through my mind as I scanned my surroundings. I was sitting on a narrow steel bench, leaning against a cinder-block wall, and my sweatshirt was saturated with nutritious moisture. You see, at least twelve hours had passed and I was long overdue for lactation. My six-month-old was still nursing and in dire need of her mommy. Unfortunately for me, I had nothing to manually express the milk into. My breasts were painfully engorged, leaking profusely, yet I hadn't received much empathy. Although there was one exception, an odd woman I shared the room with, who made herself aware of my special dilemma. This stranger briefly became my advocate and called out to stir up attention by doing what I guess she knew best, which was making a ruckus. I was embarrassed and afraid.

Someone eventually came to see what the fuss was about, which signaled the eccentric woman to audaciously demand that we be provided some towels right away, as if we'd been slighted a four-star luxury. After waiting a bit longer, we were handed a partly used roll of toilet paper, which she brought over to me without any hesitation. I quickly stuffed my brassiere with what I could, leaving some remaining tissue on the roll, perhaps as a courtesy. I didn't want to consume all of what she had rallied so hard to obtain. After what seemed like an eternity, I heard my last name being beckoned for and instructed to come through the barred doorway. The deputy said, "the magistrate will see you now." It was time to plead my case, I suppose. I had never been in this predicament. The female magistrate took one look at me, sporting a purplish-blue hued left eye, then indicated I would be released on my own recognizance. I wasn't exactly sure what she meant at that moment, but, given her telling expression, she knew I didn't belong there. It wasn't until four in the morning when I stepped foot out of the station, even though my arrival was at least six hours prior. I'd driven myself there, directly following a ten-hour shift, for what I assumed would be to add my signature to a piece of paper and leave. Of course, once I stated my name at the window, the attendant told me to wait for what would be a male officer, who emerged from behind the secure entrance toting a yellow document. He calmly said, "ma'am, I just need you to sign here," as he simultaneously handcuffed my wrist. I was caught completely off guard and confused.

I hadn't been given the infamous phone-a-friend, and no one would know of my whereabouts. Upon leaving my extended stay at the local lock up, there stood both of my distressed aunts to greet me in the parking lot. They, along with my nanna, had been frantically calling around town, because I hadn't returned to where I had left my infant in their care for nearly twenty-one hours. It became apparent that I had given everyone a good scare, especially since the week prior was the big incident with the ex, which ultimately delivered me to the clink early that evening. I'd been trying to exist in an unfamiliar type of relationship, one that consisted of mind games, gaslighting and which quickly grew into physical abuse. I was arrested because I had fought back. There was blood drawn in the last scuffle (the ex had to get stitches for only 15 or so punctures, but who's counting). Ironically, he had not been jailed for any of the other squabbles we'd had.

A few months before the *big* brawl, my arm was dislocated in a late night tussle. I managed to run out the house in my undies, holding my infant, as I was being chased. I encountered some neighborhood fellas hanging outside who let me in their home to call for help - my father. Strangers shielded me from further attack and offered their clothing. I know you are asking yourself, so why did you go back. Why do many go back? For the hopes of promised change, after all we had only been married a few months. I wasn't raised in that type of environment and was determined, after the arrest, that I would not allow my child to be either. The impact of realizing my child would suffer long-term effects is what ignited my decision. After much time, a protective order and my attendance to a women's advocacy group, I finally began to pull away from that situation.

My alarm goes off with a special ringtone at 5:30 a.m. I'm exhausted. I've barely had a solid five hours of sleep and I'm feeling some kind of way. By force of habit, I hit the snooze for 5 more minutes but I know it's not going to help me get my task done. After fumbling my way in the dark to the walk-in closet to find something to slip on, I head down the curved backed stairway with Tink, our feisty Chihuahua mix, leading the way. I'm lugging the usual heaping bundle of freshly laundered bath towels … rarely folded for stacking because it's completely pointless since we go through them daily. As usual, I'm moving a bit slow due to arthritis of the hip, knee, lower back and sacroiliac, which are referred to, as a term of endearment, "my Sacagawea" because of everything *she* went through. Crash car dummy tryouts from my teenage years would be the culprit. I came around the kitchen corner to meet my little furry friend, who had paused mid-stride to make sure I'm still in route. She gives me this look as if to say "let's get it poppin' cause we are on a mission boss."

I'm often reminded of how astonishingly strong-willed mom was - up until her last breath. I remember well over 10 years ago now, her showing me the ropes, as one would say. Shortly after my caregiving lesson, I would be so unbelievably taken aback at the mere fact that she would stand in the kitchen, gaze out the window above the kitchen sink, chomping on a very crispy piece of buttered toast. I would ask her, "how in the world can you eat now" after doing a bowel program regimen and she, with that rapid fire tongue, would shoot me down without blinking an eye or pausing in mid-chew, to say "I've been doing this for over 16 years!" Need I mention the faint shimmy that was included in her body language, oozing of sass that only she could eloquently exude. Never raising her voice or saying anything further, she just continued to finish her toast as some of those dried crumbles fell like snow into the sink. I would just look at her in awe, mostly because I was utterly disgusted by what my caregiving lesson truly entailed. But honestly, I had the utmost respect and insurmountable admiration for her. I wish I could have told her *then* versus allowing my emotion of the circumstance to supersede any level of empathy toward her.

Not even a year after that lesson, life for me came to a hard screeching stop. Mom passed on the morning of Mother's Day of 2013, leaving me heartbroken, and the task of caregiver to my disabled brother, who suffered a catastrophic high school football injury over twenty five years ago that would leave him permanently in peril. I chose to give up my own personal passions to become a full-time caregiver for my brother. Despite what many others may have done, I made a choice. I would have it no other way, although the unspoken burden is extraordinarily great. His freak accident left him a quadriplegic, meaning he would need everything done for him by someone else for the remainder of his existence. Having to tend to someone's beckon call continuously is not an easy undertaking, especially when you are an entrepreneurial mother of three and a doting spouse, who all, regrettably, fall within a rotating pecking order. I have somehow managed the job, however, not without inner turmoil and, often quite begrudgingly. Being a caregiver is an extremely selfless act. Being someone's everything is more than what many of us would be prepared for. It's all-consuming and all-encompassing. I've had to force balance, time for those in my life, and not to mention, time for myself. There is an ongoing battle within my heart, my soul, my mind, and my whole spirit. It is a constant feud, similar to the McCoys and Hatfields!

I have often wondered what God was preparing me for while in the midst of each challenge I've faced. At times it was unveiled right away, other times the reveal comes well after managing my way through the challenge. Although recently my soul has become weary, the saving grace for me has always been to figure out how to best handle a situation. We have all heard of fight, flight or freeze. We're hardwired to respond to danger and stress when presented with it. I've taught myself to pull from a toolbox of skills that I have learned over the years throughout my life. Instead of allowing myself to remain saturated with utter dread, I remember to revert back to those basic skills. Rediscovering my toolbox has been a Godsend. Adjusting my mindset and tapping into my own emotional intelligence was what caused me to stop and think that I was in charge of my own thoughts and response to any situation at hand. Having this allows me to pivot, become steadfast in resilience and triumph over most of my challenges.

The stories I have shared with you reflect real life snippets of challenges I have conquered. I use affirmations and meditation now, as well, to hone my toolbox of skills. First, for example, the highway accident was a terrifying ordeal which scarred me inside and out, but I managed to pull from my proverbial toolbox, the skill set of motivation to push myself to walk and eventually walk without a cane. Then, the altercation that reluctantly landed me in an undesirable place, both physically and mentally, resulted from my being constantly thrust into fight mode. I was not self-aware and could not regulate my own behavior until I was removed from the dysfunction and had time to look back inside at the person I was before losing myself in the relationship. And finally, being a caregiver by choice. Although this is an ongoing challenge, I had to pull empathy and revisit my mindset from my toolbox to get through the days where I struggled with certain tasks. Empathy allows me to look within, at how humbling it would be not to have control of my own faculties. Regulation of self reminds me that as the caregiver, I had a choice, but he does not and is fully dependent on someone else to help with most bodily functions. It is as trying for me, as it is humiliating for my brother.

Now, make no mistake - I have driven the doggone "struggle bus" on many occasions. This is the bus without seat belts, zero power steering, two tires so deflated the blazed rims spewed sparks - *and* on course to hit a speed bump traveling 99 miles per hour. But guess what, amazingly enough, I have not crashed. That speed bump gets moved further and further out, and willfully the bus shall be removed from existence. Until that time, I will continue to keep pushing through life, triumph after triumph.

WITH INTENTION COMES TRIUMPH.

* * *

Tam Smith

Tam Smith is a serial entrepreneur, author, and through life's experiences, a mentor who advocates for personal growth. Having owned a corporate event management franchise, the entrepreneurial spirit summoned Tam early in her career. It was seeded by her mother, as a young girl, to become an accomplished businesswoman. Infused with this mindset, she has successfully taken on various leadership opportunities. She was a founding board member of the Central Virginia African American Chamber of Commerce and was Managing Director of the Richmond Chapter for eWomenNetwork, backed by a tribe of premier business owners. She wholeheartedly enjoys seeing women and aspiring young creators flourish. Whether it's local volunteerism, or support of a national non-profit, Tam thrives in serving others. She's an incredible wife (just ask her spouse), an inspiring mom of three humans, plus one deranged fur baby, and is a dedicated caregiver to her brother. Downtime includes long conversations with her daughters, watching nature programs, pondering ideologies of ancient extraterrestrial theorists, and nourishing her brain with fruitful information.

You can keep up with Tam Smith on
Instagram @Tam.Smith
Facebook @TheRealTamSmith
LinkedIn: TamSmithRVA
Email: Info@TheRealTamSmith.com
Web: TheRealTamSmith.com

So, What's Next?

I truly hope that you have enjoyed the powerful stories and wisdom of THE WISDOM G.I.F.T.S. book!

If you are ready to unlock the wisdom of your story, I have a free gift for you. My "What's Your Story?" course. In this course I share some key techniques for unlocking the wisdom you have.

This course is designed to get you on the journey to discovering more about who you are and why your story matters. I want you to find your story and embrace the lessons and wisdom you possess.

Your wisdom is meant to be shared with the world... take the "What's Your Story?" journey now! Access it at storywithkim.com

Connect with me on Instagram and LinkedIn @kimcoles and Facebook @realkimcoles or visit kimcoles.com.

⁂